WAR MEMOIRS

1916

WAR MEMOIRS
1917–1919

SECOND EDITION

Wilfred R. Bion

Edited by
Francesca Bion

Introduction by
Chris Mawson

KARNAC

War Memoirs 1917–1919 first published in 1997 by
Karnac Books, London.

This second edition published in 2015 by
Karnac Books
118 Finchley Road
London NW3 5HT

Copyright © 2015 by The Estate of W. R. Bion
By permission of Paterson Marsh Ltd and Francesca Bion

The rights of Wilfred R. Bion to be identified as the author of this work has been asserted in accordance with §§ 77 and 78 of the Copyright Design and Patents Act 1988.

"Introduction" by Chris Mawson first published as "Editor's Introduction" in *The Complete Works of W. R. Bion, Vol. III*. London: Karnac, 2014.
Colour reproduction of maps by DL Imaging Ltd, London.

All rights reserved. No part of this publication may be reproduced, stored in a retrieval system, or transmitted, in any form or by any means, electronic, mechanical, photocopying, recording, or otherwise, without the prior written permission of the publisher.

British Library Cataloguing in Publication Data

A CIP record for this collection is available from the British Library

ISBN: 978–1–78220–358–2

Edited, designed, and produced by Communication Crafts

Printed in Great Britain

www.karnacbooks.com

CONTENTS

INTRODUCTION / *Chris Mawson* — vii
EDITOR'S NOTE / *Francesca Bion* — x

DIARY
France, June 26, 1917, to January 10, 1919

INTRODUCTION / *Francesca Bion* — 2
1917 — 5
1918 — 71

COMMENTARY

INTRODUCTION / *Francesca Bion* — 192
1972 — 193

AMIENS

INTRODUCTION / *Francesca Bion* — 206
Prelude — 207
Fugue — 209

AFTERMATH / *Parthenope Bion Talamo* — 299

REFERENCES — 303
INDEX — 305

INTRODUCTION

Bion's war diary, which he kept with him during combat, covered his years fighting in tanks in France during the First World War. He was just twenty years old when he began writing it. *War Memoirs* constitutes the final part, after *The Long Week-End* (1982) and *All My Sins Remembered* (1985), of Bion's autobiography. It comprised three hardbound notebooks written soon after he had been demobilized from the Army and had begun his studies at Queen's College, Oxford. He wrote it for his parents as compensation for having found it impossible to write to them during the war. It has been aptly described by Winship (1999) as a "book about the blood and guts of a youth who cut his teeth in the most devastating of circumstances".

Bion begins it, with the entry on 26 June 1917, by stating,

> In writing this, I cannot be absolutely accurate in some things, as I have lost my diary. In the main it will only be my impressions of the various actions. I do not intend to write much about life outside of action except in so far as it will give an idea of the life we led. My dates of events out of the line cannot be accurate. Actions are, however, accurate as they are very clearly stamped on one's memory! [p. 5]

The actions he describes in the *War Memoirs* are terrifying and detailed. They form the basis for his later understanding, as a psychiatrist and psychoanalyst, of the inner torments faced by the patients he treated. In *Band of Brigands: The First Men in Tanks* (2009), Christy Campbell, referring to a segment of Bion's descriptions, wrote: "Bion (who later became a psychoanalyst) looks repeatedly in his account at how sentient human beings continue to operate when everything around them is dissolving into violent chaos" (p. 290). Such is the detail recorded by Bion that they have been found valuable by military historians of the period. Brigadier General Sir Hugh Jamieson Elles led the action of 20 November 1917 in which Bion was nominated for the Victoria Cross and earned both the British DSO and the French *Légion d'Honneur*. Colonel Mackenzie sent a detailed report – which Bion called 'flowery' – of what he termed "the show":[1]

> Some of the tank crews had miraculous escapes. One tank was pierced in the front by a shell which knocked off the driver's head, flung it on the knees of the officer sitting beside him, killed the two gunners in the right-hand sponson, and then went clean through the back without bursting. Whilst attacking nests of machine-guns near Flesquières, tank Edward II, commanded by Lieutenant Bion, received a direct hit by a German field howitzer, which put it out of action. The tank commander gave the order to abandon ship. The sponson door, on the side away from the enemy, was jammed tight, and to evacuate by the other door meant being exposed to heavy machine-gun fire. Private Richardson, however, did not hesitate. Seizing his Lewis gun, he courageously jumped out of the door, and, flopping to the ground amid a hailstorm of bullets, got his gun into action whilst the remainder of the crew clambered speedily out and found refuge in a communication trench.
>
> Lieutenant Bion then reopened fire with his Lewis gun from this trench, where his little garrison was, not long after, strengthened by the arrival of ten men of the 5th Gordons. One enemy machine gun, in a hidden position, annoyed him so persistently that Bion crawled out of the trench, with a Lewis gun, climbed up to the top of the tank, and, sheltering behind the huge fascine, blazed away until the nuisance had abated. Seeing that there was only a handful of men in the trench, the Germans emerged from the village and attacked the position with about 200 men, but Bion's guns, firing in rapid bursts, soon nipped this attempt in the bud. Unfortunately this encounter exhausted all his ammunition, and if another attack took place his tiny garrison would be overwhelmed. But Lieutenant Bion was a man of resource.

---

[1] See also Bion's comments on p. 51, this volume. An abridged account can be found in Liddell Hart (1959), p. 143 fn.

> He searched round in the trench and found a German machine gun with ammunition. He switched this gun round and kept the Boche at bay until, a few hours later, welcome reinforcements arrived in the shape of a company of Seaforth Highlanders. Whilst discussing the position with Bion, the company commander was shot through the head. Once more Lieutenant Bion stepped into the breach by taking command of the company, and remained in charge until another lieutenant of the Seaforths arrived. [in Wilson, 1929]

Various authors have attempted to make meaningful connections between the young Bion's extreme experiences in tanks and his later psychoanalytic ideas – for example, those about the explosive and compressive relationships between container and contained – and some of these seem plausible. Souter (2009), for example, writes of what she felt was a hallmark of Bion's psychoanalytic capacity: "The alarming gift – an entanked capacity, as it were – of being able to continue to think while stuck within horror and suffering, or at the very least, to think about not thinking".

For the most part, however, it probably is true that attempts to analyse the text of *War Memoirs* is, as Winship (1999) has suggested, "a defence against the unthinkable horrors that Bion portrays. To give way to the narrative is to face up to the fuller force of the bleakness and deathliness of the war and the frontline" (p. 94).

Winship (1999) has also made the interesting point that in reading *War Memoirs* one has the distinct impression that, "Bion's life-impulse was fuelled by his blatant anti-authoritarianism":

> He berates many of his fellow officers and superiors for their downright abstention of duty in the face of his enemy, cowardly wriggling their way out. However, Bion later admits that he no longer wished to go out of his way to meet a hostile enemy; he comes to see the war as futile and the precious turf as meaningless. Indeed, at one point Bion recounts being chastised by a senior officer who all but accuses Bion of shirking. Bion rears up, and the commanding officer, rather sensibly, lets it pass. Shortly afterwards, Bion was allowed to go back home. One has the impression that, even at 22 years old, Bion was not a man to take on in an argument. [p. 95]

The introductions and commentary to *War Memoirs* by Francesca Bion, and the 'Aftermath' section written by Bion's eldest daughter,

Parthenope Bion Talamo, are valuable contributions. The 'Aftermath' is, I think, crucial. In it, Parthenope reveals a clear, penetrating insight into her father. Beginning from the question Bion poses in his *War Memoirs* – "Had everyone gone mad?" – she explores the role of mental regression:

> This vision of the mind as a palimpsest with a continual potentiality for almost instantaneous regression can be seen to tie up to the theory of beta-elements, a continuous flow of unprocessed pre-mental sensory data, which then have to be subjected to alpha-function in order to be used for thinking at all, in the sense that these two theories deal with the rock bottom of mental and pre-mental life. I also feel that it is no mere coincidence that although the diaries were dedicated to his parents, it is his mother alone who is invoked every now and again as reader, as though Bion felt that she was a fundamental participant in an internal dialogue. It is perhaps not too fanciful to suppose that the fact that he had not 'written letters' during the war had not only been part of a desire to spare his mother pain, but was also an unconscious attempt to preserve her in his own mind as a container as undamaged as possible by hideous news, and hence as a part of the personality capable of alpha-function. [p. 300]

Chris Mawson
2015

EDITOR'S NOTE

I wish to express my gratitude to Cesare Sacerdoti for making possible the publication of this book of war memoirs to mark the centenary of Wilfred Bion's birth. It is not only especially apt at this time but also a valuable addition to the already numerous and wide-ranging Bion writings.

Francesca Bion
1997

DIARY

France,
June 26, 1917, to January 10, 1919

This is Bion's factual record of his war service in France in the Royal Tank Regiment between June 1917 and January 1919, written soon after he went up to The Queen's College, Oxford, after demobilization. Hand-written and contained in three hardbound notebooks, it was offered to his parents as compensation for having found it impossible to write letters to them during the war (see 'Commentary', p. 191). It has none of the nightmare quality he so vividly depicted in The Long Week-End; he would have been unable to express his very recent painful experiences, especially to his parents. But it is evident that he had them in mind throughout: detailed descriptions of tanks and equipment, explanations of battle strategy, photographs and diagrams were included for their benefit – and 'bloody' became 'b___y' in deference to their disapproval of swearing, a by no means unusual attitude at that time; Shaw's 'Pygmalion' had been first performed only five years earlier, shocking audiences with Eliza's 'not bloody likely'.

He writes in the immature style of a public-school boy of that period, using 'awful', 'terrific', 'beastly', 'absolutely', 'frightfully' and a liberal peppering of 'verys'. But one must remember that it was his first piece of descriptive writing: he had entered the army at the age of eighteen soon after leaving school; he was catapulted, like millions of others, from schoolboy to combatant soldier in a few months. The horror of that war inflicted on such young men did not contribute to their maturity; it destroyed their youth and made them 'old' before their time. Bion's remarkable physical survival against heavy odds concealed the emotional injury which left scars for many years to come. (It was clear that that war continued to occupy a prominent position in his mind when, during the first occasion we dined together, he spoke movingly of it as if compelled to communicate haunting memories.) The nightmares to which he refers (p. 90) still visited him occasionally throughout his life. He grew old and remembered.[1]

Francesca Bion

---

[1]Laurence Binyon, 'For the Fallen'.

In place of letters I should have written!
— from Wilfred.

In writing this I cannot be absolutely accurate in some things as I have lost my diary. In the main it will only be my impressions of the various actions. I do not intend to write much about life outside of action except in so far as it will give an idea of the life we led. My dates of events out of the line cannot be accurate. Actions are however accurate as they are very clearly stamped on ones memory! I don't intend to write much about the general scheme of action except in so far as it touched on our particular affair. For one thing you can get that in nearly any report. For another the general scheme touched me very little & in the action itself everything is such terrific confusion that you can only tell what is happening in your own immediate neighbourhood. I shall try to give you our feelings at the time I am writing of as, although now one sees how unfounded some of our fears were, yet at the time we could not tell & it was just the uncertainty that made things difficult to judge & unpleasant to think about.

1917

In writing this, I cannot be absolutely accurate in some things, as I have lost my diary. In the main it will only be my impressions of the various actions. I do not intend to write much about life outside of action except in so far as it will give an idea of the life we led. My dates of events out of the line cannot be accurate. Actions are, however, accurate as they are very clearly stamped on one's memory! I don't intend to write much about the general scheme of action except in so far as it touched on our particular affair. For one thing, you can get that in nearly any report. For another, the general scheme touched one very little, and in the action itself everything is such terrific confusion that you can only tell what is happening in your own immediate neighbourhood. I shall try to give you our feelings at the time I am writing of. Although now one sees how unfounded some of our fears were, yet at the time we could not tell, and it was just the uncertainty that made things difficult to judge and unpleasant to think about.

Our battalion in England was known as 'E' Battalion. As a result, all names began with 'E'. A short time after we got out, the letters were abolished, and we were known as the 5th Tank Battalion.

We had a good deal of training, and I had a very good crew indeed. The crew consisted of the tank commander, a first driver, and, since my tank was a male tank, two 6-pounder gunners, two loaders, and two gearsmen. The gearsmen were also second and third drivers. They were supposed to be able to drive in emergency. Their actual job was to help to steer the tank. The drive of the tank was connected to each track through what were called secondary gears. Thus if you wished to turn to the left, the left gearsman or third driver put his gears in neutral. The officer (who helps to drive) then puts the brake on the left track, and the right track then drives the tank round. When you've turned enough, you signal to the left gearsman, who puts the track into gear again. That, and looking after the engine and seeing that nothing is going wrong, is the gearsman's job. You can see the positions of the crew and the tank equipment generally from the diagram (Figure 1). It is of course a very rough one.

I was in No. 8 Section of 14 Company (afterwards B Company). My first driver was L/Cpl A. E. Allen – a very good man but slightly built and not very strong. My second in command was Sergt. B. O'Toole, an Irishman who was a very good man indeed. He was left gearsman and third driver. He was an orphan and a rather lonely fellow. He was absolutely straight and conscientious and an excellent disciplinarian. He was very popular with the men when they got to know him. I could always rely absolutely that he would do his job. If he had a complaint, he always let me have it. He was an extraordinarily moody fellow in some ways and was not at all popular with the officers at first, as he was very brusque in his manner and his outspokenness was misunderstood. But it did not take people long to realize his absolute worth. He was also Section Sergeant. My second driver and right gearsman was Gunner W. Richardson. He was an old man who had been a frightful invalid before joining, but the army made all the difference to him. On parade he was very nervous and always in trouble for making mistakes. He looked rather like Bairnsfather's 'Old Bill' [Bruce Bairnsfather's trademark character, in comic drawing sent from France during the war] and was indeed called 'Bill', as his name was William! He was a very kind-hearted fellow. Later, in France, when I knew him better, he showed me photos of his 'missus' and the kids. He explained he was once a pawnbroker's assistant and went into lurid details of the trade! He said he'd never go back to the old life after the open air of the army. My left gunner was Gnr. Allen. He was a Portsmouth chap and an absolute boy. He was absolutely street-bred really and rather a grouser. He had very little self-respect, and he always seemed rather a weak spot. With him was Gnr. Hayler. He was a small farmer in civilian life and the reverse of Allen. He was very independent in spirit but always did his work conscientiously and well. At first he used to talk a lot about 'bad officers' and so on, and I was more than doubtful of him and wondered how he would turn out. My right gunner was P. M. V. Colombe. He was a very cheerful and good fellow. He had gone to quite a good school; he was a clever man at his work, and one could always rely on him. He formed

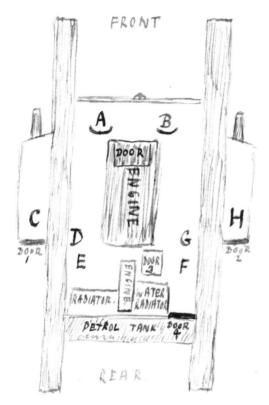

Positions of crew:
A Officer
B Driver
C Left gunner
D Left Loader
E Left gearsman
F Right gearsman
G Right loader
H Right gunner

Door 1. Left door in sponson
Door 2. Right door in sponson
Door 3. Rear door in roof
Door 4. Rear door in side

The petrol tank is OUTSIDE the tank and heavily armoured

Figure I
Male tank.

a sort of common-sense element in the crew. With him was L/Cpl Forman. He was a fellow whom I disliked. He did not do his work really well and always had a terrific opinion of himself. He did an enormous amount of talking. He was, however, absolutely trustworthy.

The other officers in the section were 2nd Lieuts. Despard, Broome and Owen. Broome was a foolish and rather hearty kid. Owen was a good fellow, and so was Despard. Despard was a cheery Irishman – absolutely outspoken and very popular with officers and men. The section commander was Capt. Bagshaw, a very easy-going and hopelessly slack fellow who had been with the original tanks. He was good-hearted but weak-minded and incompetent and got in the wrong set. Cohen was in another section when we left, and Quainton

7 Section with him. Sergt. Reid, a Scotch fellow, was the
[ser]geant in No. 8 Section and in Despard's crew. He was a
[fine] fellow indeed, and although he had a bullet in his lung
[was] fit for general service.

The Company Commander was Major de Freine. He was very slack and incompetent, but good-hearted. On the whole we didn't fancy our chances as a section as our Company Commander and section commander were notorious throughout the battalion as hopelessly slack.

The Battalion Commander was Lieut. Col. Burnett. He was thought a great deal of in England but became very unpopular in France and lost his command after Cambrai.

The battalion as a whole had a very good name indeed and had a fine spirit, but the officers were, I thought, patchy. There were good ones there, and more came out to the front when we got to France. The others were largely men who had seen a good deal of fighting and had gone into Tanks to avoid it. Later, when the Tanks got into action, their low morale etc. let them down, and they were gradually weeded out – particularly after Cambrai. The men were a very fine lot indeed. We got a lot of training, and a good deal was expected of us from the Staff at Bovington Camp. My crew practically held the record for efficiency in their courses and had done two battle practices in which they came out very well. The course consisted of driving over a field about three-quarters of a mile long, where there were various targets. Each gunner fired ten rounds. In the last and final test, in France, over a rather harder course, my crew got the Tank Corps record of 100% hits.

On June 25th the battalion marched out of camp in full battle order at 9 a.m. and entrained for Southampton at Wool. The whole camp – about 5,000 men – turned out and cheered us off. The band played us out. The Brigadier saw us off at the station and shook all the officers by the hand. As the train steamed out, the band played 'Auld Lang Syne' and 'Home Sweet Home'. We reached Southampton at about 2 p.m. and embarked at about 5 p.m. on the *Australind*. We steamed out an hour later, and it was getting dark as we lost sight of land. We had to lie down where we could below decks. Most people were pretty miserable, and there was not much talking. We had some bully beef and biscuits and then got to sleep as best we could.

We woke at about 2 a.m. and found we were anchored outside Le Havre. It looked a dirty, miserable place as we ourselves were not too happy! However, when the daylight came and at last we got into the dock, we felt better. We disembarked at about 3 p.m. and a little later marched up to the rest camp. Here we got quite good meals again and went off to sleep expecting to shift on up the 'line' shortly. We, however, stayed at Le Havre a week and had a very good time. We had bathing parades every morning. Here our sergeant-major of the company got into trouble and was returned. We were thoroughly glad to see him go, as he was a rotter. The next one we got was better, but he wasn't much use.

At last we got orders, and one afternoon we marched to the town and on to the station. Here our train was waiting. It consisted of red cattle trucks and very red third-class carriages for the officers. We realized later that cattle trucks were better as you can lie down and get to sleep in them, but can't do that in ordinary compartments. We moved out at dusk and passed through Harfleur just before nightfall. We didn't know where we were going except that we were going up towards the 'line'. We tried to get to sleep as well as possible, but in those days we didn't know the value of getting to sleep when and where you can, so some of us didn't bother very much. Fortunately on this occasion it didn't matter very much.

At about 2 a.m. we reached Abbeville and here had hot tea, which was made in large cisterns on the platform for passing troop trains. At about midday we reached our destination, which, we found, was a small French village called Anvin. This was quite near St. Pol, the great railway junction, and about thirty miles behind the 'line'. It was a very pretty place, and we were very comfortable in huts. There were an enormous number of wildflowers in the fields, and it was very pretty. As evening came on and it got quieter, we heard the guns for the first time. They sounded just like very heavy thunder in the distance. We often heard them afterwards even in full day. When the artillery opened up at all, it sounded just like the continuous but rather muffled roar of heavy transport over cobbles. On these occasions the windows used to shake and shudder with the concussion.

We did a good deal of drill and so on at Anvin and also went to Merlimont Plage, the Tank gunnery school, for battle practice courses. We had a very pleasant time there. We left the battalion in groups of about four crews and stayed at Merlimont a week. The parades were very short, and it was by the sea. When we came back from Merlimont, we drew tanks. For this we went to Central Workshops at Erin. You were given a tank, which you looked over and ran a little to see it was all right. You then drew all its equipment – telescopes for the guns, periscopes, tarpaulins, tank compass and a thousand other things. You then loaded up your tank and drove off.

As soon as the whole battalion had got tanks, we prepared to go forward. We drove our tanks to Erin from our park and there entrained them. Entraining is very heavy and tiresome work and takes an enormous time until a battalion gets expert at it. You first have to push in the tank sponsons (gun turrets), and this is heavy work if your tank is a male (with 6-pdr guns). If it is a female, you have far smaller turrets (for machine-guns only), and they are hinged and just close back into the tank, but both kinds are liable to stick. At first we used to batter them in, but later we used to get another tank to shove its nose against the turret and drive it in that way. After your sponsons are in, you drive on to the train by an end-on ramp, as per the diagram (Figure 2). The train is specially constructed, and the trucks are 8'1" broad. As the tank is 8'½" broad, we had to steer carefully. You can, as a matter of fact, overhang quite a lot, but you must finish up with your tank flush. You will see in a later picture how they should be. Later the battalion got pretty expert, and from the time we were all ready to go on (sponsons in etc.) to the time we were all on and chocked up was a little under two minutes.

We set off at dusk and arrived at our destination – Beaumetz – at about 1 a.m. This was about ten miles from the line, and we arrived just as a raid was going on. The whole place shook from the heavier concussions, and the roar was terrific to our inexperienced ears. Very lights [flares] and star shells, together with the gun flashes, helped to light up the horizon. The company (we came in a separate train from the two other companies) detrained as fast as we could. Thanks to the absolute lack of arrangements by either battalion or company commander, we were very tired. No orders had been sent by the O.C. Company who had gone on ahead, and so we prepared there and then to drive five miles to our camp. This was a frightful strain on all as we had had little experience of tanks and none of night driving. Everyone was tired. However, we got to Wailly, our camp, at about six. We were absolutely tired out.

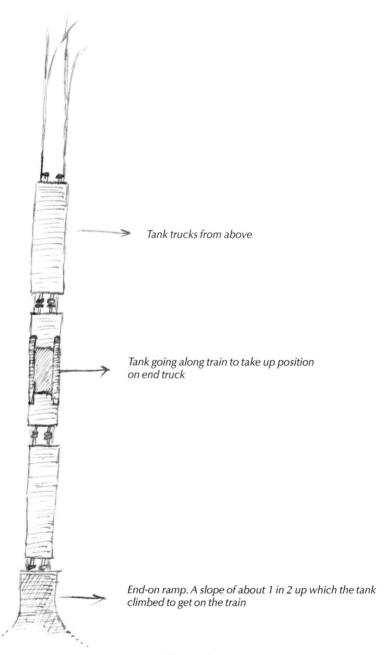

Figure 2
Entraining tanks.

Wailly was at this time a tank corps driving school. It was an old British front-line village, which the enemy had retired from in the early part of the year. We thus had actual old trenches to practise on. The only thing was that, as it had been a peaceful part of the line, there were few shell-holes.

Our section had billets in an old ruined house. We were very well off and quite appreciated it. We were about four miles south of Arras.

We stayed at Wailly, driving our tanks and so on, for about a fortnight. The whole time was spent in teaching our drivers how to drive and tinkering up the engine so as to get the best possible from it.

It would be as well here if I described the tank. At this time we had the most modern tank there was – the Mark IV. Mother saw one when she was at Wool. There were two types. The male had 6-pdr guns and four Lewis guns (machine-guns). The female had six Lewis guns only. The crew was the same number in each. The tank weighed between 35 and 40 tons when ready for action. Its fastest was about 4½ m.p.h., and at night, owing to difficulty of driving, it did about 19 yards a minute. Its slowest would be anything – a barely perceptible movement. The armour plate was 3/8" thick. The male tank took 200 rounds of 6-pdr ammunition into action and a large quantity of .303. The female took in .303 only and, later, some armour piercer. The engine ran down the centre of the tank. It was a 105-h.p. Daimler sleeve-valve engine. There was just room to squeeze past the engine and the side of the tank in the passage. You could not stand upright. You looked through flaps in the front of the tank for driving. You can see these in the picture (Figure 3). When in action, these were shut down, and you looked through small flaps in those flaps until you came under fire. Then you shut down even these and put your forehead against a leather pad on the side of the tank and looked through three small pin-pricks to each eye. When you did that, you got a small complete vision. There was a Lewis gun mounting between the front two flaps for the officer and driver to fire from. There was also a mounting in each 6-pdr sponson, but this was not much good as you couldn't fire 6-pdr and Lewis together. Then there was one in the rear.

The female simply mounted the same but had two Lewis guns to each sponson instead of a 6-pdr. The picture (Figure 4) shows a female tank with Lewis guns mounted. The tracing paper shows important points [see diagram]. As the tank got run in, the tracks stretched and got loose. These had to be tightened up by the track screws (in the

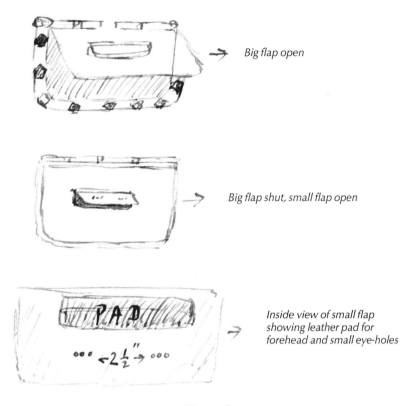

Figure 3
Tank flaps.

photograph). If the tank got stuck, you 'unditched' it by fixing the large oak unditching beam to both tracks. The tracks slipping round then carried the beam under the tank until it gripped and forced the tank forward – like a gigantic scoop. The gear all told weighed nearly one ton. You can imagine the terrific force it had dragging under the tank. You would think the tank would come out of anything.

The rear part of the inside of the tank was filled with the radiator. There was a large fan cooling this and sending the hot air out at the back. When the tank was fully closed for action, it got very hot inside, and the petrol fumes were very bad at times. In this respect, however, it was nothing like as bad as later tanks. On a still night you could hear tanks about 1,000 yards away. The later tanks were noisier by a long way.

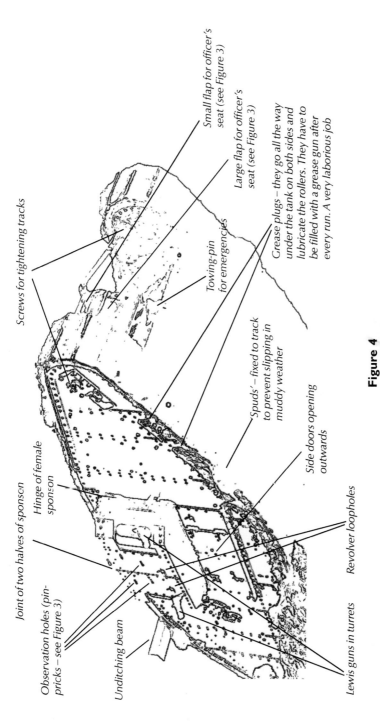

Figure 4

Female MK IV tank (crossing a trench). The tank is ready for action and is crossing a trench with Lewis guns ready for firing down it at enemy.

One very great disadvantage of this tank was that whenever you wished to turn, you had to stop the tank and then turn – I described the secondary gear system earlier. This made you a sitting target, and sometimes, when the gear took a long time to get in, it was very dangerous indeed. Well, I think that is all I need explain about the tanks at present.

At last rumours began to grow about a big battle up north, and we were told we should be going up. We had one very big advantage by our long pause before going up the 'line'. We had got to know our men far better, and they had got to know us more. Also, the grousing at small discomforts was disappearing as they saw more of what they were coming towards. The stay at Wailly had shown them artillery in the distance, and they realized they could be worse off than they were. Then again, as each crew had a tank of their own, they had learnt far more than in England, and they were working together as a crew.

Two companies (A and C) moved off before us, and then on July 30th we entrained. We knew we were going north but did not know where. The picture (Figure 5) gives a good idea of entraining. The tanks have been put aboard and covered up. The leading tank in the picture is a male. It would be about 5 p.m. The men are wandering about in greatcoats, and some are trying to get a wash – there is one fellow under the nose of the front tank. They are all pretty tired and very quiet as they know they are going up the line and are far from cheery. They have a tin of bully and two biscuits issued them, and that does for the day's rations. Tea is made just before the train goes. They have just had theirs. Before long everyone will get up and lie under the tanks. You can make yourself fairly snug with the help of a tarpaulin. There are no trucks at all owing to shortage. Everyone simply goes with their own tank. We thought this a great hardship at first! You will see the tank does not rest on the truck itself but is 'chocked up'. You drive it first well on the front beam or 'chock' and then reverse it onto the rear 'chock', which is slipped in behind, and so suspend the tank.

We moved off at about 6 p.m. and travelled all night. The train, of course, went at a snail's pace. The next day we pulled up just outside Hazebrouck. We were told that we were going up to Ypres and that we should take no part in the first day of the battle. The battle had begun that morning (July 31st). We were to detrain that night at a railhead that was frequently shelled. So we were to get our tanks off as soon as possible, and if shelling started while we detrained, the train would pull out again. Those tanks already off were to make off as soon as possible away from the ramp. This did not make us too cheerful. We then went on, and as we went through Hazebrouck, which was then fourteen miles behind the 'line', we had our first experience of shell-fire as the enemy were trying to hit the station with a heavy long-range naval gun. We passed through all right as he was shooting badly. Night now began to fall as we approached the 'line', and progress was slower. We kept on stopping, and we could hear the guns thundering away. It was, of course, terrific fire. By this time it had begun to rain – the rain that was to wreck the whole Third battle of Ypres and Passchendaele, although we did not know it then. The horizon was simply lit up with gun flashes and flares of all colours. As we went on, we passed a Casualty Clearing Station – a sort of advanced hospital – and we smelt quite distinctly the anaesthetic.

It was a very exciting business to one who didn't know what war was. The older hands were, however, very quiet and tried to get to sleep. At last we reached our ramp – about four miles from the front line. It was not being shelled, and we got all our tanks off as fast as possible. It was raining quite hard by this time, and thanks to that we got no bombing. We drove our tanks into a wood quite near called Oosthoek. Here we had to camouflage up. This consists of suspending a net, which has rags painted brown and green tied on it representing leaves, right over the tank. It completely hides the tank from aerial observation and in a blank field looks just like an innocent shrub in an aerial photograph. But you must be careful that no part touches the tank, as that would form a hard line and give the show away (Figure 6). The job was a very difficult one for us who were inexperienced. It was absolutely pelting rain, and the men were wet through and half asleep. Twigs and roots got in our way the whole time. At last we got the job done. It was now about 3 a.m. and pitch-dark. Of course we could show no lights.

We were then told we were to leave our tanks here with one man on each for a guard while the rest were to go to a camp about five miles by lorry. We went off at last and got into our camp. Again we were let down by the inefficiency and slackness of our senior officers. No one was there to meet us or tell us anything, although the O.C. Company had gone on two days before with an advance party. At last we found our camp. The tents were pitched in a wood – so as to be

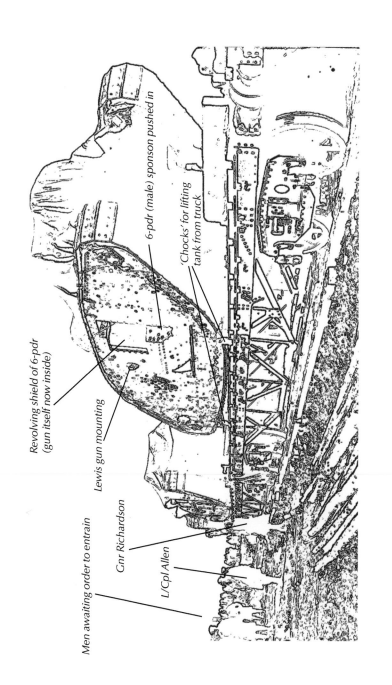

Figure 5

Battalion entraining. Note that the tank just fits on the train.

Figure 6
Camouflaged tank in a field.

safe from aerial observation. No brushwood had been cleared away, so that stumps and thickets were sticking up in the tent. The mud, even inside, was almost ankle-deep. There was no tea or anything for us. There was nothing for us to do but spread groundsheets in the mud and get to sleep. It was about 5 a.m. now. We got up about 12 midday and had a meal of some sort. It was still raining hard, but we tried to get the camp into some sort of shape. The result of the whole business was to confirm us in our ideas of the incompetence of our senior officers. The men, of course, thought that the officers cared about nothing so long as they were all right, and looked forward to action less than ever. As Tank commanders, we tried to do our best. But the selfishness of the senior officers was too appalling for words.

The rain continued practically without stopping for about three weeks. All fighting was stopped except for tentative attacks and the repelling of enemy counter-attacks.

In the meantime we continued to go down to our tanks and make them ready for action. We loaded on our ammunition and 'swung' our tanks – just as you 'swing' a ship for putting the compass right and allowing for variations. We spent our time tinkering them about. It was a bit of a nuisance marching from our camp at La Lovie to Oosthoek each day, but otherwise it was all right. The more we saw of the poor blighters coming down from the firing line for rests and so on, the gladder we felt that we were not in it, and the less we groused about our own particular little troubles.

At last we got a spell of fine weather. Rumours started that the battalion was going into action. Finally, about the 20th September, A and C Companies went into action. The ground was hopeless, and they all got stuck at once. Fortunately casualties were very few, but they lost nearly all their tanks. We were naturally keen to go in now that they had been in and wanted to show them we could do better. We got our order on the 23rd and were told we would be in shortly in an attack on Zonnebeke. The attack was to be on a six-mile front – quite a big affair really – to capture the ridge in front as a preliminary for attacking Passchendaele. Our company was going in alone with the 3rd (regular) Division and the 8th Brigade.

The company was now at Oosthoek, as we had moved our camp there. That afternoon (23rd) we drove our tanks to Reigersburg Château and got there without mishap.

In the morning Cohen and I went up to reconnoitre our route to the front line. We had to go to Reigersburg Château (on the outskirts of Ypres) and then across the canal to English Farm and from there to Spree Farm, which was in the front line and was about 100 yards from the starting-point of our attack.

The reconnaissance was fairly interesting for me, although I was wondering how I should turn out. The country up to the canal was simply a mass of mud roads, paths, transport roads etc., and the nearer we got to the canal, the thicker got the guns. All over the place there were 12" howitzers, 9.2" and so on, firing more or less erratically as it was a quiet day. We got to the canal and there entered on complete desolation. The pictures (Figures 7 and 8) are typical of the whole countryside. Light railways pushed up as far as possible. They took up shells and brought back wounded. There were no trees with a leaf to be seen – although the front line was nearly four miles away now. Old houses were simply mounds of bricks. Here and there guns were firing. The stench was terrible in places, and every now and then you came across dead horses and mules. Some had been scattered with chloride of lime, and the stink of chloride of lime will always bring the whole business back again.

We reached English Farm at last. There was nothing to see but some hedge. We noted our route there carefully, as when we came next it would be pitch-dark, and a mistake would mean that the whole lot would go to the wrong place, and that would mean awful confusion.

From English Farm we pushed on again. We were now where the front line had been on July 31st – the commencement of the battle. The ground was absolutely torn up, and roads were blown to pieces. No signs of trenches remained at all. The shell-holes were filled with stinking rain water. We followed a road (so-called) known as Admiral's road, that led into Wieltje. This had been a village but could only be told owing to the peculiar-shape entry, onto the Wieltje–St. Jean road, of the Admiral's road and No. 5 Infantry Track. The road was constantly shelled by the enemy, and men were employed the whole time repairing it. Every now and then they had to lie down as the enemy started shelling.

We pushed on down this road very fast. We were within a mile of the 'line' now. Everywhere the desolation was complete. You would see small parties of men hurrying over duckboard paths – no one loitered but tried to get out of the danger area as fast as possible. We were now going down the Wieltje–St. Jean road, which led to the Steenbeck. The road was formed out of facines [sic].[1] Facines were bundles of brushwood laid across the mud. This formed a foundation for traffic etc.

We reached the Steenbeck at last. This stream, which figured so largely in the battles, was simply a dirty little dribble through shell-holes. It shifted about 40 yards a day, according to the heaviness of the shelling – if the ground got very badly churned up at one part, this little stream of putrid water used to trickle down into this new channel. It was very impressive to think that this thing had done so much to hold up the attacks. Of course, it was the absolute morass formed by the original Steenbeck valley that was the great obstacle. At this point many tanks were lying about. They had been knocked out in the first attack and lay there as they were. They were a terrible sight. There would be one or more holes where shells had entered and the blackened ruin of the tank itself. No one would go near as the enemy still shelled them at the slightest provocation. In any case, they were too horrible to look at. We now reached Spree Farm. This was in the front line. It was on the enemy side of the Steenbeck and was approached by this rising road. So we were out of sight of the enemy, who were on the other side of the rise. The situation of the farm is important as it played a very serious part later, when we came to commence the battle. There was, of course, nothing left of the farm. The road was sunken, with walls of about six feet high on either side formed of slippery chalk. At the point of the farm itself there stood gaunt, shell-stricken trees pointed into the sky – a very good landmark. The ground on either side of the road was impassable for tanks. If you left it, your tank would inevitably be stuck

---

[1][Bion misspelled *fascine* as 'facine' consistently, including in his handwritten labels for Figures 13 and 14. *Ed.*]

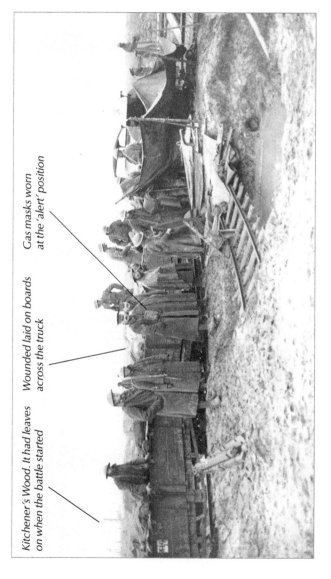

Figure 7

A light railway at Ypres. It brings up shells and takes back wounded. They are put in the hammock and then laid on the train. Note the isolation typical of whole Flanders battle. Note that although it is only about September 20th, men are all wearing heavy coats and that the shell-hole in the foreground is half full of water. All have got their helmets handy or are wearing them, as this is within a mile of the front line and light railways were frequently shelled.

in the deep mud and waterlogged shell-holes. The road itself was being specially constructed for us and was at this part only nine feet broad – just wide enough for a tank. It resembled nothing so much as a sort of springboard over a bath – the staff told you to go to the end of it and then get to your objective as best you could. The Boche, of course, watched the building of the road with great interest. Beyond occasionally shelling a too-daring working party, however, he held his hand – and to some effect as we learnt to our cost. At Spree Farm we were to turn to the right, climb the side of the road and start the attack diagonally across the front (see plan, Figure 9).

When we had examined the ground, we left for home – very relieved, as each step took us away from the dangerous area. We got back later in the afternoon, pretty exhausted. The tanks had been taken to the Reigersburg Château, and a guard had been left on them. The next day we did little. We studied our maps and plans and went over to the infantry we were to work with and discussed things with them. That night (24th–25th) we went to Reigersburg and drove our tanks to English Farm. Here we had to camouflage very carefully indeed, as there were bits of scrubby hedge. We again left a guard of men who were not going into action and returned to camp at Oosthoek again. On the 25th we slept the whole morning. In the afternoon our pigeons arrived. These were to be carried in the tank. Then, when a message was to be sent, you attached the chit to the pigeon's leg in a small container and let it go. They were the surest and best communication there was. They could take a message back from a battle very fast. It was generally reckoned that, if all went well, the bird would deliver a message at its loft, and it would get sent on to H.Q. five miles behind the line in less than two minutes from the time the bird was released.

Figure 8
Ypres battlefield; Dickebush Lake in the distance. This again is typical of the district. The wood is again shattered although far behind the line. It is a very good photo of a shell-burst. Note the debris lying around – coils of wire, etc. The ground has not been lately shelled and is covered with thistles and weed of all sorts. For a shell bursting so near you would have to lie down, as it is very dangerous. Shell splinters from an instantaneous fuze *can* kill at 800 yards. Note that there are very few people knocking about.

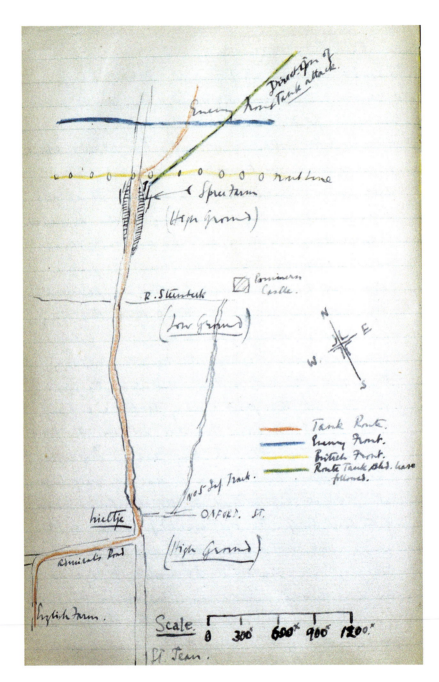

Figure 9

We went over all our plans again. Everyone was very quiet and in a high state of excitement and nerves. It seemed to be an incredible time before evening came. We had a hot meal at about 6 p.m. Most of us could eat very little. Later we got so callous about these things that we used to eat like anything before action.

At 7.30 p.m. we got on board lorries and were to be taken to the canal. The tension was beginning to break, and the men were very cheery and so on, and were singing. Going through Ypres shut them up though. We were stopped and had to put on our steel helmets and wear the gas masks at the 'alert' position. The desolation began to tell on us all, and from now on very few people spoke at all. We stopped at the canal as it was no longer safe to go by lorry. It was a beautiful evening, and the sun was just setting. We marched by crews to English Farm and got there by moonlight.

We were all given our rum ration for each tank. We couldn't take this before action though, like the infantry, as it tended to put men to sleep in the heat of the tank. The mess had already dubbed rum as 'canal-crosser', because it was supposed to give you sufficient courage to cross the Ypres Canal! The name stuck to it ever afterwards.

By this time, the usual nightly bombing started. English Farm was notorious as a pet spot, and tonight the Boche lived up to his reputation. We all lay down scattered about the ground and got no casualties. They fairly shook the place up though.

When they had finished, we got aboard and set out. I was told off to lead. There were six tanks of the company following me. The senior officers weren't to be seen. Bagshaw (the section commander) stayed with the last tank. This was quite right, as then he could always turn up if one of the tanks of his section went wrong. There were four tanks of his section and two of another (No. 7) and one of another (No. 6). The moon went down fairly early. I had a white piece of paper pinned on my back so that L/Cpl Allen (the driver) could see to follow. The crews were all in their tanks. We got to Admiral's Road and then down that to Wieltje without much trouble.

When we reached the Wieltje–St. Jean road the trouble started. Although orders had been given that this road was to be left clear, the place was blocked with transport. Mules, guns and ammunition were all going up this very narrow road. There was only just room to pass, but even then the tanks would touch the transport. I leave you to imagine the position as well as you can. It was now pitch-black.

The transport *had* to get up and so had we, and it was getting late. The jam was apparently hopeless. Many of the transport were hopelessly lost and were in the usual desperate state of nerves and dejection. They knew that if they were late, the infantry to whom they had to give ammunition might be in a very dangerous state. No one knew what was going on ahead and what had occasioned the jam. All knew that at any moment the enemy might begin to shell the road, and we trembled to think of the result.

Finally we decided to push past regardless of anyone else, as it was now very late and vitally important for us to get on.

The road was very winding and very hard to steer on. The steering had to be very delicate and careful – a matter of inches, or we might stampede the mules and horses and knock transport off the road.

After five hours of this, we got to Spree Farm – a distance of about a mile – so you can see it was not fast progress. It was now 4.50 a.m., and we were to start the attack at 6.20. All watches were synchronized and the tanks were greased and oiled-up and we tried to rest.

In the meanwhile Quainton had stuck and got out with great difficulty. He turned up just in time for the attack.

All our nerves were in an awful state, and we tried not to think of what was coming. The waiting was awful and seemed to be almost a physical pain – a sort of frightfully 'heavy' feeling about one's limbs and body generally.

Our guns opened up at about 4.50 as there was to be a preliminary bombardment of the enemy's organization. This, of course, gave the show away, and the Boche began to reply. We decided to push off to our starting-points at once, before he started to shell our own road.

Everyone got in the tanks except the tank commanders, who led them outside. The section commanders Homfray and Bagshaw were in the tanks as they didn't know the way and were no use outside anyhow. Cohen came up in front with me so as to make quite sure we went the right way, but we were too late.

As we set off, the shelling began, but I got to the place where we were to leave the road without getting a shell near. As we reached it, a shell burst right in front, and the concussion knocked me over. I picked myself up and ran round to the right side of the tank after signalling to Allen to turn to his right. As Cohen and I got to the right door, another shell burst, and we both flattened out by the tank. The shell had knocked a lot of splinters off the tank, it burst so close, and had sent off a shower of sparks inside the tank. We both got in as fast as possible, as now we could go on without being outside. Allen fortunately had the sense to drive over the crossing without further orders – it was great presence of mind, as the next shell could have got us on the crossing. We then drove to our starting point, and Cohen left us to go back to his tank – he had a supply tank, and his job was done now, for he did not have to come into action.

We shut off our engine when we got to the starting point. It was now 5.30, and we had forty minutes' wait.

In the meanwhile the rest of the tanks did not get on so well. It was very slow going, and they had to go down the road through the shelling. Two tanks got knocked out, and the crews became casualties. Quainton got a glancing hit, but it did no more than cut about some of the crew. By this time the general bombardment had developed, and in the silence of the tank we could hear the shells screaming overhead from our own guns, and bursting near from theirs. The shelling was simply one continual roar. Your own guns sounded a sharp crack behind. You could, of course, distinguish nothing. You simply had the deep roar of the guns, which was continuous, and imposed on that was the shrill whistle of the shells passing overhead – just as if it was the wind whistling in a gigantic keyhole. One very big German shell that burst near us could be distinguished above the rest. It sounded like an express train coming through a tunnel – a gradually increasing roar as it came nearer. Then a deafening crash. As the nearer shells burst, the tank used to sway a little and shudder. This was very beastly, as one had previously felt that a tank was the sort of pinnacle of solidity. It seemed as if you were all alone in a huge passage with great doors slamming all around. I can think of no way of describing it.

At 6.15 we started up our engine – we had previously shifted a little, thinking we were going to get a little away from a large shell that kept bursting very near! At 6.20 (zero hour) the real bombardment started, and the barrage came down. This simply excelled everything that had gone before.

We pushed off steering by compass. It was pitch-black still, and we could distinguish nothing outside. Unfortunately my compass was quite inaccurate. The shell that had burst in front at Spree Farm had knocked it right out. So, when I thought I was steering due east to my objective, I was going north.

At last it got lighter, and I distinguished what I thought to be a wood. As I got nearer, I found it was our infantry. We were supposed to follow till they got held up and then to go ahead and clear the way. I discovered from my map that I was now hopelessly lost (see Figure 10). I was following a ridge that I shouldn't have been on. I decided to hang on and do what I could there till I got more certain. The ground was absolutely ploughed up – like fine flour.

We now came on a German pill-box – you can see what it is like from the photo (Figure 11). The infantry were held up by cross-fire from a pill-box on my left. As I pushed forward, a big shell hit near the base of the pill-box, and the whole thing simply turned over on its side. You can get some idea of what the force of a large shell is when you realize that a pill-box is solid concrete and about six or more feet thick. This effectually cleared the place in front, but the infantry could not advance because of the cross-fire.

At about this time the sun was getting up, and I decided to steer straight into it. The tank, however, was in very serious difficulties. The ground was so bad, and so badly shelled, that one gun (the left) was below the level of the ground and was simply ploughing through the earth. The tank was on a slope and couldn't right itself, so we went on like that. At last she became permanently stuck. We fixed the unditching beam, but this only shifted the tank a few inches each time it got right underneath. We travelled literally no more than one foot to each revolution of the tracks. I left the tank at this stage and went over to a bunch of infantrymen in a shell-hole to ask my whereabouts. I didn't realize I was under machine-gun fire, I was so dazed, and they shouted at me to get down. From them I learnt, by yelling in each other's ears, that we were at Martha Louise Farm. It had been a farm but was now a German pill-box. I went back and decided to steer to the right. We simply kept the unditching beam on and so went on for about an hour, in which time we did about 200 yards. In the meantime the infantry went on as the pill-box on the left was mopped up. The German guns now got on to my tank, and shells were bursting very close indeed. Finally we had to shut our front flaps for lumps of mud and shell splinters that came in. We expected a direct hit at any moment, but our slight movement apparently baffled them – they were firing from indirect observation. At last the ground got a little better, and here I took off the unditching beam as we couldn't steer with it on. The beam is attached to both tracks, and so you cannot

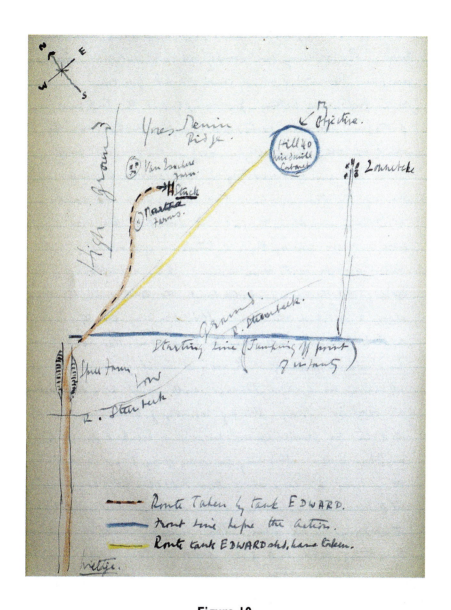

Figure 10
(See *Maps*, p. 44.)

x-ref

Derelict German field-gun Door – always facing away from British line

hold one while the other goes on. But it was hopeless, and we had to fix it again. I decided to go straight ahead and do what I could where I was, but this proved too much for the engine. The steering brakes broke and the transmission broke. As a direct hit was merely a question of seconds, we abandoned the tank and formed a strong point with the guns from our tank about 50 yards in front. A strong point is a kind of fort. Here we stopped. The enemy opened feeble rifle-fire on us as we got out, but we had no casualties, although Sergt. O'Toole had a very narrow escape – a bullet struck the tank by his head as he got out. I sent off the pigeons, reporting the situation.

It was now about 10.30 – I felt more as if it was about 4 or 5 in the evening. We simply hung on as we were. I saw a tank stuck on my right; this was Quainton's. And another on my left; this was Despard's. He came over to me, and we arranged some plan to stick to in case of an enemy counter-attack. He was frightfully cheery, and so was Sergt. Reid with him. As far as we could make out, all objectives were reached.

At about 1.30 all was pretty clear. I checked the distress signal to aeroplanes on my tank and stated the number of the tank. Several planes came over flying very low and saw it. A bit later some enemy planes came over and fired on us, but their shooting was rotten. The shelling was still very heavy, but our light guns were coming up, and the enemy were withdrawing theirs. They tried a counter-attack, but nothing happened. A little later, as all was clear, we got permissions and went back. Despard had withdrawn earlier, as his tank, like mine, was a hopeless wreck. You can get some idea of a stuck tank from the photo of one of ours at Ypres (Figure 12), only mine was right under on the left side, and finally it disappeared from view! We got back to No. 5 Infantry Track safely. This track was well wrecked by the Boche and was littered with dead mules and men and was a terrible place. We got back to Wieltje now comparatively safe – with much relief. Here, we were so dead-beat we went to sleep. We were laden

---

Figure 11

German pill-box, captured on Sept. 26th 1917 at Ypres. Notice the slight effect of shell-fire, although it had been the mark of many guns. This pill-box was on my left in the Sept. 26th attack.

with our guns etc. as we brought them back, and had put our 6-pdr guns out of action.

When we awoke, it was about 4 or 5 p.m. We pushed back to Reigersburg Château. Here we reported to Company H.Q. and then went back to Oosthoek Wood. We had a hot meal and then turned in for the night. We were all in a fairly shaky mood. The next day we heard what had happened to the company. Two tanks had reached their objectives and done fairly well. The remainder had all had the same luck as mine. In our section Broome and Owen had both got shell-shock and were in a fearful state. Despard had been killed by a shell just after he left me in the action. He was a great loss to the section, as he was always cheerful and kindly. He had said before going into action that he was sure he would not come back. But it didn't seem to worry him at all.

In the morning we were interrogated by the intelligence officer and told our stories of the action.

At about 5 p.m. they decided we would have to fetch our tanks back from the line if we could. This does not seem a great hardship, but it was. The crews had all been very badly shaken up, and the effects were now at their height. As I was the only tank commander left in the section, the job fell on me. They decided the only tank in the company that could be fetched back was Despard's. I was given Sergt. Reid from his tank, a boy named Foster, Colombe from my crew – he volunteered – and Hayler. Foster had been very badly shaken up by the action. He was only 18 and had been in France in the infantry previously. He had been wounded and knew what it meant. Sergt. Reid told me it was better not to take him. So I decided to leave him, whereupon he insisted on being brought along. The result was that I had a very willing and good lot with me, and I felt I needed it. For

---

Figure 12

Tank after direct hit. Note how it has sunk into the ground. The holes are very small as the shell has gone in and burst inside. The worst of it was that the splinters would usually kill or wound the crew and set the tank alight. The wounded often couldn't get out and simply were burned to death. The petrol would catch at once and then the oil. After that the ammunition kept on going up, as the sides are just honeycombed with it. They look like large squibs going off when they are burning as you get the continuous 'pops' of the 6-pdr shells.

the action I had felt more or less prepared, but I didn't feel at all ready for this and found myself in such a state that I didn't think I should manage it.

We set out at 9.30 p.m. The nightly air raids had just begun. As we left, two bombs fell in the camp. The whole time we went up the road, the place was lit up by bursting bombs and ammunition dumps going up. We expected to be bombed at any moment, as they always had a few shots at roads – especially Brielen at that time.

We reached the canal without mishap. The night was pitch-black, and we then began the rough part of our journey. The nauseating stench of chloride of lime, dead mules etc. was everywhere.

We went along the St. Jean–Wieltje road, which you can see marked on Figure 9, and joined the route we went into action by at Wieltje. But here we branched off and went up No. 5 Infantry Track (the one we came out of action by). By this time we were amongst the field guns again. We simply stumbled through shell-holes and over bits of barbed wire that stuck up in the ground – the remains of old entanglements that had simply been turned into the ground by bombardment. It was very tiring and demoralizing. We came upon the remains of an old strong point. I was horrified to find that we were treading amongst men and thought that something had knocked them out. I then found they were simply machine-gunners who were lying there in the mud and shell-holes asleep, resting. With them were some artillery men. I wanted to make sure of my way, so I shook one fellow. I could make no impression on him for a long time. At last the shaking had some effect, and he sat up. I asked him if it was No. 5 Infantry Track, whereupon he answered some absolutely un-intelligible gibberish, as if he was delirious. I never struck such a nightmare in my life. But it gives you some idea of the state of infantry, gunners etc. in the glorious Third Battle of Ypres. At last I got an officer. I told him what I wanted, and he said he would show me. The guns had now opened up heavy fire, and the Germans replied. As we went along, this officer said I should never get to the tank, as the Germans had counter-attacked and the position was uncertain. They were opening up then, as there was great restlessness and the situation seemed very critical. As it turned out, he was right, and we need not have bothered to go any further. We had now got onto duckboards, and there was little chance of missing the way. So I turned to thank the officer for his kindness; as I turned, the moon shone out behind a cloud, and he saw my face and said, 'Great Scot! Is that you, Bion?' So I said 'Yes', whereupon he said he was Bonsey, and then I saw his face and recognized him as an Old Stortfordian. There was no time to say anything except goodbye and good luck. Poor fellow! He was killed just a week afterwards. We got back to Martha Farm and then found we could get no further. The bombardment was very heavy, and it was foolishness to risk going on. We had been told not to take risks, so after a bit I decided to go back. The track was now (as usual) being shelled, and we went as fast as we could. It was a frightful business.

I don't quite know how we got back to the canal, but at last we did. The crew were very done, and it had proved too much for me at least. As we went along and began to feel safer, a gun by the road was fired and proved the last straw for Foster. He simply fell down on the road and struggled and fought, shouting, 'Keep them off! For God's sake keep them off!' We had to get his arms and legs and carry him back to a dressing station. He struggled like fun, but we tried to talk quietly and soothe him down. We left him at the first dressing station we found and then went on to camp. As I went along, I talked to Sergt. Reid. He was a Black Watch man originally, and this was the first time I really got to know him at all.

We were naturally thinking of our recent show and our losses, and so we spoke chiefly of that. We both found we were by no means keen on the war and its justice and glory and so forth – which is obvious a good distance away, but not quite so obvious close to the real thing. He said he could see no sense in it all, and when I said that the usually accepted views of right and wrong appeared rather out of place when compared with the death of a man like Despard, he startled me by saying that it was really rather hard not to believe that the conscientious objector was right, while we were all deluded fools. So you will see that some, at least, of the much-maligned Tommies were not the brainless and inhuman automatons that the staff and British press liked to paint them.

We got back to camp at last, and I reported. They were quite satisfied, and next day's battle reports confirmed me in my decision.

We had a few days' rest and were then sent down with skeleton crews – i.e. officer and drivers – to draw more tanks from Erin to replace losses. I went down with Cohen to Erin. It was a wonderful change to get away from our ghastly Ypres surroundings. We went straight into the peace of the country. The trees had all the lovely autumn tints, and it seemed quite strange to see trees that were not shattered and leafless stumps.

I will not bother you with details of drawing tanks. We came back the next day, having drawn our tanks and tested them superficially.

After we got back to Oosthoek, we ran our tanks into condition and oiled and geared them. In about three days they were practically fit for action again.

The ground was still in a ghastly condition as rain had fallen once more, so you can imagine our surprise when we were told that we were to go into action again in a last attempt of the 5th Army to break through. Maps were issued, and we appeared to be operating under even worse conditions than previously. All ranks gave up hope of ever doing anything or of ever expecting common sense from senior officers or general staff. How tanks could be *expected* to operate seemed beyond the comprehension of anyone who had the vaguest idea of what a tank was like. However, we prepared for our show.

At the last moment they proposed to give me a rest. I made a row about it, but it was no use.

The tanks shifted up to the Pelcappelle road, and then, just the night of the action, the whole action was washed out and the next day the tanks were withdrawn to Oosthoek Wood. We were very relieved indeed.

We were then informed that the year's campaign was over and that our battalion was to go to Wailly for training and then into winter quarters.

By this time I discovered that I had a very bad tank. Engine trouble was very frequent, one of the track rollers was defective, a shaft twisted and had to be removed, and it always overheated. This was to be a source of endless trouble.

We entrained on about the 7th of November and went to Wailly. Here we tried to get our tanks into trim and exercise our drivers and crews. The defective roller was removed and the engine was tinkered up, but it still overheated.

While we were there, the 51st Highland Division came and practised with us. They were practically *the* crack division on the Western Front. They were all territorials but had a magnificent staff, wonderful discipline and tremendous *esprit de corps*. Ypres had destroyed their faith in tanks, and they were very contemptuous of us.

We carried out set-piece manoeuvres over the old trench system at Wailly. After that we were told that we were going into a new battle and that not a word must be said about it. At first we thought it was another suicidal show. But we were issued with maps (without names on), and we found the ground was to be very good and practically unshelled. It seemed too good to be true, but we began to get a little more interested. We then discovered that our battalion was to work with the 51st Division, and after going to a lecture by the brigadier of the brigade that B Company was to work with we were quite enthusiastic. It was a fine lecture and showed a grip of detail and conscientious hard work that gave us more confidence than I can say. For the first time we realized what good 'staff' work could be. Here was a general, and he absolutely knew what the details of a platoon sergeant's work was – and he gave them good advice on it too. After he had explained the plan of action, our colonel got up. His 'lecture' was a striking contrast – *he didn't even know how many guns a tank had*! Practically all our respect had gone for him by then. What little remained went a few days later, when he gave us a hectoring speech on tank work. Apparently we had not earned him enough glory at Ypres, and he now said that if any man or officer let him down, he would court-martial him, whoever he was. A worse thing to do I can't imagine. Every man had done his best and that under hopeless conditions. All fighting-men felt they had been let down by the staff, and this fellow had the audacity to talk about letting *him* down. From that time on he was the hated man of the battalion.

We met the officers of the 51st a good deal so as to get used to working together. No. 8 Section was working with B Company, of the 6th Seaforths. The company was commanded by Capt. Edwards, who came from a Scottish village called Lossiemouth. The Company Commander of their A Company came from the same village, and they had been boys together. They were terrific rivals and had great arguments as to which company would reach and take the German guns behind Flesquières village (as we afterwards found the village was called)! Edwards had won the DSO at Beaumont Hamel on the Somme, where he captured a German staff single-handed. We went into every detail with him.

At last, on the 12th, B Company had orders to shift off. I had orders to leave by midnight.

Our Company Commander, Major de Freine, had just been sent home to England for rowing with the Colonel. In his place we had a new man we didn't know, called Major Bargate. He was weak-minded, underhand, incompetent and addicted to drink. He was, however, well-intentioned and amiable. My crew had been working hard on the tank all day and were very tired. They would have to work hard all the time if they were to get off by midnight. So, as our last tank didn't leave till 3 a.m., which would have given them a chance of rest, I asked to go last. This was refused by Bargate, who seemed to think his authority was questioned if an amendment was suggested.

The men in our company were in a very bad state. They disliked and distrusted the senior officers and were consequently liable to grumble the whole time. I was lucky in my crew, and they said very little, although they had good reason to grouse.

At midnight we left and trekked to Brisleux-au-Mont, the rail-head. The tank went very badly and still overheated. We reached Brisleux at about 7 a.m. and entrained. The fact that our train was not due out till 7 p.m. simply emphasized the lack of common-sense consideration for the men. They had been kept up and tired out all night for no purpose at all.

Our journey led across the devastated Somme region, and when we stopped, we found we were at Plateau. We detrained and went into the wood there. For once we had a hot meal of stew and tea on arrival. It was now 2 a.m., and instead of turning in, the crews had to go and fetch petrol. This fatigue lasted till 3.30 a.m., when all turned in. This was the first bit of sleep they had since the night of the 11th/12th. I leave you to imagine how tired they were. Next morning (14th) we had to be up at 7.30, so we only had four hours' sleep. My tank had to be tinkered up. The trouble had simply been that the engine became red-hot in about ten minutes' running. The tuning appeared to be correct, so we could only think that the trouble was due to carbonization of the cylinders and consequent pre-ignition. The tanks are so badly constructed that to take off the cylinder heads and exhaust, we had to remove the roof to get to the bottom of the trouble. This meant more very heavy work again. We found a little carbonization, but not enough to satisfy us that we had got to the root of the trouble. We had the tank fitted up again by 5 p.m. As soon as it was dark, we drove into a neighbouring field and there drew facines – large bundles of wood bound round by chains.

They weighed over a ton. They were subsequently replaced by the skeleton facines you can see in the later photos. These facines were to be carried in front on top of the tank. When we came to a very deep trench, they were released and dropped in so that the tank could cross more easily. If you have a deep trench and do not drop in a facine, the tank falls back into it as you cross, and the tail sticks in the bottom, making it impossible to go on. A facine prevents the tail going to the bottom and sticking – you can see from the diagram (Figure 13).

It was a frightful business getting it on. We attached it to the tracks as it lay on the ground and then reversed the tank so the tracks carried it from in front of the tank up onto the top (Figure 14). We finished the job about 9.30 and got back to camp and turned in by 10.30.

The next day (15th) the crews went on working at the tanks, but all tank commanders had to leave and go by lorry to the place our battle was to start from, so as to reconnoitre the positions thoroughly. I was

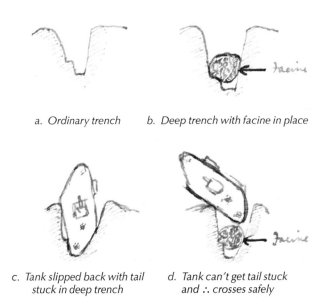

a. Ordinary trench   b. Deep trench with facine in place

c. Tank slipped back with tail stuck in deep trench   d. Tank can't get tail stuck and ∴ crosses safely

Figure 13
The use of facines.

a. Tank with facine attached to the track   b. Tank travelling back in reverse and carrying up the facine

c Facine in position on top of the tank

Figure 14
Attaching a facine.

very glad to be rid of my tank and hoped somehow that something would happen to the thing to make it go before I saw it again.

We arrived at our destination at 2 p.m. on the 15th after a ride through Bapaume and the devastated region. We were to live in Havrincourt Wood, which was about 1,000 yards from the front line. It was just in front of the village of Metz. Opposite us, in the enemy's lines, were the villages of Havrincourt and (partly in our lines) Trescault.

That same evening we went up to the front-line trenches. It was an extraordinary change from Ypres. We were now opposite the famous Hindenburg line, and the country was hardly touched. The trenches were in wonderful condition. The villages looked as if they had never heard of the war except for those behind us, which had, of course, been blown up by the Germans in their retreat. Havrincourt Wood was like an ordinary wood in England. The front was very peaceful. There was about 1,000 yards between the enemy trenches and our own, and hardly a gun fired. The great question was, should we catch the enemy napping? I will not bother you with the reconnaissances. We did two more on the next day (the 16th) over the same territory and one back to the railhead (about five miles from Havrincourt Wood). This place was called Ytres, and we were to meet our tanks there. The greatest precautions were taken to keep the enemy from knowing what was happening.

On the 17th we did one more reconnaissance, and then that evening we went back to Ytres to meet our tanks. They were due in at 7.30 p.m. As I saw them come in, I wondered if my old tank was all right, and my first question was, 'Is my old tank going all right at last?' The reply was, 'She behaves like a perfect swine'.

That put the finishing touch on me for the time. I saw the crew and found they were utterly fed up. The great thing was to get it the five miles to Havrincourt.

Well, it is hardly possible to describe the trip. Everything went wrong. The oiling system gave up and we had to mend it with the aid of what wits we had left. She overheated every 200 yards. The driver went to sleep (L/Cpl Allen) as he drove and rammed a house. I took on driving, but Allen seemed so thick-headed he couldn't lead properly. You can tell what it was like when I say we reached Metz village four and a half miles off at 5.30 a.m. That is to say, we took ten hours for four and a half miles. Walking pace isn't in it! When we reached Metz, the tank gave up the ghost. There was a terrific flash and an explosion, and she stopped. When we recovered, we took stock of the situation. We were in the middle of the village street. Daylight was coming, and we would be certain to be spotted if an aeroplane came over. The sight of a tank behind the British lines would have given the whole show away. Fortunately, another tank from C came along at this stage. In command was a fellow named Wilson. He had very little petrol and could never have towed me in. But although it was very late, he towed me to the side of the road. As this enabled me to hide the tank from aerial observation, I was more grateful than I can say. It took him about three-quarters of an hour to do and meant a lot of extra work. He was killed in the battle and recommended for the VC but did not get it.

When we got to the side, we built an imitation house over the tank to hide it. The crew were so tired that I sent them to sleep and did no more. At 11 a.m. (the 18th) we started work again. We did what we could, and that night started to get the tank to the wood. It overheated hopelessly again, but we got there somehow. The crew got sleep from 11 p.m. till 10 a.m. and so at last had a rest. Action would have been impossible without it.

At 11 a.m. we started a last despairing effort to get the engine right. We then discovered that the timing was wrong. The dead centre was marked wrong on the flywheel, so all our previous timing had been wrong! This small mistake on the part of the makers had cost us hour after hour of hard work and anxiety. We timed it by the cylinder heads and felt that we had at last got to the root of the trouble. We spent the rest of the day (19th) on running out our 6-pdr guns and preparing for action. Our facine again gave us endless trouble. We were all ready but for this by 7.30 p.m., and zero was to be 6.50 the next morning (November 20th).

Before going on, I will explain our orders and tell you what we had to do. A and C Companies had to form the first wave and take the trenches marked **A** (see diagram, Figure 15). They were to drop their facines in so we could cross. We had to form the second wave and go through them on to the trenches marked **B**, and take them using our facines to cross the **B** (or second-line system) trenches. No. 8 Section was on the left, and I was the left section. I had to deal with the strong point and small wood at Flesquières. Ribécourt village was on the right. The infantry and artillery all came up that night (19th/20th) in lorries. They had to fire by the map and could do no registering. You see, the orders were all fairly simple.

Maps

I have drawn rough maps of the action so as to save looking at the original. The Marcoing 57.C. N.E. map I am sending is the identical map I used on November 27th 1917, and that accounts for its battered and stained condition. It was with me from start to finish. I therefore don't want to mark it at all as it's rather a relic! But from it you will follow the details clearly, and also get some idea of the very great accuracy of our maps. The country was practically untouched, as I have pointed out, and therefore there were trees in existence. You will notice that even the trees are marked on the Grand Ravine. As I was the tank on the extreme left of our battalion, I practically followed the line on the left, which marks the left boundary of the battalion's activities. I therefore crossed the Grand Ravine just to the left of the little bunch of four trees marked on the map. So you see, an action was arranged in very great detail, although of course you had to use your initiative at all times. The thing was to disobey orders at the right time and in the right way. You will see Villers-Plouich marked – where we went later with Capt. Clifford [see p. 57]. [These maps are now lost. F.B.]

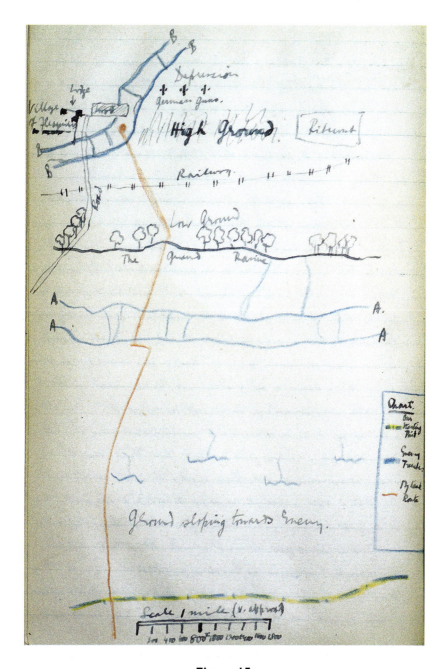

Figure 15

At 9.30 I got the crew out, as we had to start. Hayler was now so ill as to be useless, and a new man had to be put in at the last moment. He was a young fellow called Pell – aged about 18. He was a very willing and hard worker and most enthusiastic. After very great difficulty we fixed the facine somehow, and at 12.30 we set out. We reached the starting-point by 3 a.m. The crew were very tired and almost inclined to be hysterical. The engine overheated the moment we started, and it looked as if it was all up. The infantry were warned that my tank wouldn't be able to go in after all.

We started up again, however, and to our surprise it went like a bird from that time to the end!

At the starting-point we got out and rested on the ground. It was very quiet and peaceful, and only now and then an enemy machine-gun opened fire and we heard the bullets sail over. We wondered if they suspected anything. At 6 o'clock the guns suddenly opened up, and we were afraid that they had found out, but it died down. It was quite light by 6.50, when three shots were fired and suddenly the barrage came down.

All the enemy trenches were outlined in low-bursting shrapnel. It looked like clouds of white with golden rain in the bursts. It was very beautiful – and very deadly.

We started off, and everything went like clockwork. There seemed to be no fighting at all and an absolute surprise to the enemy. When I got to **A**, I had to tackle a machine-gun, but he gave up when we came near. It was the only battle in which I saw anything clearly, and it might have been a manoeuvre. The whole place swarmed with tanks and Highlanders. After a pause at the Grand Ravine, we went on – now B Company was in the first wave as A and C stopped on the **A** line. Some of the kit on board caught fire, but we chucked it overboard. When I got within 1,000 yards of Flesquières, I opened up

---

Figure 16

Our tank route to the starting-point was as follows: Q21 b, follow the sunk road in the Trescault valley from there to where it crosses the 'enemy defence' line representing the communication trench called Sherwood Avenue. Follow the 'Avenue' from there till it reaches the line representing the left battalion boundary. Follow that to the front line (Derby Trench), and there you are.

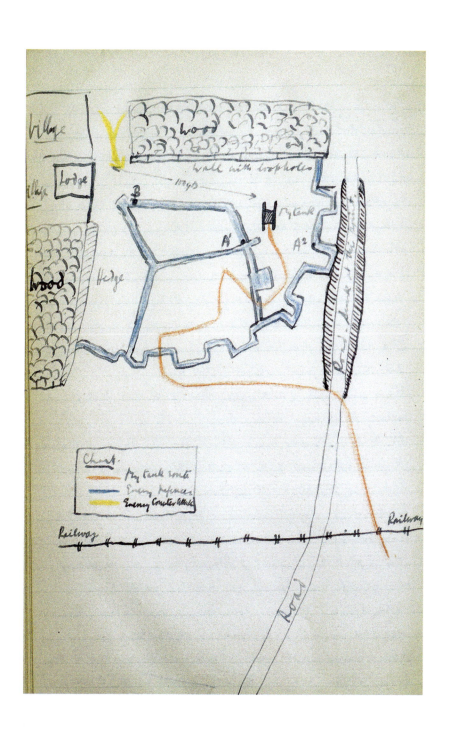

slow fire on the lodge – first the left gun and then the right (Figure 16).

I reached Flesquières at about 9.10. This was rather too early. We were greeted with tremendous machine-gun fire. In the ordinary way the noise is so terrific when the engine is going that you can hear nothing outside; but bullets hitting the tank sound like sledgehammers against your ear. Also they knock off tiny pieces of red-hot metal. These fly off and cut you about. The first thing I knew was this frightfully demoralizing row, and I had no idea what to do. The worst thing was that bullets began coming in through the gaps in the armour plate and ricocheted round the tank. Some rivets were driven in, thus leaving holes in the armour. By some mischance the left gunner Pell (the new man) got hit in the thigh by a bullet that came up the breech when the wedge was down in the gun. Allen was then left. He was demoralized and left the gun. As a result, a perfect storm of bullets came in. I shouted to them to get back, whereupon Richardson took the gun and managed to get it into action somehow, with the result that that particular machine-gun shut up. Richardson was hit in the leg doing it.

Pell then was transferred to the right side and had to lie on the floor working the gears wounded. By this time several more tanks came up, and the strong point stopped fire as we simply sat on it. But the infantry had not come up. After a while the other tanks went off and I stayed on. We simply patrolled up and down.

Suddenly there was a terrific crash, and a great chunk of stuff ricocheted round and hit me on the back. It was a piece of shell, and we had got a direct hit on the right side of the tank by the gears. This effectually put us out of action. The tank immediately showed signs of catching fire, and as it was useless to stay in – we might get another hit any moment – I decided to evacuate. Pell, who was by the gears where the shell entered, had shell-shock, and the rest of the crew were hit about. The piece of shell was afterwards found near my seat and given me. It was the one I sent home.

Unfortunately the enemy realized what had happened and opened fire on our left door. Our ammunition for the 6-pdr was finished. We tried to get out by the right door, but it was jammed. So we had to get out by the left. There seemed little chance of getting out all right, but there was less of staying alive inside. Richardson took a Lewis gun, loaded it and then flinging the door open tumbled out. He was hit through both legs doing it but opened fire and shut their gun up.

As a result we got out safe, dragging Pell after us. We got into the enemy trench near the tank and put out our Lewis guns. The enemy were up one end (marked **B** in Figure 16). Our position is at point **A1**. We opened fire at once, and the enemy shut up again. Some more of our tanks turned up, and everything quieted down again. I led one or two of them to the right corner of the wood in front, showing them where to go as all seemed all right where we were.

We had received our direct hit at 10.30 a.m., and the whole thing was over in a second or two, although it seemed years. When these tanks cleared off, a couple of Seaforth Highlanders came up with us along the trenches behind. So we knew we were going to be supported at last. But just at this time the enemy seemed to be opening fire on us again from all sides, and we didn't quite know where they were. I was very excited at this time. I had sent back Colombe and Allen with Pell to get him out of the way.

I decided the chief fire was coming from the wood in front from behind the wall. So I took my Lewis gun with two drums of ammunition (we only had four left) and got on top of the tank behind the facine. From here I could see over the wall. I ordered Forman to open fire with his gun on to the lodge to keep them from hitting me from that side. I fired into the wood over the facine and saw the enemy begin to run about and clear out. They all cleared out or stopped firing pretty quickly, and then my gun jammed and became too hot to hold.

At this moment the enemy led a counter-attack through the gap between the lodge and the wood. I only saw an officer run out in front waving a small stick and pointing at me. I decided it was time to leave, and I came off that tank in record time.

I found my crew had run out of ammunition. I shouted to them to clear out, as I decided to fall back to the trenches behind, which were easier to hold. There were only five of us now. As we ran back, I got behind a fold in the ground and tried to open fire again, but my gun wouldn't fire. So I hared back and we finally got to Point **A2** (about 80 yards behind). I found the Seaforths were already there. This was an immense relief, as you can imagine.

I met Edwards there, and he said everything was going splendidly. A moment later a sniper got him through the head, and he died a bit later. I thereupon took over the company – chiefly supported by a Seaforth sergeant named Gray. Their ammunition had practically run out, so that we were still in a rotten position. I got hold of an enemy machine-gun, which we had taken previously, and as there was a lot of ammunition, we opened fire. The enemy had stopped at Point **B** and along that line, and we kept their heads down with this fire. I subsequently took the lock out of this gun and that I also sent back to you.

About half an hour afterwards, the enemy counter-attacked the Black Watch on our left and drove them back. I got hold of the sergeant, and he said it was all O.K., so we hung on – we had nowhere to retreat to anyhow! Fortunately the Black Watch had not gone back far, so our flank was not exposed. At last an aeroplane of ours came over, and we lit our flares to show where we had gone.

From this time on the position seemed to be stalemate. An enemy aeroplane came over flying very low, and we opened fire on it. Most of our time was occupied firing at their snipers in the trees opposite.

Some time later Colonel Mackenzie, the Seaforth commander, came round, and I was relieved by another Seaforth officer. Mackenzie told me to go back as 'you are no good without your bloody tank'. Nothing more could be done that day. We went back to our rallying point – Sergt. O'Toole, L/Cpl Allen, Richardson and L/Cpl Forman. I discovered that all had gone well except on our immediate front, and they hoped that would go soon as the village was nearly surrounded.

By the time I got back to Havrincourt, it was 7 p.m. and a gentle rain was falling. It was then that I discovered that my face was covered with blood! I got an awful shock but found it was only the result of the small pieces of tank that had stuck in my face. These little chips came out bit by bit later on. I got quite a large piece from my right ear! My right hand still has some very small pieces in it; you can just see little blue spots under the skin.[1]

Quainton again had very bad luck. His tank ran out of petrol in front of the German guns, and he lost four of his men from a direct hit. He was just in front of a sunk road, and by pouring whisky into the carburettor and throwing in his clutch the engine started, and he just toppled the tank into the road safe from direct fire! It sounds rather funny, but I wouldn't have been in his place for any amount. Cohen was knocked out and very badly wounded. I have not seen him since. Stokes was killed at the beginning of the battle by a direct hit. Greene

---

[1] [Visible for the rest of his life. *F.B.*]

also was killed. The battalion had about twelve tanks left. The remainder attacked next day, and we were left with six undamaged tanks by the 23rd. The crews were completely exhausted by then.

The next day after the battle (21st), we had our interview with the O.C. Company (now Gatehouse, as Bargate had been wounded). We gave our reports of the action; Gatehouse said my report would be confirmed and that I should be recommended for the Military Cross. I was, of course, very surprised, as I expected a row for losing my tank. Well, they found out from the Seaforths what had happened and confirmed my report. To my surprise the Colonel called for me, and I had to give my report again. He congratulated me on it, and he said, 'I have decided to recommend you not for the Military Cross but the Victoria Cross'. I was too flabbergasted for words. I found subsequently that I had been mentioned in the infantry brigade report on the battle, and that is what had settled the matter – Colonel Mackenzie had sent in a most flowery report of the show!

It was now understood that we were to go into rest. We improved our camp and polished up our buttons and so on. We were all very dirty, and as we had had no change of clothes, we were somewhat verminous as well. Although the prospect of rest pleased us, our nerves were very much on edge, and we hardly spoke civilly to each other! We made ourselves fairly comfortable in our camp, which was very near our starting-point for the action – just inside Havrincourt Wood. The sound of the guns went further and further from us, and we could only just hear the explosion of our bigger guns.

On the 28th we were informed that the Germans were going to counter-attack. A feint attack was to be made on our right flank, and the main attack on our left. No danger was expected as we were well prepared.

Nothing more happened till the morning of the 30th. We then heard terrific gunfire in front of us. This died down after about an hour. At about 10.30 a rumour suddenly started that the enemy had broken right through on our right. We of course laughed it off. But a moment or two later on the crest on our right there appeared an A.S.C. wagon and horses bolting like mad with no driver. This looked suspicious. Then another appeared, and at the same time our wood was shelled by *field guns*. This *was* uncanny, as up to that time we were at least four miles out of range. The situation was obviously serious, and it seemed that the preposterous rumour was, after all, true. While

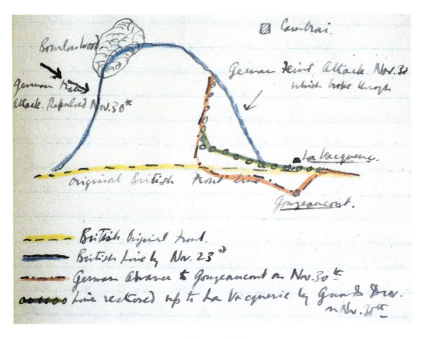

Figure 17
Rough diagram of battles November 20th–30th.

we were wondering what could have happened, the order suddenly came to our company to stand to arms.

The officers were hurriedly called together, and we were given the following information. Apparently the left flank of the salient had withstood the enemy sham attack. But the feint attack, thanks to the low morale and panic of two divisions, had given way, and the enemy were through (Figure 17). No details were known except that the Guards had gone up that morning and the enemy at that moment were advancing and were believed to be about 1,500 yards in front of us. They had taken Gouzeaucourt, which was behind the front line, as it was on November 20th. We were to prepare our tanks (the three left in our company – only six were left in the whole battalion) for action and make up crews to man them. This was done at once. The entire company was then put on to cart ammunition and so on to the tanks. All was ready in about three-quarters of an hour. This was pretty good work, as we had not a single crew complete, but just had to make them up somehow. All the tanks were unfit and had to be put into order and stocked with ammunition. After the tanks were cleared for action, we found that we had about six officers and 60 men with nothing to do. Without tanks we were useless. It was decided, therefore, that all 'unemployed' men should march back to Ytres and entrain, as had been arranged before the break-through occurred. I was told off to march back, and Quainton was to remain as a tank commander.

We fell in and marched off. It was about 3 p.m. when we left the wood, and, as we did so, four German aeroplanes came over flying very low down the road, firing their machine-guns. None of our men was hit.

We picked up news as we went. The Germans had apparently got through so fast that they had captured our guns where they fired. That accounted for the sudden cessation of the bombardment. The Guards had marched up and just stopped the gap. By about 6 p.m. news came through that the Guards had not only stopped the Germans but had driven them back to La Vacquerie – a place about 1,000 yards in front of our original front line on the right of the salient. In spite of this, the situation was very critical indeed, and the whole 3rd British Army was in danger of being cut off. With this news in our ears and with the sight of the Very lights going up in front, we lay down in a ruined village and tried to sleep. The demoralization amongst our troops everywhere was apparent. They were tired out after long fighting.

One of the most demoralizing things, which we were to experience often in the future, was the *silence* that followed the enemy breakthrough. Hitherto we always had felt that the cessation of artillery fire meant the end of the show. Now we had learnt that it might mean a complete breakthrough – the capture of our guns and the silence consequent upon the advance of theirs. The next morning we marched to a place near Ytres and entrained. We travelled back across the Somme battlefields to a place called Méaulte about two miles from Albert and quite near Brayé. It had been a mile or two behind our lines before the 1915 Somme battle. We went into a hut camp here. There was not much room, and the huts were very bad. The country was desolate, and it was very cold. But we were very thankful and slept in peace that night.

The next day we were ordered to relieve the men we had left with our remaining tanks in the Cambrai salient. I was told off to

go in the party with my crew: Richardson, who was pretty well all right – he only had flesh wounds, Colombe, L/Cpl Allen, my driver, and Forman. Allen, the left gunner, also came, but I knew he would not be much use.

The officer over us was Capt. Clifford. He was a dreadful individual. He behaved like a stable boy, was quite unscrupulous and blustered enormously. Carter was the other fellow. He had only joined our battalion recently – just before Cambrai, in fact – and had come to my section. Bagshaw was not detailed, and I was the only officer from 8 Section.

Carter was a most astounding fellow. He had knocked about East all his life and had seen a lot of fighting. He was aged about 45 and was a 2nd Lieut. I have never seen him even look mildly perturbed in the hottest action and nor had anyone else. He was an agnostic and summed up his philosophy for the war by saying that 'if it was a question of German Empire or British Empire, he backed the British, and moral issues be blowed. Fighting wasn't Christian ever before, and certainly wasn't Christian now'. He was a first-class man and absolutely straight and honest.

A fourth member of our party was a fellow named Hauser. He was about 20 years old, fussy, an infernal nuisance to his superior officers and a plague to his men. He was never seen to look frightened or in

---

Figure 18
The village of Flesquières. This photo was taken on Nov. 20th. Just before this the 51st Division took it in their first attack in the morning. The 6th Seaforths, who were following my tank, have remained in the village, while other troops have gone forward, leaving them to rest. The divisional artillery limbers are just going through Coutaing. It was at the far end of the road that runs off the left side of the picture that the Germans massed to make the counter-attack when I was on the top of my tank (see below). Note how little the village is knocked about. This shows how little shell-fire there was and what a surprise the attack was to the enemy.

To Coutaing

To my end of the village

any way worried in an action and was kind-hearted and efficient. He called himself an agnostic and talked about the war like the oldest inhabitant of the most boring club in London. He was very short and wore glasses like the portholes of a battleship. I will give you a story of him that is typical: we were up at Ypres and owing to the shocking weather and conditions generally, had been told not to take our tanks out for the usual daily test. Hauser said the order was rot and took his tank out. He spent half the morning making his crew potter about the tank while he stood on the roof and swore at them. While he wasn't looking, he stepped backwards off the tank and fell about 6 feet. This didn't worry him, but it amused the men. At last he drove out. The place was a quagmire, and it was about 12 midday. His driver warned him continually they would get ditched. 'I don't care if we do. We are going out', was his comment. The driver kept up his complaints, and at last Hauser lost his temper. He got out and beckoned to the driver to follow with the tank. He then led the tank smack into a gigantic quagmire. Opening the door of the tank, he bawled out, 'Now you jolly well *are* stuck!' It took them till 2 p.m. to get out. The men got back, cursing and swearing, for their main meal two hours late.

In spite of all this, he was respected for his absolute fearlessness in action and the fact that he never gave a man a job to do that he wouldn't do himself. He was a useful fellow to have.

We had all got clean clothes and were feeling cleaner, but nevertheless very sick at having to go up. We entrained that night and arrived next day at Havrincourt Wood. We took over a line of tanks. They were stretched across the country about two-and-a-half miles behind our front line – in fact, on just about the line that our trenches took before the opening of the battle. The tanks were about 300 yards apart and so formed a kind of line of small forts – like the German pill-boxes at Ypres. If the enemy broke through, we were to allow our troops to pass through and were then to fight a rear-guard action. Such were our very vague orders.

The troops we relieved were D Battalion, who looked in pretty poor spirits and didn't cheer us much. Since all our tanks were in the open, they had camouflage nets over them. Every night these had to be taken off so the tank could get into action without confusion, and at dawn they had to be put on again.

The crews took over their tanks and saw everything was correct. It was now 6 p.m. I had a tank opposite the extreme right of our battalion front at the start of the November 20th action. We felt a bit lonely in our little bunches of eight scattered over the wide front. We ate some bully, made a bivouac close against the tank and, after arranging sentry duties, went to sleep. It was very cold, and we had not much to keep us warm – a very thin blanket each. We were woken about 1 a.m. by a bombing raid. This is a very unpleasant thing to hear, especially when you fear a breakthrough. It sounds just like an artillery duel, but you don't get the scream of the shells. It sounds very near. It ended in about three-quarters of an hour. (See map Marcoing 57.C. N.E. The place where we stationed our tanks was Q18 b.q.o. approximately. The trenches we sheltered in to cook food and avoid shells were old British ones and therefore not marked on this bit of front. They were never put in unless of vital importance, and then only the small bit needed, e.g. at our jumping-off place for November 20th.)

We stayed like this for two or three days and began to feel confident. The days were all cold and cloudy and the country rather desolate. There is something uncanny about being camped on an old battlefield – particularly when you yourself have fought over it quite recently. We were not visited during these days. Capt. Clifford remained by one tank and wouldn't budge. The food was poor – eternal cold bully and biscuits. This, combined with the strain of a breakthrough at any moment – which always threatened us – and the cold, made us very miserable.

Then suddenly we received orders to move forward. It was about 6 p.m., and we had just started getting ready some hot tea. Unfortunately we could not do this job and have something warm, as apparently the matter was urgent. Clifford put in his first appearance, accompanied by Col. Hankey (later Brigadier – he now commanded the composite battalion of which we were a part). Apparently a breakthrough was expected. The Germans had massed even more troops, and the 61st Division, who were in front of us, felt they wanted us to support them much nearer their line. It was now growing dusk. We started up our tanks, and the four that were under Clifford started to go forward as soon as we had collected. Our task was easy, as we could nearly see the place we were aiming for – Villers-Plouich. We arrived there at about 8 p.m. and camouflaged our tanks. We were about 1,000 yards from the front line and *just* out of sight of the German lines. No fires were allowed.

Our tanks were already prepared for action, so we simply gave orders that men were to eat some bully beef and biscuits and then, after posting sentries, go to sleep. Clifford went to infantry brigade H.Q. in order to be in touch with the infantry. The moment an attack was opened, he was to come back to us (a distance of about half a mile) and warn us. With this news, he disappeared. Carter, Hauser and I then went to sleep in a small hole in the ground. The men slept under the tanks. We felt very miserable, as we had no idea what was going to happen, and really felt quite useless if the enemy did attack. We didn't know the country, we had no orders as to the direction in which we were to retire in the event of retreat, and our tanks were quite useless for defence anyhow.

It was freezing cold that night and next day. At 11 a.m. we managed to get some hot stew going over a fire we made in a disused trench. We decided this was safe from view and were careful to use nothing damp. With the aid of large doses of petrol we kept the fires smokeless. We all, officers and men, collected round this and simply swallowed it. It was our first hot meal for over 30 hours and the first meal proper since mid-day the day before. We felt absolutely changed after it! We washed it down with scalding hot tea and felt warm and comfortable for the first time that day. The sky was a grey, leaden colour and the air was bitterly cold, so we felt really grateful. In order to keep men from moping too much, we put them on to the work of digging holes to lie in. The idea was that if we were shelled, they would be safe from all but a direct hit. Also, they would be much warmer. This kept them busy and made them anticipate a good night. The feeling of comfort and security did much to improve their spirits. After dark we drove the tanks over the hole that had been dug and so made a roof. This unfortunately proved a very dangerous thing.

When we awoke next morning, we found the crews apparently dead under their tanks. We hauled them out and to our intense relief they began to show signs of life. We broke small tubes of very strong ammonia under their noses so they inhaled it. This made them violently sick, but it did what we wanted. As soon as they could swallow, we poured a diluted dose of ammonia down their throats. This finally pulled them round, and two or three hours after they were all right. What had happened was this: the tank engine had been run and had simply poured petrol fumes and carbon monoxide from its exhaust into the hole it was over. When the men got in to sleep an hour or so later, these heavy fumes had sunk to the bottom of the holes and stupefied them. Another hour or two, and we should have lost two crews. As you can imagine, we were very thoroughly frightened by this business and took great precautions ever afterwards. The experience was certainly very valuable to me, as this particular form of poisoning was to become a common thing in the later tanks. I now knew how to cope with it and was saved from some very awkward scrapes in 1918 by applying the same remedies to men who were apparently done for.

The rest of the day passed more or less uneventfully except for the fact that the Boche smelt a rat and started to shell our little area. We took cover and lost neither men nor tanks. We simply had the misery of enduring an hour and a half's desultory strafe from 5.9's.

In the evening we were cheered by the arrival of three artillery officers who were going up to observation posts to reconnoitre. They stopped to talk, and we had the usual flow of 'news'. The artillery are notorious liars and always cheerful liars. They assured us the enemy would attack the next morning and that they would suffer hopeless defeat; King George had been assassinated and Horatio Bottomley had seized the throne; the Germans had sued for peace, which would probably be signed within three days. With this and earnest protestations of truthfulness they departed! It's a funny thing, but cheeriness was every bit as infectious as gloom, and these yarns, with the method of telling, quite set us up for the night. But we were to have a rude shock. Clifford had not been near us since he had departed to Brigade H.Q. in a state of panic. We had been left entirely to our own devices. All matters of water, rations, orders for possible defence, routine orders etc. had been settled by Carter. Carter as senior officer simply carried on as commander of the section. After our first morning we talked things over and gave Clifford up as hopeless. We first sat down and decided to draw up, to the best of our abilities, a set of operation orders. It was a matter of vital necessity that we should. If we did not, there was nothing to prevent our straggling everywhere and losing touch hopelessly. We thereupon arranged what to do if the infantry held fast and also what we should do in the event of a general retirement. We mapped out a line of retreat. We then drew up routine orders and sent orders to the rear, giving particulars of rations and so forth.

Thus, as far as we were concerned, Clifford might not have existed, and we forgot him.

That night we had just turned in when suddenly we heard a great puffing and blowing, the tarpaulin was dragged off our hole, and we saw Clifford's face peering at us out of the moonlight, 'I say, you chaps' (puff–puff!) 'the Germans' (puff–puff!) 'are going to attack!' He was nearly in tears. Carter slowly sat up and looked at him and then said 'Well, what about it?' Immediately an incoherent shower of words rushed out as we got up. Clifford said all the men were to be turned out and tanks manned at once. This we did. It was bitterly cold and a very quiet night. We all got into our tanks and sat and shivered. After a bit I went round to Carter's tank, and we then went on to Hauser. Here Clifford was. Carter turned to Clifford and said, 'Now that we've got all those poor devils out of their holes and frozen them to death, what orders have you for us?' Clifford said, 'I don't know. How on earth should I know? I only know they are going to attack. You know as much as I do.' 'But aren't you going to issue any orders? What are we to do?' 'Oh, I don't know – just keep amongst them and shoot 'em down, shoot 'em down'. We then asked if he knew when the attack was supposed to come off. 'In the morning or any time between now and then probably'. We simply couldn't get an atom of sense out of him. The whole time his teeth were chattering and he was just whining away. So we just shrugged our shoulders and proceeded to go over the plans we had previously thought out together. After a little, Clifford attempted to assert himself but was met with a stern, 'Will you kindly refrain from shoving in your oar?' from Carter, so that ended him. It's really rather funny looking at it now, but it was far from funny then. We were very cold and very miserable. Our orders were nil, and if anything went wrong we should be blamed for it, as we made up our plans without considering Clifford. The enemy had apparently at last decided to attack. We had an absolute fool in command. Added to this, the officers and men were not at all fit for scrapping. We were all more or less demoralized, and personally I was fit for nothing.

We stayed up all night waiting for dawn. Nothing happened, and finally at midday we were told the attack wasn't coming. Clifford cleared off to the H.Q. dugout again, to our intense relief.

The rest of our stay here passed in much the same way as the early part. We could do very little moving about as the Germans would shell us, so we had to lie pretty tight. L/Cpl Allen was nearly killed. A shell landed near him and knocked him over with concussion. He was fortunately not wounded but was struck dumb with shell-shock. He stayed some time in England and then came back to the base in France. As he was no good, he was sent back to England and was still stammering in January 1919. I haven't heard from him since and cannot get into touch with him. So I lost a jolly good man. At the time, he was about the best tank driver in the battalion. He was not strong physically, but he had any amount of pluck, and he really knew his job very well. He had been very slow and too careful when he first came to France, but after the Ypres action had given him experience he was very good indeed.

At last we heard we were to be relieved. We moved back one evening to Havrincourt Wood, and our tanks were taken over by a section of the 4th Battalion. With intense relief we said goodbye to Havrincourt Wood and trained back to the rest of the battalion at Méaulte.

We spent about four days here when again orders came that our battalion had to send a detachment to man some tanks at Flims in Dessart Wood. This time Quainton was to go up and so was Hauser and one or two others. I volunteered for the job as I wanted to be with Quainton and drew the line at keeping Clifford & co. company at Méaulte. We trained up to the wood at Flims (a ruined village just behind the right flank of the original front of attack on November 24th) and there took over from 4th Battalion some awful old derelict tanks. We were now some two miles to the right of Havrincourt Wood.

The whole country was very desolate and snow-covered and cold. The wood was not very much shelled. We lived in tents and were very well off. We were about three miles behind the line. Our stay was uneventful. We had to drive our tanks to Havrincourt one day for a false alarm, but we came back very shortly afterwards. Winter had set in hard, and there was little chance of a German attack. The wood was frequently bombed by aeroplane, but that was really all the war we saw. This was a great relief to us as the 4th Battalion had to make nightly expeditions to no-man's land to haul 9.2 guns that had been lost in the retreat and were now lying between the trenches,

back behind the lines. It was a bad job, as you had to drive a tank into no-man's land on a pitch-black night and then get out, possibly under machine-gun fire, and make these terrific howitzers fast to a hawser. You then cleared out under a storm of bullets etc. with the gun bumping along behind. I didn't fancy the idea at all myself.

On December 21st we heard we were to go back to rest at last – the rest promised ever since October 10th! We got our tanks ready, and at last we entrained on the afternoon of December 22nd at Flims. We detrained at Plateau – our halting-place from Wailly to Cambrai when we came down to the Nov. 20th action – and started to trek to Méaulte. Our tanks were hopelessly out of order, and it took us the whole day to get from Plateau to Méaulte – about four miles. Thus we got into camp at about 5.30 p.m. on the 24th December. When we got in, we found all preparations made for Christmas and most people feeling very considerably cheerier than they had done previously. There was no chance of the battalion having to go up to the line again till the next year's campaigning opened. We were really and truly in winter quarters at last. Our battalion had had its first taste of war.

Christmas Day dawned in a heavy snow storm, and I think it will be as well to describe it to give you some idea of our happy life behind the lines and the morale of our battalion after its adventures.

First, as to personnel: Major de Freine, our Company Commander at Ypres, had gone and so had Bargate his successor. He

---

Figure 19

British defence on Nov. 30th, 1917. This picture shows the Villers-Plouich Front. The Germans have just been held up by the Guards Division's counter-attack and are opening up with their guns. The front line runs about 500 yards in front of the man taking cover here. This was the part we were knocking round under Capt. Clifford. Our position (which we took up some eight days later, when we came up) was over the crest and about 500 yards in front of the man. Thus we were just about where the front line was when this picture was taken. By then the front line had gone on about 1,000 yards. The picture gives a good idea of the deserted appearance of a show in recently 'inhabited' country. The white chalk you see everywhere added to the cold, miserable look of the place.

had been slightly shocked at Cambrai but was now back again. The Colonel had been very strongly condemned by the G.O.C. 51st Div. for his behaviour at Cambrai and was almost certain to be recalled, although he fought hard against it. A and C had had several changes in officers. Gatehouse, our second in command, had gone over to command C Company. B Company were left with Bargate in command and Cook second in command – he was formerly company reconnaissance officer and was a bit later in hospital. Clifford, Bagshaw, Homfray, and Harrison were our section commanders. They were all, except Harrison, regarded with contempt and deserved it all. Homfray was Quainton's section commander and was as wildly incompetent as any man I ever met. He was so bad that, in order to get rid of him, our company were determined to promote him to second in command to a company – such promotion meant he would have to go to another company. In the end C Company got him. By August 1918 they had had enough of him, and he was promoted to O.C. Company in order to get rid of him again. He was thus transferred to the 1st Battalion!

All these section commanders were very little better than animals in talk, in action or in manners.

The men were in a fairly bad way also. They had had bad fighting and poor rations. The camp was on top of a bleak and desolate

---

Figure 20
Tank breaking through German wire. This photo gives you some idea of German wire. It is typical of the defensive wire at Cambrai. At Ypres the wire had all been blown up by weeks of ceaseless bombardment. At Cambrai they relied on tanks to crush paths through it for the infantry. This is how we did it. You can also get some idea of the country at Ypres when you realize that all this kind of stuff – sometimes belts 50 yards thick – was all churned into the ground. You seemed to have barbed wire sprouting out of the ground like weeds. In 1918, when we held parts of the old Ypres battlefields, we simply stumbled through old shell-holes overgrown with thistles and with the remains of this kind of wire protruding to trip you up. Of that I'll write later, though. You get some idea of the power of a tank when you realize that this wire, with its iron knife-rests and so on, was simply squashed out flat without affecting the tank in the very slightest!

hill. The whole district was on the edge of the devastated Somme area. There was nothing to do. It was very cold and blowing hard the whole time we were there. Snow used to come in through the cracks in the huts and cover the floor about an inch deep.

The combination of all these things proved too much. The men were given unlimited food and beer. No attempt was made to organize anything or do anything decently. By 10 a.m. Cook (the second in command of the company) was carried to bed dead drunk. Homfray was hopelessly maudlin and collapsed a little later. By about 11 a.m. Quainton and I felt as if we were in solitary state. Men were just shouting about and lying drunk round the camp. No one interfered.

The 4th Battalion, encamped near us, were even worse. It took them about a week to get sober.

The whole day was just spent in an orgy of eating and drinking and beastliness generally. Quainton and I were about tired of it by 6 p.m. and left camp to walk out in the dark and snow, as that seemed considerably more cheerful than staying in camp. On the distant horizon we could see the never-tiring Very lights rise up, flicker, and die away again. We came to a Y.M.C.A. hut and found a service going on. We went in. The place was bare and feebly lit.

Figure 21
Ribécourt on Nov. 20th. This was taken during the Nov. 20th attack. It was on the right flank of our battalion and so did not affect me personally. I have put it in as it was one of our landmarks and, more particularly, because it gives you a very good idea of village fighting. Note again that the village is hardly touched. When this photo was taken, machine-gun bullets were coming down the street and one grazed the camera. So you see that an advance was no fun. You can see no enemy, and yet death may not be far off if you aren't careful. You just creep round corners hoping for the best. As a matter of fact, in this you can just see two Germans far up the street scuttling across the road. Neither side shells the village as they don't know who's in it. The place is very quiet except for the crack of machine-gun and rifle, and an occasional tile that clatters down. I have put this in very largely as you can get some idea from this of our 1918 fighting, which I will describe later. All the points I have mentioned are typical of what we got then, so when you read of our village shows of 1918, look at this.

About twenty men were present, and all crowded up at one end of the hut. The service dragged on. No attempt was made to sing carols or Christmas hymns – that would have been more than we could stand. The sermon came – the text, 'Peace on earth, goodwill to men'. It was proved, apparently to the satisfaction of the preacher, that this was idealism – our real task was to hate evil and so, presumably, to hate Germans. We sang a closing hymn and cleared out.

We got back to camp, after trudging through snow and slush, at about 10 p.m., and thus ended our first Christmas in France. Had everyone gone mad?

Such was our battalion at the end of 1917 – dazed and brutish without hope or care. Another year was coming, and we all knew it would be the most desperate fighting yet. But 1918 was still far on the horizon. Few thought of it, and few cared. But for those who did, it was not a pleasant outlook. A hopeless set of officers in France and a country at home that realized nothing – that seemed our support. As for religion – well, that was nothing to do with war.

Figure 22
The devastated area. The old Somme battle resulted in the capture of this country – after it was thoroughly destroyed by the enemy. It now formed the 'rest' area for British troops.

1918

After the battalion had recovered from Christmas and New Year, we settled down to ordinary camp routine. Each company had a few tanks, all in very bad condition. These were at a tank park about a mile from our camp. Our chief work in the very cold weather we were having was to keep tanks in condition. They had to be run constantly to prevent freezing in the cooling system. Also they had to be moved, as otherwise even the tracks froze! You see, mud always got in between the actual chain track and the rollers which the track ran on. This mud would freeze and become like cement. This was so powerful that if you started your engine and tried to run the tank with the tracks frozen, all that happened was the complete destruction of the transmission. We had enormous trouble with this in all our tank shows in cold weather. All the time we had been standing-to behind Cambrai it had been a constant source of anxiety, as you can imagine, for we were always supposed to be ready for action, and any mistake with this would have meant possible disaster if an attack started.

The work was dull and usually carelessly and badly done. A section from each company would go down each morning and simply clean up the tanks and break up frost by using improvised petrol flares. The remainder of each company was employed in squad drill and so on. This was the official side of our life. But off parade was another thing. Amiens was quite within reach of a car, and an occasional trip to Amiens used to lighten the burden of existence for the officers. Quainton and I went in once or twice and had quite good meals at the Restaurant du Cathedral. The whole time we were at Méaulte we also walked to the officers' club at Albert – about two kilometres off.

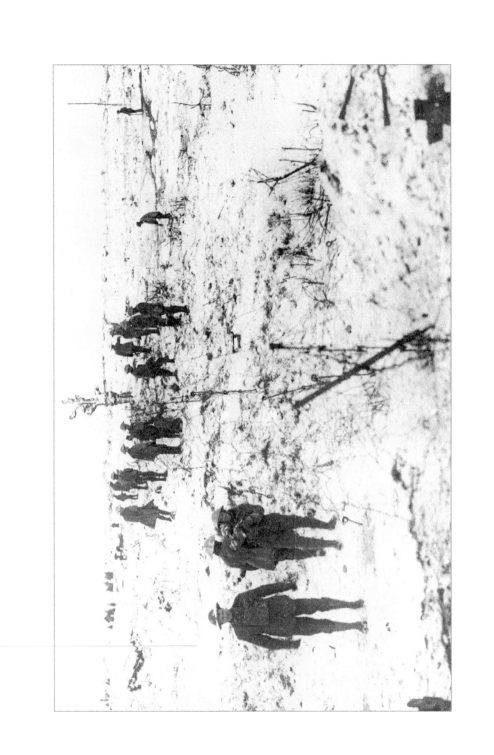

The whole battalion was in rather an unsettled state. The personnel was changing and promotions were in the air. Jealousy and whispering became prominent as we unthawed and began to realize we were safe from the enemy for a bit. Clifford, who had been dubbed hero and awarded an imaginary medal (the V.P. – for distinguished bravery at Villers-Plouich) began to fear he would not be made a captain, and was afraid Quainton and I would, as I at any rate had been promised a section. At last Quainton and I were sent on courses. He was to go to a tank driving school at Wailly, the place we were at before we moved down for the Cambrai action. I was sorry for him, as it was a desolate spot and he would be little better off there than at Méaulte. I was sent on an instructor course to Merlimont, the place where we had done our battle practice before we went into the Ypres battle. An officer named Johnson, a tank commander in 7 Section (under Clifford and with Hauser) came with me. He was a very good fellow, I found as I got to know him better. He had been in the battalion a bit longer than I had and was a bit senior to me. He was very slightly built but had endless courage and could stick it like the best. He was made section commander later. We went to Merlimont, which is on the coast about five miles north of Étaples, by tender (a fast motor lorry for carrying small spares etc.). We found ourselves part of a number of officers sent from each battalion. Curiously enough, all the people seemed to be jolly good fellows and not a rotter there. We had a house to ourselves and very short hours of work. The whole time we were there we had blue skies and golden sands, and not a breath of war. It was simply magnificent. We never worked in the afternoon, but just sat in the shade on the veranda, smoked our pipes and watched the sea.

As the result of the exam, I was made gunnery instructor to the 4th Tank Brigade. General Hankey, the brigadier, came down once or twice to see how brigade training was going on. Every week a

---

Figure 23
Cambrai front under snow. Preparing wire for the defences against the March attack. The scene was very much like this when we were 'standing to' at the end of 1917 after Nov. 30th.

company from the 4th Brigade came and went through a course, which I mapped out and supervised. So he came down to supervise *me*! He spoke to me two or three times and at last suggested that I had had enough fighting and would do better to take on a job as permanent brigade instructor at Merlimont. This I refused. I explained that I thought it was a job for a fit man and not for me, and he saw my point and agreed. The first week a company from D Battalion came down. It was commanded by a Captain Nixon, who was afterwards to be transferred to our company as second in command. I got on quite well with them. The next week, A Company from our battalion came, and all went smoothly. Then suddenly I was ordered back to the battalion. We were going up to the 'line'. The rest was over. This was about the end of February.

When I got back, I had the D.S.O. ribbon pinned on me by Ellis, G.O.C. Tank Corps in France. I had been told previously that I had been awarded it.

The battalion then drew tanks and prepared. Quainton had gone on leave and was due back. But he didn't come, and I heard from him to say he was down with shell-shock. This was a big knock for me, as I felt now that I was almost alone in the battalion. I knew very few officers, and of those I did know, the majority were rotten and very unpleasant.

We entrained and went up – the same old business. Again, as we approached we saw the Very lights rise up, flicker and disappear. As we drew nearer and our train went slower, acute depression and nerves settled on us all. Whenever we stopped we could hear the guns. Once, when we stopped, we found it was because of bombing. We waited and saw bombs being dropped by the line in front. They came nearer, and suddenly we found them dropping round us. By this time we were all lying on the permanent way. Fortunately, all fell at the bottom of the bank, and we had no casualties. The train went on at last. We arrived at Tincourt, our destination, and drew our tanks up to a wood about two miles off.

Our stay here was uneventful. We were in the 5th Army and in the devastated regions again. We were five miles from the front line. The weather was awful – snow and slush everywhere – and there was no escape from the devastation. We lived in huts in the wood.

At last I got leave. I need not say much about it, as you probably remember it, Mother. When at last we came up to town, we heard the news of the start of the March battle. We had been warned it would start on the 11th at first, so I knew it would not be long. The first news we got was when Mother and I were walking in Hyde Park. I bought an evening paper and saw '16,000 prisoners taken by the enemy', and above everything else my eyes were attracted by one passage. 'The enemy have taken Tincourt and we are holding him in our battle positions.' Now Tincourt was our camp. I also knew that there weren't any battle positions there. When I left – and I found they were never touched again – the trenches were just marked out by flags, but they had not been dug. There simply were no defences whatever at Tincourt, and I knew the thing was a lie. Also, Tincourt was five miles behind the 'line'. That is to say, the enemy had advanced five miles on our bit of front alone and had passed all our defences. I never had such a shock in my life, and I knew we were very near disaster. I think I told you, Mother, that it was all right and so on. But it was almost incredible to me. We saw 'Chou-Chin-Chow', but of course it meant nothing to me, and I've no doubt it was the same for you, as I was to go back to France next morning. I had had two days' leave extension to get my medal as it was, but even then I never felt sure I should go straight into action, and I knew the battalion must already have had its show.

I need hardly say that I didn't sleep that night. I simply walked about the room and didn't dare to think what was happening. At last I saw the sky grow grey and knew my leave was over. I shaved and went down to the dingy early breakfast. I don't think any of us were very lively! The cab came, and the driver made a forced attempt at being cheery by saying, 'Back again soon, sir!' and off I went. Victoria was the usual scene – men lying asleep on the platform, women rushing about, and khaki everywhere. But everyone was frightfully cheery. All were convinced it was the end, and all were cracking jokes about going back to camps and trenches now miles behind the German lines.

When we reached Boulogne, we found all were stopped from going up the line, owing to congestion. The rail services were completely disorganized by the enemy advance, and there was no knowledge of the whereabouts of the units of most officers and men. We were sent up to the camps on the hill outside Boulogne, and there we did odd parades and things while waiting. Many officers flouted all orders and left Boulogne by various stratagems, determined to rejoin their units by hook or crook – working their way up on transport lorries and so on. At last orders came through for Tank Corps. We had to report at depot. This was at Le Treport, and there we went. It was a very fine camp, and very finely organized. We had very little to do there and spent most of the time harassing the orderly room for news of our units and permission to rejoin them.

On the 7th April I heard that our battalion – now called the 5th – was to be relieved. They were in the 'line' as infantry near Amiens. On the 8th they came out, and on the 9th I rejoined them at rest in a village near Blangy (where they had gone after Méaulte and while I was at Merlimont). I found them all very cheery. Nearly all the old stagers were there, but nearly all the reinforcements had been lost again. The tank commanders had nearly all gone, but most of the people who came out with me had been acting section commanders and so on in the battle and had missed the worst part of the show – trying to save a tank with engine trouble from a rapidly advancing enemy. They told many amusing stories of the retreat – most things are funny when you are safe. Promotions had come through in some cases, and we all knew how we stood. I was not yet a captain but was a section commander, and it was just a question of time before I got gazetted. A certain Fairbanks, who had led a very chequered and shady career as a civilian, was commander of No. 7. Bagshaw had been sent off on some safer and more congenial job; and I had 8 Section in his place. Clifford was in command of No. 5 Section, and an American named Robinson had No. 6. He spent most of his time talking. He was really harmless but was subsequently put under arrest for something or other and lost his job. The men were much as before. Carter had gone from 8 Section to be company reconnaissance officer, Cook was still second in command and Bargate O.C. Company. Our colonel was new – O'Kelly from King Edward's Horse. He was a kind but voluble and excitable old liar, who was determined to get the D.S.O. at all costs. His reputation, outside the battalion, was terrific. The battalion complained bitterly that all through the March battle he had dashed about in absolute safety in a car, offering to hold the 'line' everywhere and anyhow with his battalion – the troops of which he was too frightened to go near. But these things were only subjects for amusement, for we could only see prolonged rest ahead of us, and Amiens seemed to be safe. In order to minimize the effect of the enormous casualties we were having, the battalion was arranged on a new plan.

A certain number of officers and men were to be earmarked before each action and kept behind as a nucleus on which to build up the battalion from reinforcements. This gave scope for resting men who had had heavy fighting, but in practice you wanted good men too much to leave them out. So as usual the brunt fell on the best.

We lived this happy and contented kind of life without a care. News came of the German breakthrough up North on April 9th, but we remained calm and serene. But suddenly on April 12th at 5 a.m. I was awoken by Parkins, my batman. The battalion was to parade at once.

This did not look like amusement, and it wasn't. By 6 a.m. we were all out. The troops had to be inspected for action at once. We went through all the weary paraphernalia mechanically – gas masks, tin hats, iron rations, identity discs (the most suggestive of all) and the rest. At 8 a.m., as we stood on parade overhauling everything and doing the hundred and one jobs that had to be done, a large staff car rolled up, and General Ellis got out. He made no inspection but a short speech. The situation in the north was, he said, very serious and critical. The enemy had broken through and had not been stopped. The Tank Corps had been called on again and this time as infantry – there were not enough tanks ready and no scope for them if they were. Our record as a battalion made him confident we would do our best. Our job was to hold out in small isolated posts and stay there even if the enemy got through. Then we were to open fire and cut them off.

Such were the words of encouragement for us, and I suppose they were the best that could be given. But none of us was in the mood to cheer or feel we had been done a great honour – that time was past.

By 1 p.m. we had sorted out the 'nucleus', and the battalion was ready. But we had no rifles. We were simply armed as for tank fighting (with Lewis guns), but we had no tanks. We had a midday meal, and at 2 p.m. there drove up a large convoy of lorries, bearing, as a sign, the red sun on a yellow circle. It was the mark of the G.H.Q. Reserve.

The sun had gone in, and it was now becoming cold and miserable. We climbed onto the lorries, waved goodbye to the lucky blighters who were to stay behind, and off the lorries went. The journey was very dusty and beastly. We lay down in the bottom of the lorries and bumped about and tried to keep comfortable. And on we went.

As it was getting dark we arrived near Hazebrouck. But it was not the same bustling town we knew in 1917. Streams of miserable people trailed off along the roads, carrying bundles. The roads presented a weird sight of misery and poverty.

At last we came in sight of the town. The flare of bursting shells could be plainly seen. The Germans must have made a tremendous advance, and this brought it home to us. We were now looking down onto Hazebrouck. Somewhere amongst the trees beyond were the enemy, and only the Guards Division between them and the town. But we had not reached our destination. Hazebrouck marked the nearest point of the enemy – we were travelling across his front.

We skirted Hazebrouck to avoid the German shelling and went on. One had a curiously deserted feeling. You felt you were being pushed into the unknown – into the terror all the inhabitants had been flying. But we had passed even them now. To complete our loneliness, we saw, along the railway, all the signals down and no signs of life, but a very heavy train drawn by two immense goods engines going away from what was now the front line. I suppose it was about the last train, saving army stores, to get away.

Night had now come on, and still we followed roads parallel to the front line. The stars were out, and it was freezing cold. At last we stopped. We had reached a rifle dump. We all got out and filed past three piles. At one we were given a rifle each, at the next an oil bottle and pull-through, and the last a bayonet and scabbard. After a short pause we climbed in and went on. Almost half an hour later we reached our destination and tumbled out of the lorries.

Our company, very sleepy and tired, fell in by the roadside. After a pause we were marched to a farm and allotted a barn. We posted sentries and went to sleep. It was about 2 a.m. At 4 a.m. orders came through to the company, and we were awakened. Our men were to stand to arms at once.

It was pitch-black, so we tried to relieve the darkness by candles. The huge barn just showed up in the dim light as we pulled through rifles, rolled up puttees, tightened up our equipment and swore. It was probably a picturesque scene, but with two hours' sleep in twenty-four and the immediate prospect of action, we let the artistic side look after itself. As soon as the officers had pulled themselves together, we were assembled outside in the courtyard and given

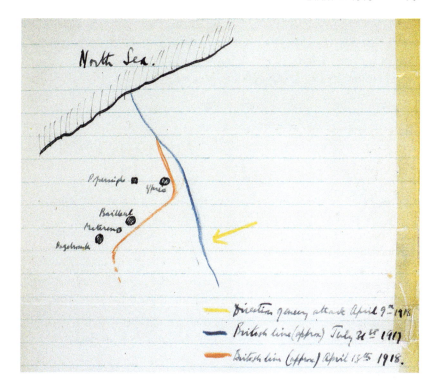

Figure 24
General position after March '18 and April 9th–13th attack. This rough diagram will show you what had happened. The enemy had broken right through and made Ypres the point of a terrific salient. We were now fighting or about to fight in places which were miles behind the line when we were up at Ypres in 1917.

maps. We discovered then that we were near Bailleul and in what had been perfectly peaceful country until the enemy advance. So, for the first time, we were to have fighting amongst houses, gardens and green fields. Briefly, the position was this (Figure 24): the enemy, when last heard of, were being held by miscellaneous British troops some two miles in front of us. There was no shelling and no signs of war, simply because we had very few guns and the enemy had not yet got theirs up – the advance had been too quick for them. They were gathering themselves for the next spring. The position of the front line was unknown. But we were to reinforce at once as the urgent need was for troops – as troops came, so they were being flung into the gaps.

With this, the Colonel gave us his blessing (by messenger and not in the flesh), and we went off. We didn't march, for the following reasons. We had had no sleep. We all carried (i.e. everyone below the rank of captain) a rifle, the full infantry kit, eight drums of Lewis gun ammunition per man and one Lewis gun per six men. Full marching order was bad enough, but this was hopeless.

We trailed on and on and stumbled and cursed as dawn slowly broke on us. What we were going into we didn't know and didn't care – we hadn't 'any b – – – tanks anyway, thank Heaven'.

We went on through peaceful and quite pretty country, and at last stopped at a perfectly good barn. We made tea and ate bully and tried to sleep. The sun, which had come out earlier, was now overclouded, and the air grew chilly.

The second in command of the company, Cook, and the company reconnaissance officer, B. Carter, went to get into touch with the infantry. They found Brigade H.Q. and went from there to Battalion H.Q. In the meantime we persuaded ourselves we should not be wanted in action at all and lay on the straw and stared at the barn roof.

At last Cook and Carter came back, and we watched them talking to Bargate and rustling maps. This did not look hopeful – and it wasn't.

Carter came to me and said I was wanted. I joined the conference and was informed that the infantry wanted a section of Lewis guns *at once* – the rest of the company would follow at night. I was the lucky section commander for the job. So my luckless section fell in, and we went through the old wearisome examination of kit all over again, had tea and pushed off. We were only 800 yards from the front line, so we kept off the road and went over ploughed fields etc. for safety. I halted the section after a time and left them behind a hedge while I went to Battalion H.Q. for orders. I discovered the C.O. was Colonel McNeil – known in England as 'Sapper', the writer of the short war stories. He was commanding the remnants of a Middlesex pioneer battalion – they act as Engineers to their brigade or division as wanted usually, but now had to hold the 'line'. Briefly, the position was as follows: his men held **B** (see diagram, Figure 25). Other

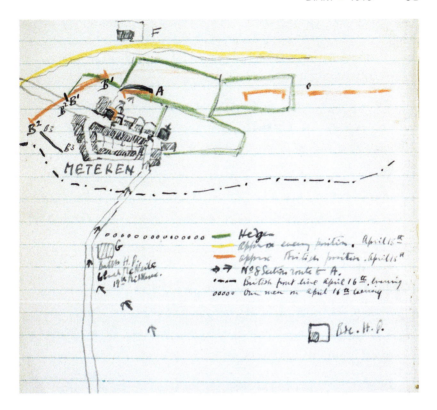

Figure 25

Meteren position. Meteren was on a hill and overlooked the enemy position. It was about 20 feet higher than the surrounding country and very important as it commanded many enemy positions and safeguarded Bailleul. At A my guns could sweep right and left from the left of B to the right of C. It was a very fine position. D was Section H.Q. where I went, and about 20 yards from A. Infantry Battalion H.Q. (G) was about 800 yards from A. No scale given as it is not all to scale.

British troops were along **C**. He wanted us to go to **A** and do it *at once*. An attack was expected at 3 p.m., as the enemy had got a good many guns up now and was in a hurry to break through. It was 2 p.m. now and vitally important that we should get there at once and *stay* there at all costs. The only way was to go there down the main road – quickest and easiest for heavily laden men.

I left at once, and as I was going back, the enemy shells began falling in Meteren. So he *had* got his guns up – that part of the instructions was sound enough at any rate!

We went down the road for all we were worth. When we got into the village, I broke the section into four parties – making one Lewis gun each. We then set off – a gun team at a time to double through the village. I went with the first lot, and Bridges – the other officer in the section – came with the last. It was hard work with all our kit. We stumbled forward as tiles and glass tinkled down all round. Coils of telegraph lines which had been shot down helped to trip us up. After an age (so it seemed), we reached **D**, dashed through the house and lay down panting at the far end of the back garden. In time the remaining lots arrived. Behind cover of the garden hedge, **E**, we opened into extended order. We were just ready to dash forward to **A** when the enemy barrage opened onto Meteren properly and the village began to go up in smoke. We were only just in time. I gave the signal, and we got through the hedge unseen and then dashed forward. As we ran, the enemy opened up heavy machine-gun fire, but they were very wide of the mark, till suddenly they began to hit up the ground in front. But we had practically reached **A**. Once behind the hedge, we fetched out entrenching tools and dug small shallows to sit in. So each man had a kind of hollow to lie in. After about an hour we had each of us made a place about one foot deep, and we began to feel safe. But at the same time we had to do some firing. We had our Lewis guns posted in the hedge, and with these we opened up on some of the enemy we could see moving about by **F**. The shelling grew heavier and heavier, but none of it came our way. At last it died down, and everything grew quiet again. So the enemy attack was not to come after all.

The sun was out again now and just setting. Behind our hedge we proceeded to make ourselves comfortable. It was a beautiful evening, and our business kept us from thought or worry. We dug down about two feet, and up came water. So we started to put up a kind of breastwork. It was like a pleasant little job in somebody's back garden. The sunset on the green fields and the red tiled roofs in the distance looked too pretty to be a battlefield scene.

For reasons best known to themselves, Company H.Q. insisted the actual section was to be left at **A** under Bridges, my second in command, while I went back and saw to arrangements generally.

Actually the idea was not bad – two officers to 16 men was absurd. But it annoyed me at the time, for I still hadn't learnt to appreciate good luck when I got it. As a result I was withdrawn to Company H.Q. – the barn the section had started from. I got back at about 8 p.m.

When I reached H.Q., I had two petrol cans of hot tea made. These were then put into infantry packs stuffed with straw. A stew was also made, and this was similarly put into a petrol box, which was packed with straw.

I then went up with four men, taking this to the section. When we arrived, it was bright moonlight and bitterly cold. The tea was absolutely boiling – too hot to drink at first – and the stew was the same. I felt very proud of myself, as this was about the only part of the line where men were not eating cold bully and biscuits. I really think it set the men up properly, for it was bitterly cold that night. When I got back to H.Q., I made application for Very lights, S.O.S. signal lights and barbed wire. We could have none of them.

In this way the section really was left in a bad position. But they were not the only ones, for the rest of B Company (minus the superfluous officers) went into the 'line' that night. They were in the position **B1 – B1**. Bargate nominally was in command. But he had soon reduced himself to a state of happy insensibility by frequent applications to the bottle. Carter therefore did most of the commanding there was to be done, and if we had only had enough whisky to keep Bargate dead drunk, the British army would not have lost Meteren. But of that later.

I went up to the section next morning (15th) and stayed there all day till 5 p.m., when I came back for orders. I also obtained permission to stay at **D** (about 50 yards behind the section), so I could be in touch with my section and with the rest of B Company. I took up my abode there at 8 p.m., when I received a message from Bargate. He said the enemy had broken through near Bailleul, but that no retirement was to take place on our front. But his part of the company was shifting to **B2 – B2**, and his position was being taken over by some Middlesex. So actually the position of British troops on this front was as before, and we had no real cause for anxiety. I was again ordered back. I decided to return in the morning.

At about 4 a.m. Bridges came, saying that an Argyle and Sutherland patrol had been out and found the British positions at **B1 – B1** *unoccupied*. This news was almost incredible, as it meant about 800 yards' gap in the British line. The enemy could walk into Meteren when they liked. I decided I had better report the situation at once, so I went back. I left Bridges the runners so he could send back messages if anything happened. I went back to Brigade H.Q. (Infantry) as fast as I could and reported. The General at once said the situation was most serious and told me to take up troops at once if I could find any. I collected a few men at our former Company H.Q. and started off. It was about 5 a.m., and so far I had acted over the heads of my immediate superiors. I was rather frightened of them, but as I now had the General's orders, all was well.

I started up the same road that the section had first taken. But no sooner did I get on the road itself than an enemy machine-gun opened on us – from Meteren itself!

I immediately extended the few men I had so as to avoid casualties, and we pushed on with our left resting on the edge of the road. We were just in front of **G**. At this stage I could see in front of me some British troops. They were our front line retiring. They stopped on the dotted line (see diagram, Figure 26) and held the enemy there. In the meantime we took up a position where we were, in partially dug trenches, and waited to go on at once if we saw the enemy attack. But as it grew darker the enemy fire died down – they had taken the first step towards Bailleul.

I now had time to take stock of the position. I had about 15 men, with about four of Bargate's men and one of my runners – Buchanan. The latter had been sent back by Bridges to say the enemy were attacking and had bumped into us as we went up. He knew nothing more than that. It was clear that Bargate must have left **B1 – B1** before he had handed over the position – a thing that was expressly against all principles of war at all. As it happened, the troops who should have taken over hadn't arrived, and so his mistake did not pass unnoticed but meant the loss of Meteren. As I found out afterwards, this is exactly what had happened. The full story, as told me by Carter, was as follows:

Bargate had left the trench and gone to the left before he was relieved. That morning they suddenly found the enemy advancing, and at the same time fire was opened on them from behind by the enemy who had gone through the gap. Hopeless confusion followed, and they just cleared out anyhow, being shot down as they went.

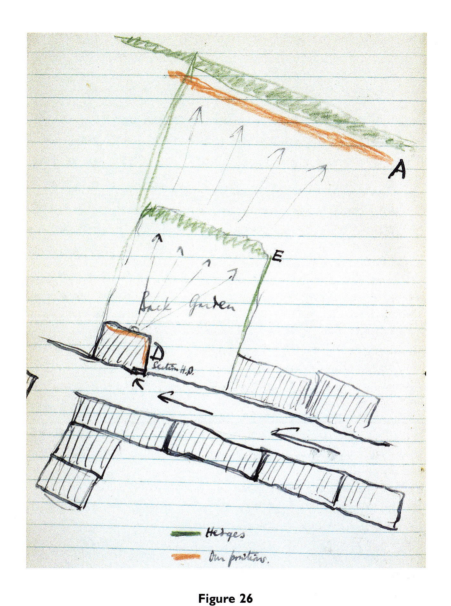

Figure 26
Meteren position. This is a large scale of Figure 25. The lettering is the same as on Figure 25.

Carter rallied some, and they formed a defensive flank **B3 – B3** and so held up the enemy advance. For this he was given an M.C. In the meantime the rescue of the 33rd Division (the Argyle and Sutherland Highlanders) had centred the line on *our* side of Meteren. This finally held the enemy advance. Bargate was last seen wounded. He had several shots that went through the shrapnel helmet but missed his head. In the end he got back to England, and they kept him, I think – anyhow, he never came back to us any more.

I spent the day in the trench by fortifying our bit as best we could. It was very harassing, as the enemy were keeping up a fairly heavy and accurate 5.9 bombardment on our trench. We had no casualties. By midnight we were in a pretty strong position and had fetched up more ammunition. At 4.30 a.m. we were relieved and trailed back to Company H.Q. (the old one). The relief was absolutely unexpected, but we were of little use, and they prepared to put in a proper unit rather than have isolated detachments all over the place. They could afford it now, as apparently French troops had relieved the British on the right and thus strengthened for the 33rd Division reserve. On reaching Company H.Q., we halted for a short space.

We then left and marched back still further. We were to be billeted at the Convent des Trappistes on Mont des Cats. As we marched, it grew lighter, and we could now see the 'line' as it was on our right where the French were. For the first time we saw some guns. The French had their front supported by what seemed an enormous number of 75's. Our journey up Mont des Cats was quite pleasant. The fact that we were resting, the clear, fine morning and the cheery sound of the 75's all helped to make us cheerful.

We reached the convent, after some delays, at about 10.30 a.m. It was a big building and imposing in appearance. We had often seen it away on our right rear from La Lovie and Oosthoek. But it was a jerry-built construction and offered small cover, as we found to our cost later.

The whole battalion was withdrawn, and we were assembled together at the convent. In the afternoon we were spread about the building in the cellars for safety. But we had not done this long when the enemy commenced shelling. We watched his shells come nearer, when at last there was a terrific roar, and a 5.9 crashed through the chapel roof, through the cloister floor, and burst in the cellar. No very great damage was done. Cracks appeared in the cellar roof, and one man had his leg very neatly amputated. He was taken off calmly smoking a cigarette. He was laughing and joking and seemed to feel no pain at all. This accident did not leave us as confident and cheerful as we had been. But there was nothing to be done. We wanted shelter, and we were determined to stay where we were, as it was quite possible they would not shell the convent for long.

After rifles had been cleaned and we were all ready for action again we turned in. The men slept on the floor, but the officers discovered great luxury in some mortuary boards, which we used for beds.

The next day was spent in kit inspection and so on. Sometime during that day Hauser, who was now under me in my section, and I had a talk. I mention this conversation as it will give some idea of the state of affairs in our battalion. Our battalion had, as a whole, done very well at Meteren and earned the praise of the Divisional General. But that fact was due to C Company and not to ourselves. *Our* show had been disastrous. I had lost the whole of my section but one man, and although it was hardly my fault, I was not doing my duty at all as a section commander by being so far from my men. I never let that mistake occur again and subsequently fought the question out with the O.C. Company when he wanted me far behind the men. The example set by Bargate was appalling, and the rot he had caused spread rapidly and was increased by the ill-behaviour of Clifford, who had again distinguished himself. In short, the general effect of the action was a lowering of the morale of our company. This was extremely serious as at this time morale was all-important. Hauser and I talked over all these matters and resolved to counteract these tendencies as best we could by pretending, in future, to enjoy action and to discourage in mess and elsewhere all talk of 'wind up' and that kind of thing. We had seen already where casual joking in that way led to, and from this time on, whether as tank commanders or as section commanders, we never gave up this policy. By degrees we got new officers who came to do the same, and, looking back on it all now, I can see how the standard rose as a result. It was no longer funny to talk of 'wind up' and 'beating it' and so on. In course of time people discovered that such talk was not expected of an officer. But this all took time. There was little chance for improvement till bad senior officers like Clifford & co. were cleared out. Later, as we gained in position, things became easier. I really believe this was the start of a better fighting spirit in the battalion. I don't mean to suggest that *we* were responsible for courage or anything in others. But I do think that we gave good officers who came to our company a chance to show their mettle. They did not immediately have their spirit undermined by foolish and beastly talk. We also spoke to officers of our age in A and B Companies, and we all worked more or less together in the matter. Before this there was much discontent, but we were all too isolated to do anything. Now we felt that there were many people backing us up. As I have said, this took time. At this date things were very bad. It is very difficult to stop in a line for days and expect an enemy attack at any moment. The strain on the nerves is very great, especially when you know there is nothing between the enemy and the sea but your line of troops. Idiotic jokes in mess and open talk of fear all contributed to lower one's spirits, and, as you will hear, I was already in a very low state.

The night's rest and the good food made us feel very much better. We were hardly disturbed by the enemy's shelling of the convent as his fire was erratic, and although there were casualties, they occurred in a different part of the building.

At midday we had orders to move, and the battalion marched out by companies travelling northwards. As we went, we saw the enemy shelling Mont Noir and Mont Rouge on our right. As we went along, orders were explained. The battalion was going in to support the 9th Division at Wytschaete. The remains of B Company were going into the 'line' that night, while A and C took up positions in a new camp. B Company remnants were to be combined in one section, as there were only 36 men left. This meant we could man six guns. These six guns were to be under my command. I was to take this section into the line and occupy three 'farms' to the left of the great crater at Wytschaete (see Figure 27). We would thus form three 'strong points' with two Lewis guns in each and so strengthen the left of the 9th (Lowland Scottish) Division. The distance between the left farm and the right farm was about 1,000 yards. I was to make Section H.Q. about a quarter of a mile behind the centre farm. At this I objected and finally had the distance reduced to 200 yards. This was better, but still useless, as it was too far to allow effective control in action. Such control is always difficult. A distance of 200 yards made it almost impossible. The ridge (the plan, Figure 27, will show you the position) lay between us. The enemy's position was not certain.

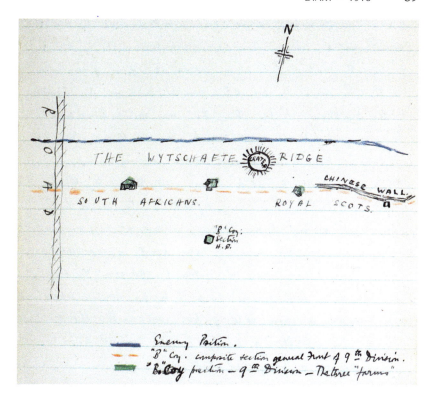

Figure 27
Wytschaete Ridge position.

Sometimes he was on our side of the crest and at others on his side of it. Generally speaking the ridge was in no-man's land. When we reached A and C Company camp, they halted, and we boarded lorries and were taken up to a point some 1,000 yards behind our 'line'. Here we disembarked.

We slowly stumbled up to the line, and after about half an hour our guides brought us to the left 'farm'. Here I left two guns and went on to the second 'farm', and from there to the third.

This operation seems simple enough. In point of fact it is about as simple an operation as one is likely to get in war. But there is more in it than there seems. Imagine very tired men and two very tired officers all carrying heavy loads. The country was simply a wilderness. In front, where the enemy was, we could see a ridge with a few stunted trees standing stark against the sky. The ground was torn up by the shell-fire of the old battles of Messines. The craters were still there but were now overgrown with rank thistles and weed. The remains of old buried entanglements sprouted through the earth and now and then hurled someone headlong as they caught his foot. The deeper shell craters were filled with blackish water, which stank.

The physical difficulty of going on through this was not our only trouble. We had just had a nasty knock. Officers and men were mystified by a kind of fighting they could not understand. We knew very little of our work, and here we were, stumbling on to heaven knows what, led by a guide who probably didn't know his way and would only admit it when he had got us thoroughly lost. These worries harassed one the whole time. So you may judge of our relief when we were finally installed where we hoped to be.

The farms were practically non-existent: only one had anything to show for itself and that had the remains of an old cellar.

There is nothing much to say about our stay here. We had no fighting, and it is only important as it was one more step towards misery and defeat. At night I used to stumble across wire and shell-holes from farm to farm – this was not possible in daylight. (Imagine this occupation. The photo – Figure 28 – will help you to do so; see also Figure 27.) There were no trenches, and except on our left and right, there were no troops other than our six gun crews. I simply have a vague memory of painfully trudging my 800 yards and wondering whether I was going in the right direction for one farm or another, or whether I was just going straight into the enemy lines. Now and then a Very light would flare up fitfully and die away. At such times I stood still – not so much to avoid being shot as because it seemed to be the right thing to do.

I used to do most of my work at night and usually stayed up at one farm or another then. But in daytime I used to go back to Section H.Q. according to orders in case anyone came round. The days were fairly awful. There was a blazing sun most of the time, and this used to beat down on the piece of elephant iron that made my H.Q. and make the inside intolerably stuffy and hot. Here I used to lie, tired out after the night, in a kind of stupor, which served instead of sleep. It was a weird business – the heat, and the nightmares out of which one started up suddenly in a kind of horror to find the sweat pouring down one's face. It was almost impossible to distinguish dream from reality. The tat–tat–tat of the German machine-guns would chime in with your dream with uncanny effect, so that when you awoke you wondered whether you were dreaming. The machine-gun made you think everything was genuine, and only by degrees you recovered yourself to fall into uneasy sleep again.

It did not take long for interest in life to die out. Soon I found myself almost hopeless. I used to lie on my back and stare at the low roof. Sometimes I stared for hours at a small piece of mud that hung from the roof by a grass and quivered to the explosion of the shells. Then suddenly one day I heard that the South Africans on our left were playing the fool. They used to crawl out onto the road on their left at night and try to get hit by the German machine-gun that fired down the road. This news had a curiously bracing effect. I don't know now whether the tale was true – certainly it had been common enough in the earlier part of the war – but I felt things now could get no worse and that actually a gleam of hope had appeared – it was always possible to get badly wounded or perhaps even killed.

This may seem hardly possible to you. But the fact remains that life had now reached such a pitch that horrible mutilations or death could not conceivably be worse. I found myself looking forward to getting killed, as then, at least, one would be rid of this intolerable misery. These thoughts were uppermost with me then and excluded all others – and I think many were in the same state. After all, if you get a man and hunt him like an animal, in time he will become one. I am at a loss now to tell you of our life. Such worlds separate the ordinary human's point of view from mine at that time, that anything I can write will either be incomprehensible or will give a quite wrong impression. Briefly, I felt like this: I didn't care tuppence whether we held the 'line' or not. Germany's victory or defeat was nothing. Nevertheless, I would do my job by my men as well as I could, as there was nothing else to do. I wasn't interested in religion or world politics or any rot like that. I was merely an insignificant scrap of humanity that was being intolerably persecuted by unknown powers, and I was going to score off those powers by dying. After all, a mouse must feel that it is one up on the playful cat when it dies without making any sport for its captor.

With this new idea before me, I felt better. I didn't feel afraid any more, and I walked about doing my job feeling as if I had scored off Providence.

Our section was moved further to the right a few days later (I had lost all sense of time now). We evacuated the farms and manned Chinese Wall as one strong point (see Figure 29). This was far more satisfactory than before, from a defensive point of view; our isolated posts could have done nothing. While we were at Chinese Wall, we were much cursed by enemy aeroplanes. There was none of ours to be seen. This had a very bad effect on our morale, so one morning I determined on a demonstration. We loaded our six guns, and I gave instructions that, when I gave the signal, they were all to open fire on the next Boche that came over. Very soon a low-flying aeroplane appeared. As he drew nearer, I drew my whistle and blew. At once all our guns opened together. The aeroplane immediately swerved off, and it looked as if several pieces were knocked out of it. I feel sure it was damaged, as we had no more visits that day. The great thing was, the whole show cheered the men wonderfully. They felt they had at last got their own back a bit. The Colonel of the Royal Scots was very

---

Figure 28

The Wytschaete position. A photo of the road in Figure 27. The left 'farm' of our position was about 100 yards up, on the right-hand side of the road, as you see it here. We had to march up this and then turn to our right and go down a path. The path, of course, was simply a track running round the lip of the craters. The photo does not give a good idea of the ridge. But the road dips into a valley a little further on, and from this valley the ridge stood up quite clearly. As you can see the ridge wasn't much of a thing – but it had held up the British Army.

This photo will give you some idea of our life in this sector. Imagine this 'road' peppered with M.G. fire. Then imagine the shell-fire. And in this district every gun and every shell echoed and re-echoed, until at last the noise died away in weird booms and groans utterly unlike the original sound. The sound was quite different from anything I know. If anything was needed to complete the horror of that place, those echoes did it; for it needed no great imagination to think of those shuddering reverberations as the wails of spirits still tortured by the memories of their misery, still lamenting the incredible folly that doomed their successors to the same fate.

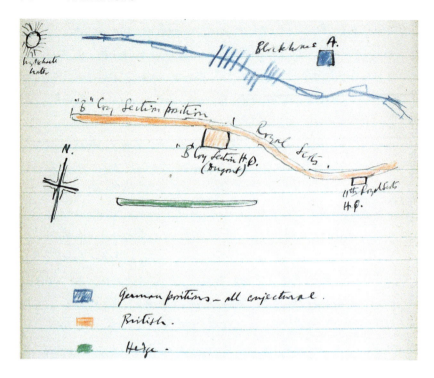

Figure 29
Chinese Wall position.

pleased, as he said it had cheered his men too. This colonel was a very good chap. He was about 42. I used to go and see him occasionally, and, to keep ourselves going, we used to talk about Addison's essays. In the evenings when the enemy would open up with his 5.9's, we used to hold our literary meetings. He would say he couldn't stand that infernal row – the enemy would be practically hitting our breastwork (Chinese Wall) by this time – and so he would hail me, and we used to stand by Section H.Q. dugout and watch developments while we talked hard about Sir Roger de Coverley. Poor fellow! He was killed a few days later. He seemed a very sound fellow and stuck it out, although you could see his nerves were nearly gone.

Although we now felt better than when we were scattered over our three farms, the position was not really satisfactory. Our position

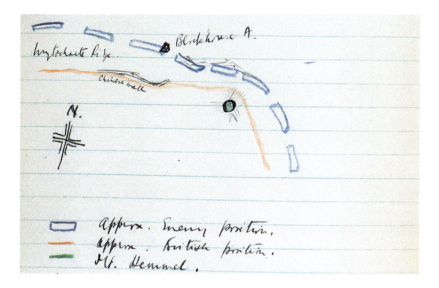

Figure 30
April–May '18, general position, Wytschaete–Mt. Kemmel. Letters are the same as on Figure 29.

at Chinese Wall was useless if the enemy attacked from the Kemmel side (see diagram, Figure 30). This was *the* real fault of the position, and it was not a merely local defect. When in the end these positions were taken, that is how they fell – the enemy took Kemmel and came down from the flank. But our own troubles were many. The enemy swept our positions very thoroughly with machine-guns – especially from blockhouse **A**. No movement from Chinese Wall was possible – as soon as one left the shelter of the breastwork, one was sniped. As the Royal Scots Colonel said, it was a good thing that sniper couldn't shoot. He always potted, and he never hit anyone while we were there. Added to these little difficulties, the enemy shelled us with gas. We slept at night with our gas mask tubes in our teeth. The food was quite good, but water was scarce. What little we had came in badly cleaned petrol tins and tasted filthy. One fellow complained that he felt like a petrol lighter after a dose of water from the supply.

On the whole we spent our days in greater comfort than we might have done. We were pleased to note the arrival of a French mortar, which soon made a mess of blockhouse **A**. This did not end harassing fire at night though; it earned, on the contrary, a very heavy 5.9 bombardment for us that night.

At last news came that we were to be relieved. We made all preparations for departure, but with no real hope, for we had already been fooled by that story. The section pessimist prophesied an enemy attack before we could leave.

At about 6.30 p.m., the enemy suddenly commenced shelling far on our right. We watched the bright white light of our guns flickering across the sky as our barrage answered theirs. The red glow of their shrapnel bursting and coloured lights of our S.O.S. signals made a weird and terrible sight. But the unpleasant part was the fact that the barrage zone seemed to be extending towards us. Before many minutes, the enemy barrage had opened up on our immediate right, and I gave the order to stand to arms.

The sentries had to stay up and watch carefully all that happened. The rest of the men kept at the bottom of the trench, ready to spring up as soon as the barrage lifted and the enemy advanced.

By this time the barrage was on to us as well. The Royal Scots Colonel at once sent up the S.O.S. – a red light over a green over a yellow. These lights are fired out of a pistol and float across the fields tied together, looking somewhat like a ship's riding lights. When the infantry send them up, it is a signal to the artillery to drop their barrage. It is very weird on a quiet night to see the S.O.S. suddenly soar into the sky. Almost at once the whole place rocks and sways to the roar of our guns – for the speed with which the barrage falls is most important in defence. A peaceful night is at once transformed into a scene of indescribable chaos. I have no time here to go into the question of S.O.S. signals. The colours were frequently changed so that the enemy did not know them. Each part of the line had its own colours.

In reply to our S.O.S., our barrage came down. While the opposing artilleries amused themselves firing at the opposing infantries, the opposing infantries took as much cover as they could and swore gently to relieve their feelings.

We waited an hour or two like this while the S.O.S. went up more and more on our right. There seemed to be no movement on our immediate front. At about 9.30 the enemy fire slackened on our front, and we began to feel that it was all over. But the fire on our right seemed, if anything, to have increased in intensity.

At 10.30 our relieving troops arrived, and we went out feeling very thankful. Even so, it was no night for relief. We had to go over roads that were being shelled and through fields across which the enemy was dropping a shrapnel screen. It was noticeable at this time that his shrapnel fire was a great deal more accurate than it used to be.

As we trailed back, we heard the roar of the guns grow greater and greater while the enemy's harassing fire on our communications seemed to have redoubled. It was now quite clear that a very big attack was coming off.

After about two miles of very toilsome marching, we reached lorries that drove us back to camp. The place where we embarked was in the enemy's hands an hour and forty minutes later, for he had taken Mt. Kemmel and swept down the flank of the Wytschaete position.

So we had missed the loss of Kemmel by the skin of our teeth. You can tell how fortunate we were when I explain that the survivors from the Royal Scots numbered one officer and two men, and, of the 84 men that relieved our 56, there escaped only one man.

These things were not, however, known for some days. At first the loss of Kemmel was by no means certain. The French had been on its right and the British on the left. The French claimed still to hold the summit, and it was known that the Cheshires had retaken Kemmel village, which lay on the enemy's side of Mt. Kemmel. What we did not know was that the French had been cut off and the Cheshires cut to bits in a disastrous attempt to retire from a position that was too far in advance to admit of adequate support.

On the whole, then, we felt fairly pleased as we turned into camp that morning. The big attack we saw seemed to be held – according to all the news we could get.

That evening was rather a pleasant one. The men were pleased with life and had all had a change of clothes, decent food and a good sleep, My gramophone, which I bought at Cheltenham, had arrived, and I lent it to them. In the officers' mess we had an especially elaborate disguise for our bully beef and also fresh meat stew and a sweet. There was also some beer from the E.F.C. [Expeditionary Force Canteen]. So we had a palatial meal and sat down round the fire of the farm house that was our billet to enjoy a really good smoke. One officer fetched out a violin and played accompaniment to songs and, occasionally, a solo. It was, I remember, while he was playing 'Träumerei' that a messenger entered and handed Cook (now Company

Commander) a chit from the battalion. We paid little attention, for the music and the unaccustomed luxury of good food and a cheerful fire had thrown us all deep into memories and dreams of our own. When the music ended, Cook spoke. 'Sorry, you fellows, bad news, I'm afraid; B Company is to stand to arms at once and proceed up to the line. Lorries will be at the camp in half an hour to take you up. I have sent out to warn the men already. Apparently the Boche have got Kemmel after all.'

We got up and looked at the pleasant room and the cheery fire and wondered why we had ever been such fools as to believe they were real.

It was a bright starlight night and cold. We inspected the men as they stood there with chattering teeth, and then we got on the lorries. This time Hauser and I were to command a company composed of two crews from B Company and two from C. It was a composite section really. Cook was to be in command of the whole. Actually, this meant that he was about 800 yards behind the line and looked after supplies and so on while Hauser and I looked after the combatant side of the business.

Hauser and I sat in front of the first lorry while Cook went up with Carter in the bike and side-car. As we went up, the enemy were shelling the roads. It was very unpleasant as you could not hear the shells coming. First you would see a mass of hot little sparks fly up on the left, and as you drove past a second or two later you would smell that peculiar warm earthy smell with a touch of acetylene gas. Then the same would happen on the right. You waited to feel the splinters hurtle through the side of the lorry and kill you.

At last we reached Ouderdom. Here we disembarked and enviously watched the lorry drivers turn round and go home as fast as they could.

We picked up our kit and trudged wearily up the shell-pocked road. We seemed to be marching straight to destruction, for immediately in front the Very lights were flaring up at intervals and we could see each other's faces in the pale glare.

At last we reached a cross-roads called Millekruisse, and here we met Carter with orders from Cook. Company H.Q. were about 100 yards to the left of the cross-roads. Carter led us to a point about 100 yards in front of the cross-roads. Here we struck a trench. This was the left of our allotted section. A point 800 yards to the right was the right of our sector. I put one gun on the left point, one on our right, and the other two at good points for cross-fire between these two. Hauser was to look after the left and I the right. But I was also in command of him and his two guns. We took over from Windle, a young C officer who was so dazed and idiotic he could tell us nothing and do nothing – and that when there was no fire.

The sketch map (Figure 31) will show you our positions, and Figure 32 will show you where we were in relation to our Chinese Wall position. I think you will get the idea of our position fairly well from the map, but I will point out one or two important features. Between the enemy and ourselves there was a ridge of high ground

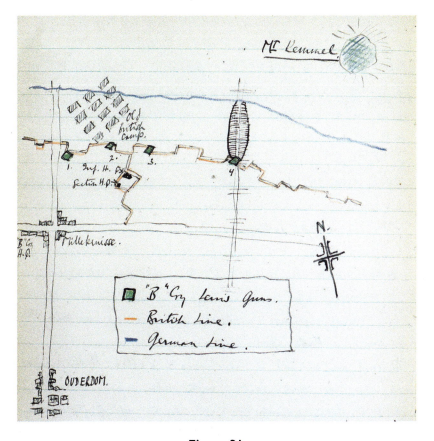

Figure 31
May '18, Mt. Kemmel.

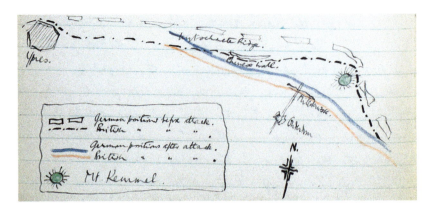

Figure 32
Enemy advance in capture of Mt. Kemmel.

(see diagram). So we were invisible to each other's front-line troops. *But* in our case we were at a great disadvantage for artillery fire, as the enemy had direct observation onto us from Mt. Kemmel. The British camp I have marked was an artillery camp that had been taken by surprise by the enemy advance. As a result a lot of horses had been left in it, and these were killed by artillery fire. The stench was awful for the weather was hot.

The camp was a great nuisance, as the enemy used to creep out of their trenches and snipe us from behind the huts. The K.O.L.I.s [King's Own Light Infantry] on our left returned the compliment, but it was no real consolation to us.

Our trenches were very poor. They were not more than 4 feet deep and did not allow one man to pass another with any ease. There was a certain amount of water in them. There were no barbed-wire entanglements, and no wire could be obtained.

No. 1 Lewis gun was in a good position, and so was No. 2. No. 3 was very bad. There was little or no protection, and water was coming up in the trench. The only thing to do was to build a breastwork, and for this sandbags were necessary. I indented for 500 but could get no more than 50 and these only when it was very late – almost too late to be any good. The 4th Lewis gun position was good. It was on the railway and so commanded the cutting and the ground to right and left.

Section H.Q. was in the corner of a square of trenches about 20 yards behind the actual line. There was one dug-out in this square and that was occupied by some infantry officers who commanded the few troops in the line with us. This whole square of trenches was very clearly defined. Although it was a spot of no great importance, it looked important, and as a result the enemy had it marked out for destruction under the impression it was a strong point.

The troops in the line with us were the 21st Division. This division used to be a good one, but it had been far too knocked about to be much good by this time. On our left we had the K.O.Y.L.I.s [King's Own Yorkshire Light Infantry], and actually with us there was the Duke of Cornwall's Light Infantry Band, i.e., a small collection of young boys and unfit men with no knowledge of arms or anything else. Their officers were hopeless. On our right – by the railway cutting – were a few of the 10th Cheshires.

Our life here was dull. The weather was hot, and the place stank. We were usually shelled by 5.9's at fairly regular hours, and then we took cover. For the rest of the day we sat about and listened to the desultory fire of our guns and the sudden crash as part of the tin roof came down in the old camp. These falling bits of tin would set us wondering if the enemy were crawling about, and occasionally we would give a more than usually suspicious spot a burst of fire.

The enemy aeroplanes held undisputed sway and droned away above us. The only relief we had came one day when our aeroplanes did a demonstration. Complaints had grown so violent about the enemy aeroplanes that the authorities sent over 36 aeroplanes one evening. These simply cleared out every enemy for miles and went about bombing and doing just whatever they pleased. The effect on our morale was really wonderful. For the first time we felt as if we were top dogs. There's an extraordinary feeling of security that comes over you when you see a sky apparently covered with aeroplanes and reflect that they are all yours. It is as if a child had flaunted a toy in your face, and for a long time you could do nothing – till one day you suddenly flaunt a far more magnificent toy in *his* face. You feel you have scored and that all past humiliations were worth it.

The effect of this demonstration was most pronounced, not only on us but on the enemy. They felt sure it was a great reconnaissance preliminary to a big attack. Let us hope they felt suitably depressed.

Hauser and I did what we could to build up defences. But we could get no Very lights, no S.O.S. signals, no barbed wire and no sandbags. The situation really was appalling.

After about four days we obtained 50 sandbags, and these we used for No. 3. gun position, making it very much better even with these few.

By this time the French had taken over the territory on our right, so we were now to see something of the work of our allies. The most noticeable thing was their terrifying use of coloured lights. These they would send up all day and all night. I am inclined to think they did it for no reason at all except to hoodwink the enemy – at any rate, they did this most successfully. The day after they arrived, they treated the enemy to a fireworks display that, I should think, was unrivalled on the British Front. Immediately after breakfast they put up showers of 'golden rain' all along the line and for about ten miles behind it. Having completely mystified the enemy by this, they opened up a desultory and extremely exasperating artillery fire – it all sounded like the nerve-racking performance of one of those irritating toy spaniels. Their fire increased in volume, and then suddenly, without any warning, all fire stopped. This sudden silence worried our orthodox friends over the way very considerably. They promptly opened up heavy harassing fire on lines of communication. The French maintained a dogged silence.

Much the same happened later. It was becoming dusk when the French began to put up streams and streams of coloured lights. This was all the more mysterious as there was hardly any firing going on on either side. All was peace and quiet, and yet the French persisted in sending up a series of signals which, if they meant anything at all, must have been quite sufficient to report an entire battle. As soon as the enemy recovered from this they dropped a really good barrage – and the French discovered what they wanted to know – i.e. exactly where the enemy fire was directed. Thus, with a happy feeling that they had done their duty, our allies packed up for the night and, let us hope, slept the sleep of the just.

The next day we heard the glad news that we were to be relieved. I was thankful, as I was very tired of Millekruisse and standing to generally. For some time we had been unable to sleep except in full equipment. Unfortunately lying in your full kit with revolvers etc. stuck all over you is by no means comfortable. The first time I did it I woke with an awful taste of blood in my mouth, and you can imagine the effect of that on a very sleepy man who has been dreaming action.

The afternoon again was very hot and beastly and made us feel all the more pleased at the idea of relief. There was one very disquieting feature about this day, however, and I had grave doubts that we should leave Millekruisse unmolested. The whole of that day the enemy had hardly fired a shot – either artillery or rifle.

It is an extraordinary thing, but this 'sulk' is typical, and you may be sure that there is mischief afoot when the enemy withholds his fire. I have not struck anybody yet who did not find this silence a sign of coming trouble.

My fears were fully justified. At 6 that evening his 5.9's opened on our position. They were firing in triplets – you only hear the first one coming, and the other two burst when you don't expect it. Within about two minutes of the start his bombardment had reached its full intensity. This was an attack for a certainty, and up went our S.O.S. – red over red over red.

The peaceful dusk had changed in a moment. The whole ground rocked and swayed, and the sky was hidden by a cloud of dust and smoke. It seemed as if night had suddenly come upon us. It was almost impossible to distinguish anything in the darkness. The weirdness of it all was increased by the sight of our three reds as they floated calmly through the dust and smoke. There was something very menacing and ghostly in their smooth progress through that inferno of flying earth and fumes. When the bombardment opened, Hauser and I were standing together. As soon as the S.O.S. went up, I drew my revolver and loaded it. (Hauser said afterwards that there was something very amusing about the calm way I did this – as if I was going to shoot the fellow who had disturbed my afternoon!) We then both waited, crouching down to see what would happen. It was quite clear that our attack was coming – and incidentally quite clear that the enemy had some guns concentrated onto our little square. What was not clear was the amount of support we were to have from our artillery.

A few moments after our S.O.S. went up we received our answer. The British artillery opened up very promptly, and down came our barrage. What its effect was we didn't know, but there seemed to be more guns than we had hoped for. All at once we noticed a new sound in the crack! crack! of our guns. There seemed to be a very short, sharp, tinny kind of bark in it. We both knew what that meant – we were supported by the French artillery, and the short cracks were simply the famous French 75's in action.

The defensive barrage was a fine one, and, as we heard afterwards, it was responsible for very heavy casualties to the enemy. Hauser and I stood in our trench and peered out into the dark-ness. We were giving up hope of distinguishing anything when suddenly, quite close to us, we saw men running. They were British troops apparently clearing out.

Hauser and I drew our revolvers and bawled at them. They didn't hear us, of course, but they saw us and our revolvers and stopped. Poor fellows – they were out in front and had received no orders, and the whole thing had become too much. I suppose they got a bit panicked. Anyhow, they settled down very cheerfully when we made them stop, and the moment they had orders they seemed quite prepared to stick where they were and fight it out.

The whole of this time we saw none of the infantry officers. Hauser and I now began to wonder what to do. It seemed imperative that we should get to our men. For my part, as I said before, I cared too little about the whole business to mind the idea of getting killed. This, and, I think, a curious kind of excitement that used to come over us in action, combined to influence me. I told Hauser that I thought the only thing we could do if we were to be any use at all was to get out of our place and get with our men. He agreed. I may as well say now that from the point of view of sheer unadulterated lunacy what followed was the maddest and most dangerous thing I ever did. I must have been very nearly mad to do it. But I never *thought* more clearly in my life.

Hauser cleared off towards the left, and I went to the right. The trench communicating with the firing line was obliterated, so I crawled out on my stomach. It seemed very unlikely that I should get to the front line, as, literally, the whole earth seemed to be going into the sky. Finally I decided it would be just as safe and rather quicker to walk. So I got up and was promptly knocked down by concussion. In this way I stumbled on and had nearly reached the line when I got chucked into a piece of trench. I didn't feel hurt much and picked myself up feeling rather dazed, to find I was in the remains of the front line. I remember feeling very trapped and stuffy in the trench.

I had a longing to walk along the top so I could see what was happening. So I got out and walked along the top till I saw our men. They seemed very bewildered but were sticking to their post and had everything ready to open fire. I can tell you I felt very proud of them when I saw this. One reason that decided Hauser and myself was the fear that our men might lose their heads as the few infantry we saw coming back had done.

I decided that the best thing to do was to stand on the top of the trench and talk to them. It was a wildly foolish thing to do, but I felt quite clearly that at this time a little foolhardiness would look well and would pay out of all proportion. They seemed very cheery, and I pretended we could knock the stuffing out of the enemy, and so on, and I then went on; I was knocked over once or twice as I went, but fortunately the enemy shooting was nothing like so concentrated here as it was on our little square of trenches at Section H.Q. I felt as if I was in absolute safety compared with the old place. As I walked on, I watched to see all I could, and I saw that from the enemy line they were sending up red over red all down the line except just to our right, and there they were sending up two greens. Now, the idea we were given was that two reds meant 'held up' and two greens meant 'all's well'. So it seemed that the enemy had come to grief on our barrage nearly everywhere. But I did *not* like that place with two greens.

I went on down to the right, and now I became very worried, for from my right and behind me a machine-gun was firing. This gun's bullets were hitting up the ground near the trench. This mystified me completely. It seemed to mean that the enemy had got round behind us after breaking through our right.

At about this same time I smelt a sweet nauseating scent in the shell gases. The enemy were using their blue-cross gas shells. I put the mouthpiece of my gas-mask between my teeth and breathed through that. I didn't bother to put the mask right on as the gas was not very strong and I wanted to see as clearly as I could.

At last I reached the 3rd gun. They were very well off as the sandbags protected them very well and their defences were really sound. I talked to them as I had to the others and went on to the right. I found this crew also very cheery but somewhat anxious about the machine-gun behind. I assured them it was one of our own doing 'overhead' fire and explained that it was quite capable of aiming as badly as that.

Although I wasn't quite so confident about it, I felt this was probably right as the gun sounded too fast for a German. Afterwards I discovered it *was* one of ours. To make sure that all was well, I crossed the railway and spoke to the Cheshires. Their sergeant was very worried at my standing on top of the trench. I talked some time to them and assured them my guns were good to stop dead any enemy attack, and in the end they assured me they had licked the enemy before and would do it again now – so I went back to the 3rd Lewis gun crew!

To my intense relief I now saw the two reds going up all along the enemy line. Although it was by no means certain that we knew the real meaning of these signals, yet I clung to the belief that two reds meant failure. It is curious how one hoped for the best when one had the chance.

Unfortunately their failure meant the increase of their artillery on our line, and up went the earth more than ever. I went back to the 2nd gun and talked to them some time. I then went on to see how Hauser was getting on on the left. The shells were now breaking up lots of trenches. I found him with the 1st gun. He had stopped there as they were rather shaken up; they had had their emplacement knocked to bits and their crew commander Cpl. Smith killed right at the start. I exchanged notes with Hauser, and he came to the conclusion everything was going well. I then went back to the 3rd crew. I looked at my watch and found it was 10.30 p.m. So we had had 4½ hours of it!

From now on the enemy fire died down, but far on our right the artillery kept at it hammer and tongs. We gave up all hope of being relieved that night as it seemed that it would be unlikely that the French would come up under such fire.

But they came after all. They took over our line in very great strength – at least 20 men to every one of ours. They manned a front line and support and seemed to do everything in the most haphazard way imaginable. All the same, they had those trenches manned with the least fuss and bade us goodnight with cheery assurances that they would hold the line for ever. We left them with our blessing and departed weary but very pleased to be going!

During all this time A and C Companies had had their share of fighting and had both done very well. Gatehouse, our old company second in command, who now had C Company, did not allow that fact to pass unnoticed. From this time on the war became purely a fight for decoration as far as he was concerned. Not a shell burst but one of C Company officers had done something worth a V.C., and of course a company with such a gallant personnel was bound to reflect great credit on the O.C. Company. Thus by degrees our commanders learnt to write the convincing recommendation and hoped that their little essays would be duly rewarded.

When we came out of the line, we found the remains of A and C in camp already. Our gallant colonel also reappeared and, like the albatross, was welcomed as a sign of fair weather as far as fighting was concerned. In fact it was now clear that the battalion was going for a long rest and was to draw tanks before it reappeared to fight.

The usual wrangling broke out, and some of it touched our company very seriously. Since Bargate had disappeared, Cook, our second in command, had taken over the company and had been confirmed as Major by Hankey our Brigadier. But Cook was very junior and was hated for this. People began to pull strings, and at last Cook found that the higher powers refused to promote him on account of his junior standing. Instead, they promoted one of the malcontents from A Company – one named Aitches.

Now, whatever faults Cook had – and being human he had many – he was at least competent, and he did do his job fairly well, even in action when he was assuredly a funk. Also, he could be trusted. He did not treat you as a bad lot without first telling you he thought you were one. Aitches, on the other hand, was just an ordinary blackguard with rather more than an ordinary blackguard's share of cowardice. In England I had thought him rather a charming and pleasant fellow. But in France his reputation had grown steadily worse. He tried to curry favour with everyone and failed to gain favour anywhere. His behaviour at Le Havre, where he had worn a Sam Browne [officer's heavy leather belt with shoulder strap] loaded with the brightly polished cartridges of an automatic revolver, must have impressed the ladies as that of the true soldier. But in the battalion, where rather more was demanded than the mere outward show, he failed to impress. It was discovered that he wore body armour under his tunic when he was still forty miles from the line. What he did when he reached the line was never quite clear. But by 1918 his name was a legend in the battalion for everything contemptible.

It was to this creature, who had put up an importunate wail over Cook's promotion, that the Higher powers entrusted the lives of a company of officers and men. They disregarded the opinion of the

Brigadier and all other ranks who had met him and were best qualified to know his virtues, and thrust the crown upon him. The best comment on the promotion that I heard was made by one of the men who parodied the hymn and was heard going off muttering, 'Oh God, our help' – and then with tremendous emphasis – 'in Aitches past!'[1] Poor fellow! I suppose really there were many redeeming features in his character. He was always willing to talk about the Lanchester motor company if he felt you were bored and wanted cheering up.

The day after we were relieved, we heard definitely that we were to go back and draw tanks. This we did after the delay of a couple of days. During this time we were very comfortably off. The enemy were held, and many more troops had come up. We had a little bombing and a little shelling. One shell decapitated the best Company Commander we had and killed two other officers. This fellow, the O.C. A Company, had only just arrived with the battalion. From all accounts he was a really good chap.

I do not intend now to give you any details of our life until August (see Figure 33). From May 14th, when we left Belgium, until August 4th very little happened that you can't fill in for yourself. We drew new tanks and went up to Berle au Bois – a place south of Arras and three miles behind the front line. Here we were in the 6th Corps area and in support of the Guards Division. There were continual alarms of enemy attacks and a fair amount of shelling. This very much disturbed poor Aitches, who shifted his tent nearly every other day under the firm conviction that the enemy were trying to hit him. He did no harm, and it kept the troops amused.

I had quite a good time as I was sent off for long journeys by car to lecture to various army schools. I went once to the 6th Corps school, which was commanded by a colonel of the Irish Guards. He told me Campbell – the great bayonet fighting man – had been there lecturing the previous week. I was very worried to have to lecture after so famous a lecturer and felt that the whole thing would fall rather flat. But at the end the C.O. told me it was just the kind of thing that was wanted. Some time later I met an officer from that school, and he told me the colonel said it was the best lecture he ever heard, which remark I felt to be extremely flattering!

---

[1]'Oh God, our help in ages past, our hope for years to come . . .': Isaac Watts [1764–1748].

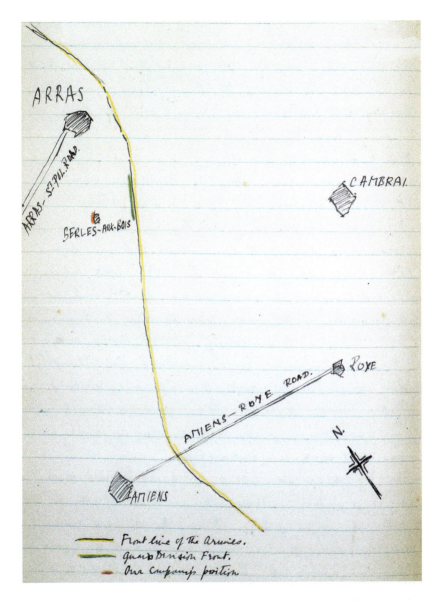

Figure 33
Our position in relation to the rest of the British Front, June–July '18.

We were now using a new pattern tank – the Mark V Ricardo. It was a wonderful machine and a great improvement on the ones we had hitherto used. The engine was far more powerful, and the steering was simplicity itself: you merely pulled up a lever on the right of the driver's seat if you wished to go right, and to the left if you wished to go left. This was done by means of the epi-cyclic gearing, which lay between the gears proper and the track.

The tank, however, had its disadvantages: sometimes the gears for steering would slip and so no power would be transmitted to the track. (I will not enter into a technical description, which would take far too much explanation). The tanks were far hotter than the old ones and gave off a poisonous gas – possibly carbon monoxide. But these defects will, I think, become clear as we go on.

The battalion as a whole was in good state. The prolonged rest at Berle au Bois bucked us up. Our nearness to the line prevented the oncoming of that weakness which always grows in great safety. We felt sure of good infantry support in case of action – the Guards Division had a name you could conjure with. Finally we had had enough testing time for our tanks to show us their good qualities. Their great superiority to the old type made us feel very much more confident. The company was well satisfied as Cook ran Company H.Q. very well indeed. He was virtually Company Commander, and he did his job well. My section was good. I had Sergt. O'Toole as section sergeant, and Cpl. Hayler as section corporal. As you can imagine, I backed these two for anything. L/Cpl Harrison, Quainton's old driver, was also in the section.

For officers I was also well off. My second in command was a well-meaning but hopeless ass called Cartwright. I am afraid I was very down on him, but one was far too harassed to tolerate a bad second in command in those times. I tried him a long time and finally gave him up as hopeless, and Asser was made second in command in his place. Asser was a young fellow of 19½. He had not been in action before and was very keen and enthusiastic. He was very useful to me indeed and practically anticipated one's orders. He could be relied on to the last and was always cheerful, however hard the circumstances. He was the most loyal fellow I ever had under me.

The third officer was Robinson. He was slightly built and not very strong. He had been in the infantry, where he was wounded, and won the Military Medal. His nerves were too far gone for him to be any real use, and his physique was not strong enough to let him stand the strain of any real tank work. But he was a good fellow and did all he could to do his job properly.

I was now a captain with seniority from March 21st – one of the most senior captains in the battalion. The section commanders in the company were Hauser, Johnson and Robinson. Robinson – an American, as I said before – had so far this year been ear-marked as a nucleus man. No sooner had he rejoined us after the Northern show than he started talking. Unfortunately he overdid it. He was over-candid to Aitches, and the worm turned. Robinson transferred his activities elsewhere after a court of inquiry which almost let him in for a court martial.

His section was given to an awfully good chap named Whyte. He had been in C Company and won the M.C. in the March retreat. He was very efficient, quiet and reserved. I think he was aged about 20.

The hopes of continued rest were becoming faint. It seemed incredible that the enemy would be passive much longer. At last on July 15th he broke through in Champagne. I need not describe the subsequent French counter-attack, as you know as much of it as I do. Only it happened that I knew of the movement of the 51st Division to that sector and was prepared for *some* of what happened. The effect of the French victory was very great on us and, I expect, on the whole British army. We felt that all was well at last.

All the time we were at Berle au Bois, our battalion had been ready for action at a moment's notice. At midday on August 4th a meeting of officers was called at Company H.Q.

At that meeting we were informed that our tanks must be ready to leave for an unknown destination at 6 p.m. If asked where we were going, we were to answer that we were off for a practice run. This excuse would satisfy most troops very well, as we had often been for them. The surprise would come when they found we had not returned, and I felt particularly sorry for poor old Sargent,[1] who was painting a picture of our tanks and had said he was coming once more! As you know, he finished it, and I have since seen it.

At 6 p.m. I paraded the section. We packed our camp and moved off at 6.30 p.m. – the time appointed for my section. With Asser's help I had all arrangements working absolutely smoothly.

---

[1] John Singer Sargent, painter [1856–1925].

We drove to a wood some five miles back and reached it without mishap by 10 p.m. – a very great change from the old business! We then covered our tank tracks in the mud by brushing them over the whole distance (to hide our movements from enemy aeroplane photography) and turned in in our improvised quarters by midnight.

The next day was spent in cleaning up and fitting out our tanks so that everything was as near perfection as possible. For there was no doubt at all that we were in for action. Near our camp was the 6th Corps Officers Club and E.F.C. This was a very fine club and very good meals. Our company decided to go and have a jolly good dinner there that night, as it was our last chance for some time probably. We collected kindred spirits in A and C, and, after all our work was done and the men were settled for the night, we set out. We only had to go across a couple of fields.

We had a very pleasant evening. The food was very good and there was a band playing. We had very good wine and ended up with good cigars and a liqueur. It was rather solemn to think of what was coming, as we sat and listened to the band. I think we all felt relieved rather than anxious, for now at last our time to attack had come and the months of waiting were over.

We sat and smoked and talked till late, for we were determined to make the best of our luxury while it lasted. At last we went out into the cold starlight night and returned to camp to sleep.

The next day we pushed in our tank sponsons and prepared for our trek. We were to move off to Santy to entrain at 4 p.m., as we were far enough behind the front line to move in daylight without giving the enemy much indication of our movements. We might simply be entraining for an ordinary relief. The train journey was, of course, made at night. I propose only to touch now on the main facts. You must fill in the detail from what I have said before. What I want you to note carefully are these two points – the extraordinarily short hours of rest we had (with consequent exhaustion of personnel) and the absolutely vital need for secrecy. If you will keep these two points in mind and realize how they acted on one another, you will get some idea of the tremendous strain that was put on us all, and more particularly on those of us in authority.

Here are the facts. We entrained and had everything done by 6 p.m. At 8 p.m. the train moved out with officers and men lying on the open trucks under their tanks (for protection from the night air). At midnight we arrived at our detraining point. We detrained and drove our tanks to a wood two miles off. The R.T.O. [Railway Transport Officer] at the station told me we were the second tank battalion to detrain that night. It was more than ever clear that something very big was coming. We covered our tank tracks and made snug at about 5 a m. At 9 a.m. we had our meal and tuned up our engines. We pushed out our sponsons and cleaned all guns.

It was now about 8 p.m. on August 6th. At dusk we moved off again and trekked about six miles. This was a very big business: no lights could be used, and the only thing we knew was that we were near Amiens; it was pouring rain; a large number of men fainted off through fumes, and here my Cambrai experience came in useful and I put straight a good many men from other corps as well as our own. We used all our men very hard as we made them cover our tracks as we went. One or two tanks broke down just before dawn and caused fearful anxiety as the whole show would be given away if a tank was seen by an enemy aeroplane. Fortunately the pouring rain stopped the enemy coming. But in case of accidents we had a powerful squadron in the air the whole time. Their orders were that no enemy aeroplane was ever to get back to its lines. In the end all the tanks of our company were in by 5 a.m., and the stray tanks of other companies got in without observation.

It was now the morning of August 7th. Orders were issued that the men were not to turn in. They were at once set to cleaning up and greasing. The safety clips from the shells were removed, and all the S.A.A. [small arms ammunition] was 'sized' for the Lewis guns. (This is done by dropping each round into the gun barrel and flicking it out again.) My tanks had done this anyhow, so all was well. By the time the job was done, breakfast was ready, and the camp turned in to sleep at 10 a.m.

This unfortunately did not apply to section commanders. I was first summoned to Battalion H.Q. and told briefly that my section was to operate on the extreme right of the British Army for the start of the battle and was then to shift a little further to the right and operate with the French. I then returned to C.H.Q., and here I was given detailed orders. The general plan was as follows. The allies were about to begin their great offensive battles. As a preliminary the 4th British Army and the 1st French Army, under the personal command of Sir Douglas Haig, were to clear Amiens (see diagram, Figure 34).

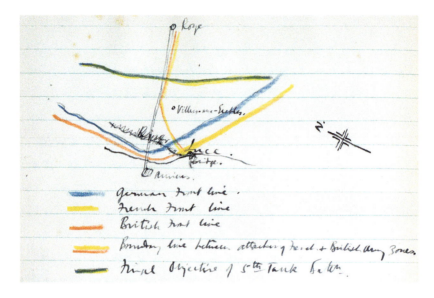

Figure 34

B Company were to be on the extreme right of the 4th Army. No. 8 Section were to keep in the British zone until the armies reached the Amiens–Roye road, and then 8 Section were to keep on the right of the road and help the French to take Villers-aux-Erables. A Company would remain on the final objective line, and the attack would then be carried on by the 1st Tank Battalion. Opposition would be stiff as the enemy were concentrated there ready to attack. We were then issued with barrage maps and ordinary maps and told details of the terrain. The obstacle of the River Luce was greatly feared. The section commanders were given good air reconnaissance photographs and dismissed with Aitches' blessing. We had one new thing to think over, and that was the [German] Anti-Tank rifle (Figure 35). This weapon fired bullets that could pierce our armour, and we had apparently no answer. But in the end, it turned out, we were saved by the enemy morale. They could not see that they were doing any damage, for if one man was hit, the next one carried on. But the biggest argument was the fact that no one likes to see a tank suddenly loom out of the mist, and you can see from the photo (Figure 36) that it is not an encouraging sight from the front – which is the enemy's view.

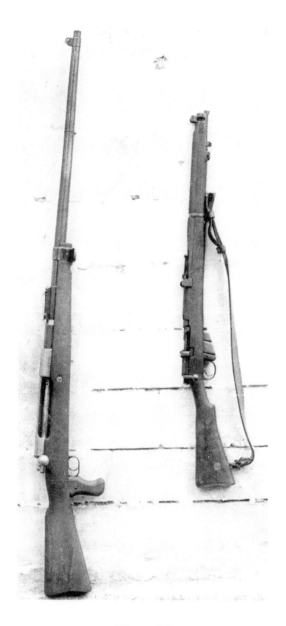

Figure 35
German anti-tank rifle compared with the British Infantry Rifle. It was really, as you see, simply a huge rifle firing very big armour-piercing bullets. It was fired on a tripod.

My job was not yet over, however. I was to meet Major Hotblack from the Tank Corps staff, and he would take me to the French Divisional H.Q. to finish off arrangements for Villers-aux-Erables and to look over the country. Hotblack is a man with a reputation. He is known throughout the British Army for coolness and pluck. He has the D.S.O. and bar and about five other decorations. He had spent a lot of his time behind the enemy lines as a spy and was dropped there occasionally by British aeroplanes.

We set out at 11 a.m. and went over very heavy country for about four miles. We then reached French H.Q. at about 12.30 and spent twenty minutes shrugging our shoulders, spreading out our hands and smiling like a party of deaf-and-dumb lunatics. I was too tired to care much or know much.

Hotblack and I then went over the Luce by a very rickety and smashed bridge and crawled about on our stomachs in the long grass in front of the French position. At the end I had a very clear idea of our route from behind the French lines to the British lines.

The weather had now turned hot and fine. One thing resulted at once from our reconnaissance. It was clear that the bridge **A** (Figure 37) would have to be seen to and built up before any tank could cross it. It was decided that I had better do it. So I was finally ordered to let Asser bring on my section in the evening while I went ahead and saw to the job.

When I got back to camp, I gave my tank commanders all the information I knew and a good deal of advice that I had learned by practical experience. Especially I warned them that if a machine-gun opened fire on the tank and sparks started flying off so as to make observation impossible, the only thing to do was to shut all observation holes and steer the tank so that the sparks flew off in front of the officer's and driver's seats. By this means you ensured putting the machine-gun out, for you knew you must be driving straight on to it. The tanks were to set out at 9 p.m.

Figure 36
Front view of a tank crossing a trench. This gives a good idea of your observation from the tank and the enemy's observation from the ground. Under M.G. fire the right-hand flap of the tank would be closed – thus giving less observation still.

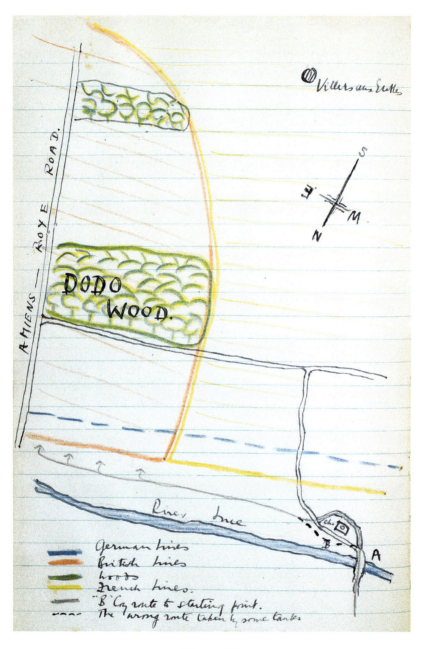

Figure 37
August 8th, Battle of Amiens.

At 3.30 I had some Maconochie stew and tea and turned in. I didn't sleep, of course. I simply watched the sky grow darker and wished in a dull kind of way that I could be spending that night between clean sheets and under a decent roof.

At 6 p.m. I got up and put on my Sam Browne. I picked up my heavy walking-stick (I had given up carrying a revolver in action now) and walked out. I saw Asser before I left.

I reached the bridge at **A** (Figure 37) and found a party of men from a pioneer battalion already there. I told them what to do and sat on the parapet of the bridge, puffing my pipe. I did not like the job for these reasons. The French had told me the Boche shelled the bridge with absolute regularity every evening. At 9 p.m. our tanks would set out, and the sound of their engines could be very clearly heard. Therefore, even supposing the enemy did not do his ordinary evening strafe, it was more than likely that he would open harassing fire on the bridge and roads as soon as he heard unusual movements behind our line. Our only protection lay in the fact that an attempt was being made to screen the noise of our engines by flying Handley Page aeroplanes. These make a noise very like tanks, so we hoped the enemy would see them and think they were responsible for the noise.

These considerations and the anxiety of my job rather crushed me. I sat still and felt numbed with an almost physical pain, which seemed to make movement difficult. At last 9 p.m. came, and I heard our tanks, five miles away, starting up. I didn't realize that my ear was well trained to their noise and that I was alert and expecting to hear it. It merely seemed incredible to me that the enemy could not hear it.

But the miraculous happened. The enemy did not shell that bridge till every tank had crossed it.

When the job was finished, I went back to meet our tanks, which were now drawing near. They were now so near the line that it was impossible to run the engines at high power without making discovery a certainty. All were put into low gear, and the rate of progression was 19 yards to the minute.

It is impossible to convey any idea of the strain this put on us all. We walked slowly in front of the tanks and waited for shells. The strain had a very curious effect; I felt that all anxiety had become too much; I felt just like a small child that has had rather a tearful day and wants to be put to bed by its mother; I felt curiously eased by lying down on the bank by the side of the road, just as if I was lying peacefully in someone's arms.

I went to the back of the column and talked to Asser. As we went past French H.Q., I went in and collected a couple of extremely tired-looking pigeons with which to send back information to the French. Whether they ever took a message back or not I don't know. When I *did* release them, they looked more like making a separate peace with the enemy than anything else.

The whole company crossed the bridge all right, and that was one load off my mind. No sooner was this done, however, than another stunt was put on me. Frantic appeals for help came from Aitches up in front. He had done no reconnaissance, and Carter had been far too busy drafting and issuing maps to get up to the line to do it. They had gone to the village and were not sure of the way as a very thick fog had arisen from the River Luce and hidden everything. I therefore pointed out to Aitches the way round by the road. Unfortunately some tanks took the wrong route and went into a swamp against which I had warned Aitches. They got out very late and after great hard work.

After this mishap I went in front with Aitches and Carter, and we worked our way forward through the mist by what I knew of the land in daylight. There was always the chance of getting too near the river and thus ditching all our tanks, and there was every likelihood that we should not end up opposite our appointed position. It was a very great responsibility, and I hated shouldering it. Aitches should have done it, and he was made a major precisely in order to take on these responsibilities. When we had gone far enough, as I thought, we stopped and turned our tanks facing the front (the section positions are marked by arrowheads in Figure 37). As it turned out subsequently, these positions were correct.

We switched off our engines and waited for zero. At five minutes to zero hour I ordered the crews of my section into their tanks and told them to start up. There was only one comment: the section wag called out, 'Those gentlemen wanting to go home to England on leave fall in here with me.'

At this moment we saw dimly the figure of a British officer flying past. 'Good luck you fellows! Good luck!', it yelled, and disappeared into the mist. It was Aitches going off back into safety. He was taking no risks of being caught in the barrage!

At a minute to zero I ordered our tanks forward. As Hauser and I stood together, we could hear the heavy drone of the tanks for miles through the still night. The tanks all along the front had commenced to move forward and our time had come.

Hauser and I walked forward as nonchalantly as possible. By the time we reached and crossed our front-line trenches, our barrage would have opened. At the moment the air was heavy with the deep drone of hundreds of tanks, but there was no other noise.

Then suddenly our barrage opened. Our guns were firing from high ground behind us, and as we looked back the mist was pierced with gun flashes and looked like a wall of fire. The earth shook as we walked. Behind us we heard the fierce crackling of our guns like a great bonfire, and overhead the shells wailed and screamed – the same fearful tornado as ever. We had been promised terrific gunfire, and this was it. Our artillery was in absolutely overwhelming strength, and it seemed incredible that the enemy could live through our bombardment.

As we walked on, the air grew darker, for the British artillery were firing smoke shells to screen the tank advance and the smoke was blowing on to us.

We wondered where the enemy barrage would fall and whether we should get caught in it. But his guns still remained silent. The noise of our guns became worrying and exasperating. Why on earth didn't the enemy fire and end our anxiety?

Suddenly I saw that one of our tanks in front had stopped. We went forward and found it was Asser's tank. His petrol feed (Autovac) had given out. It was impossible to imagine anything worse. There he was, stuck – just where the enemy guns might drop their barrage. As we stood and waited for him to go on, suddenly there was a roar and a flash and great clods of earth fell all over us. The enemy barrage had opened.

It was now only two minutes since our barrage opened, and it seemed like years. At this moment Asser bawled out, 'All right!', and his tank moved forward. It was just possible he had saved himself. We saw his tank move on and get swallowed up in the smoke.

It was now too dark to see as the smoke swirled round us and hid everything. Hauser and I walked on by compass. The first part of the attack proceeded well, apparently, for Dodo Wood was reached, and great opposition was expected there. We reached Point **C** (Figure 38)

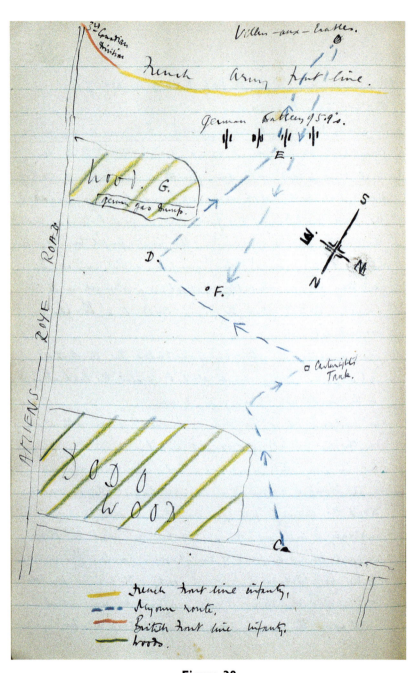

Figure 38
August 8th battle.

and now discovered that the enemy had shifted his barrage onto the road there. Their fire was so terrific that it seemed impossible to go on. We could see absolutely nothing. You will understand how thick it was when I tell you that as Hauser and I sheltered under the road bank at **C**, we thought the tall grasses on the other side of the road were the trees that lined the Amiens–Roye road! They looked just like tall trees in the distance, so you can tell how puzzled and lost we were.

While we were there, Johnson came up. He lay down with us. So now there were three section commanders together and two section runners.

At last we worked things out together and decided we had better shift forward somehow. But the shells were bursting all round us and it seemed impossible to stand up and yet live.

Johnson and I looked up for a moment, and the next thing we knew was that a piece of shell had pierced his arm. We bound it with tourniquet to prevent the blood spouting from his artery, but he was too bad to go on.

The next moment, as I and a runner named Sweeting crouched together in one spot, a shell seemed to burst on top of us, and I heard a groan from Sweeting. The left side of his tunic seemed covered with blood, and as I looked, I discovered that the whole of his left side had been torn away so that the inside of the trunk lay exposed. But he was not dead.

He was quite a young boy and was terrified, as he did not quite realize what had happened. He tried to see what had happened, but I would not let him. I pretended to bandage him, but of course the field dressing was far too small and simply didn't come near to covering the cavity. He kept on saying, 'I'm done for, sir! I'm done for!', hoping against hope I would contradict him. This I did, telling him it was nothing – but his eyes were already glazing over, and it was clear that death was even then upon him. He kept trying to cough, but of course the wind only came out of his side. He kept asking me why he couldn't cough.

He gave me his mother's address, and I promised to write. The bombardment was now dying down, so I sent the other runner to take him to the dressing station. He actually walked there with their support and reached the dressing station before dying. This incident upset Hauser and me very badly, and we were very sick.

I mention it in such detail, horrible as it is, because it had a great effect on me. The look in his eyes was the same as that in the eyes of a bird that has been shot – mingled fear and surprise. I didn't see then, and I don't see now, why that fellow and many like him should have been taken from their English homes (and their German homes) to die for a squabble they didn't understand and couldn't realize. It was simply the distrust, so frivolously sown by grown-up children who wanted to satisfy their childish ambitions, that led to Hell for us and misery for so many homes. The sooner people realize the criminal folly of their leaders the better.

The bombardment had now practically died down, and we determined to push on. Hauser went off to the left to find his section. Johnson had gone to the dressing station, and I went on straight forward alone.

The first thing I came to was one of my tanks broken down. This belonged to Richards, who was quite a young boy and had only just joined our battalion before action. At the last moment he was sent into the show instead of Robinson. I left him to get on as best he could while I pushed on.

The next thing I came to was Cartwright's tank. He had strayed off the right track and was a bit in the French lines. I told his tank by one number that showed. There was nothing else to tell it by because it had received a direct hit and was going up in flames. There were no survivors from it. Cartwright, Sergt. O'Toole and all the rest of the crew had been burnt to death.

Again I went on and reached Point **D** (Figure 38). Here there was another B Company tank, but not in my section. This was manoeuvring round just going forward when it got a direct hit and went up in flames. One man half struggled out but died before he was quite out. The rest were burnt before I could get there.

I went on as I could not get near the tank. All the ammunition was going off, and every now and then a piece of the tank would fly out as a shell went up. It looked rather like a squib in a fireworks display.

Figure 39
The effects of a British shell-burst on a German Outpost party. The photo was taken on a track leading off the Amiens–Roye road.

As I went on – I was about 60 yards behind the infantry by now – I walked into gas. There had been a German gas dump in the wood, and the British artillery had blown it up. As a result the whole wood and the valley in which it stood was one mass of gas.

I pushed on to find Asser, as I presumed he had gone on to help the French take Villers-aux-Erables. I passed the remains of a German battery at **E** (Figure 38). It was completely wrecked, and dead were lying everywhere. The German signal for hurricane fire was still stuck up by the guns, and one wondered what it must have been like when that signal was put up when our barrage fell that morning. I armed myself with a German automatic and pushed on.

I soon reached the front line of French infantry and found they were stationary. This was in accordance with the plan. The pause was of ten minutes and was designed to give breathing space to our troops. By now the enemy fire had gone completely. Only his infantry and machine-guns were fighting. Asser, so the French told me, had gone on to Villers-aux-Erables to clear up any remaining opposition.

So I stopped with them and waited. The day was now bright and clear. Our artillery was coming forward, so there was little or no gunfire. At last the French pushed on and simply walked through Villers-aux-Erables without opposition. I discovered Asser at our end of the village. He had done his job and run out of petrol.

All our work was done now, so all that was left was to get back to our 'Rallying Point' (**F**, Figure 38). After petrol had been fetched, Asser drove back, and at **F** we found Richards.

Although only one of my tanks had done anything, yet it had been quite enough to do the job allotted to the section. There were hardly any infantry casualties, all objectives had been reached, and the second line of infantry and tanks were already going through to carry on the offensive. We saw the 1st Battalion going forward away on our left – they were to take on the work we had started.

We were absolutely tired out, so we decided to sleep at **F** (Figure 38) while we awaited orders. One man was made sentry to guard against gas and so on, and in about two minutes the rest of us were fast asleep. I awoke to find Colonel O'Kelly had turned up. He looked on me with a watery eye and asked for information. This I gave him.

I asked for orders, and he told us the battalion was rallying at the wood (**G**, Figure 38) and that we should make a camp there and await orders.

This wood was now clear of gas. We fixed up shelters with our tarpaulins, and before long the cooking department and reserves, generally of our company, had arrived and started operations. A few men were told off to go and bring the remains of various crews that were knocked out.

The advance had gone so well that we were now two or three miles behind the line.

Hauser turned up at about 6 p.m. I was very pleased to see him again as he was a good man. But I had a good deal to say to him. He was very peevish at the time – chiefly nerves – but I wouldn't spare him. We discussed the day's actions, and I told him I felt I had been an awful fool and that neither of us had been very bright on the road (C, Figure 38). After a little talk we made vows not to do anything so feeble again, and we then separated for our duties. That evening we fed and made all arrangements by sections (i.e. not as a united company). Aitches and Cook came and exchanged a few remarks. Cook, who had been superintending all supplies etc. as a second in command has to do, was very fed up and complained bitterly that he had not realized how many fools there were in the British Army till that day. Aitches was fretful and looked very nervy, and so were we all.

We were all very tired but had to work till about 10 p.m., getting our tanks ready for action. When that was over, we turned in to sleep. Our wood was soundly bombed that night, but our company had no casualties.

The weather at this time was curious; it was very hot during the day and bitterly cold at night. There was not much water to be had to drink, so the heat was a nuisance; at night we only had one blanket so the cold got at us.

The morning of the 9th burst on us with a large and varied assortment of rumours. We knew all about the victory, of course. That, however, did not much worry us. The real question was a more intimate one. How long were we going to be left in peace?

At 10 a.m. it was solved. I had to take forward two tanks, Richards and Asser to act as a reserve in case of accidents. We were all assured it was the merest precaution – no chance of being used at all.

Hauser also was to come forward with two tanks, and at 10.30 we left and pushed up by the side of the Amiens–Roye road. We reached a village about two miles ahead (called Beaumont). Here we stopped and awaited orders. We had our dinner and hoped everyone had forgotten where we were. We had some indication of our advance at this time, for, as we waited, a lorry turned up towing an observation balloon through the air. This was the usual method of advance for the 'sausages' in swift open warfare, but this was the first time I had seen it done. Instead of drawing the balloon to earth and laboriously packing up, you simply started the 'anchor' lorry and casually trundled up the road.

The arrival of our friend meant that the enemy were at least three miles ahead.

At about 2 p.m. the colonel arrived in his car. He poured out a flood of instructions and sped back to his lair. We cursed bitterly. Again we were to advance – always in reserve, of course – still no fear of action. We pushed off at about 3 p.m. but soon had to stop as an enemy 'sausage' had appeared and was watching. We went on at 6 p.m. I was in command of the party.

We were all very tired indeed – so tired that when the tanks stopped for some reason and we leant against them for rest, we found ourselves asleep in about two minutes. It was bitterly cold and very dark long before we reached our destination. In the distance we saw the red glare of burning houses and dumps which the retreating enemy had fired.

We reached our wood very late owing to many stoppages – our tanks were not running so well now as they had been. When we had parked up under an avenue of trees, we oiled and greased our tanks so they were quite ready to go on. The men were all so tired that the work went very slowly. At 11.45 p.m. we turned in.

This turning in wasn't a very comfortable business. We had no blankets, and it was bitterly cold. The most important men were the drivers. We put them in the tanks so that they could sleep well by the warmth of the engines. There was no room for more than two, so the tank commanders of each tank slept inside as well. These two people were the most important of us all now, as once in action everything depended on them. The rest of us got under the tanks and lay on the ground. At 2 a.m. I awoke to find myself being pulled from under the tank. I tried to resist this extraordinary business, but found myself so stiff with cold I couldn't do anything. I was remorselessly dragged out and found my 'foe' was an officer. He was bawling something in my ear, but for a long time I couldn't make out what he said. At last I 'came to' and discovered he was delivering orders.

There was a hitch in the advance. C Company had gone ahead and needed reserves. They were being reinforced by some of A and some of B Company tanks. My two tanks were to go forward, and I was to hand them over to a Capt. Llewellyn of A Company, as they were to fight under him. I objected, saying I wanted to command my men and that I was less tired than they were. It would look ridiculous if I stayed out of action while they went in. It was no good. It was a very urgent business, and there was no time for argument. We had to reach the starting-point by 4 a.m., and there I was to 'hand over'. Hauser was to go into action with his two tanks and two of A Company's.

We had an awful time getting the crews awake. We hit the men about and propped them up against the tank, but as soon as we had awoken one and gone off to awake another the first would be asleep.

In the end we started the tanks somehow. Only the driver was allowed in the tank. We made the men walk to awaken them thoroughly. Asser and I walked in front. I condoled with him and tried to cheer him and so on, but he really didn't need it. I remember he said he supposed it was all in the game, and one couldn't grumble about having to fight. Nevertheless it *was* very bad luck. We had all been worked off our feet, and the crews really were not fit for action.

We drove up by the side of the road, and gradually the grey dawn appeared. As we advanced, our guns kept up an intermittent fire around us. We hurried forward as fast as our tanks could go, for it was very late.

At last we drew near our starting-point. When we were within 200 yards of our place, the attack started. On our right we saw the bluish figures of the French advancing. German gas shells were bursting amongst them, and we saw men totter forward and fall; here and there a whole platoon would melt away.

The enemy had got some guns up at last, and his shells were falling fairly fast and especially on the road. Our tanks deployed into line and sheared off the road a little. Richards, Asser, and I ran forward and met Llewellyn. He hurriedly shouted orders to them – all, of course, of the very vaguest description. I said goodbye and got down into a shell-hole and watched them get lost in smoke.

My orders were to report to Company H.Q. as soon as I had handed over. So after five minutes I cleared out for camp.

On my way back I saw one thing that is worth mention. I saw the British artillery do an open-warfare movement – probably the first

since 1914. I was going down the road when a battery of field artillery dashed up at the gallop and swerved suddenly off the road. I heard the commander shout 'Action Front', and within about one minute the battery had opened fire. It was an extraordinarily thrilling sight.

I reached camp at about 11.30 a.m. after a very weary march back. The Company H.Q. were still at the wood (**G**, Figure 38). I reported and went to sleep. This was midday on the 10th of August. At 8 p.m. news of the action came through. There had been no advance. Something had gone wrong. Five out of six tanks had been knocked out. The sixth tank was Asser's, and this had not been seen or heard of since the start of the battle. Richards had been badly wounded and was evacuated. There were not many survivors.

I was very distressed at the news of Asser. I still hoped he was all right, since there was no actual bad news of him.

The next day Cook and I went forward to find out what we could. When we reached the line, we found that the Division with which our tanks should have fought (the 32nd) had been relieved by the 3rd Canadian. These troops had completed the attack that the 32nd had failed in. So the line was about two miles further on. The scene of the 'advance' was curious.

In front of the line, as it was on the morning of the 10th, there were five tanks. All were facing the enemy in a neat line except one. This apparently had been following another when the one in front was knocked out. Immediately afterwards it had received a direct

---

Figure 40
Canadian infantry advancing through Dodo Wood on Aug. 8th. The first line of infantry has already passed – these are the 'moppers-up' who make sure none of the enemy are still holding out. Our tanks skirted this wood as it is very dangerous for tanks to drive through woods. It is very easy for a tank to get 'bellied' on a stump. The wood had not been shelled before the battle. Nevertheless you will see it shows distinct signs of bombardment. Actually an enormous number of shells are needed to make any real impression on a wood. To one who knows how little shelling affects a wood, this picture gives a good idea of the intensity of the British bombardment. Note the men are wearing 'battle order', i.e. no packs but just the bare necessities for fighting. At a time like this the wood is saturated with the fumes of bursting shells – a smell very like acetylene gas.

hit, which killed the crew but did not, for a little while at any rate, stop the engine. The tank had gone on and crawled a little way up the one in front.

All the tanks had carried gun cotton. This was to be used to blow up the tank if the only alternative was surrender. This gun cotton had been exploded by the direct hits, and the tanks were thus left there looking like burst toads – the roofs lifted off, the sides bulging out. Asser's tank I could not see.

Cook had gone off further to the right – on the French side of the road. After about an hour he returned and said, 'I've found Asser'. I jumped up at once very pleased and asked 'Where?' and was he all right? Cook replied that he had found him outside his tank, lying on the ground with a bullet through his heart.

We went back very miserable and tired.

On the 12th, Company H.Q. shifted up to the wood where Asser and I spent our last night together. The company was made into one section of four tanks, and I was put in command. We received orders to be prepared for action against two villages – Damery and Parvillers. The details were hopelessly vague, and arrangements were very slipshod. In the meantime we got more detailed news of the action of August 10th. It was all quite simple. Our six tanks left the line more or less together at zero. Asser was on the British right, steered on to the French Front by accident and was accordingly lost to sight. The remaining tanks went forward slowly, expecting the infantry to follow according to plan.

Figure 41

A direct hit. This photo ought really to be the Zonnebeke action of Sept. 26th 1917. This tank was knocked out there by a rather larger shell than usual. To me it is a familiar scene – and still not without horror. Of course, from a direct hit of this kind, it is quite inconceivable that any man of the crew would escape. Even with an 18-pdr the chances of escape were small – especially from a hit in the driver's or officer's seat. But this shell must have been something like 9.2". It was this kind of sight that met the eyes of the Canadian Infantry during the Aug. 8th battle. It was fear of this that made tank work unpleasant. I felt, whenever I was going into action in a tank, that at any moment one of these would come in. And the officer's seat felt more lonely and conspicuous every moment!

Actually, the infantry never left the front line. Hauser, who told me about it, said it was a most extraordinary business. There was no danger, and he himself had followed the tank. (I learned afterwards from one of the men that he did better – he went in sitting on the back of one!) When he had gone a little way, he found the infantry were not following so went back to see what was up. He found the colonel of the battalion, supposed to be supporting him, in tears, and a lot of the men also. Apparently a kind of panic had seized them. Anyway, the C.O. couldn't get the men to budge, and the 52nd Division didn't advance a foot along the whole front. In the meantime the tanks had come on a German field gun, which was behind a ridge. This gun simply put the tanks out of action, one after the other.

The whole action had been very badly managed. The tanks should have been screened by smoke, but the Infantry General, under the impression that he knew more about tanks than we did, refused to give us a smoke barrage. The account of this action was printed and handed round by order of Marshal Foch to all generals. A short note advised that in future all general officers should take the advice offered by officers in command of technical units.

The day we arrived at our new H.Q., we received fresh orders for a new attack. This attack was to be on the villages Damery and Parvillers. At the last moment the attack was called off. I shall send you the maps we were given for the action, as they are a good example of the vague orders we received from now on for the new type of surprise warfare. Rapidly changing conditions and the need for speed and secrecy put an end to such elaborate maps and detailed instructions as we received at Ypres and Cambrai. It is worthwhile to compare this map with the one I was given as a tank commander at Cambrai (1917).

The same orders that called off the action ordered the entire battalion to move. The direction of our move was away from the front, and we congratulated ourselves that this show, at any rate, was all over. The battalion had started with 40 tanks, all brand new and in fine condition. We were now left with six. But this was not all. When we first went in, we could man our tanks with crews of six men (instead of eight, as it should have been). We also had a few rescue men to fill gaps. Now we could only muster crews of five men for female tanks and six for male tanks. As you see, our numbers of men and tanks had fallen.

These six tanks were now in bad running order. They had gone very far without any real overhauling. They were supposed to be capable of 112 miles (the 'life' of a tank). Our estimated distance was already 100 miles per tank. We were guaranteed any amount of engine trouble. Since we were going home, this did not very much worry us.

On the whole we were rather pleased with ourselves. We had been highly complimented by all the generals with whom we worked, and Sir Douglas Haig specially commended us – a very, very rare distinction for a battalion. But the praise that really counted most was that of the ordinary infantry private, and the Canadians couldn't say too much of us. One private actually said he thought every man who went into action in a tank deserved a V.C.!

All this had its bad side too. The Tank Corps badly wanted recruits. But our losses in this action created a bad impression amongst the troops. The Canadians particularly were not anxious to join a new Canadian Tank Battalion that was being formed at this time. There were two actions that chiefly contributed to this besides the battle of August 8th. One was our disaster on the 10th, and the other was a fearful show the 1st Battalion were engaged in. I mentioned that the 1st Battalion took on the action on our front after we stopped on the 8th. The action was conducted by one company of the 1st Battalion, and the company proceeded in a line on the left (British side) of the Amiens–Roye road. Their ten tanks, which were carrying four infantry men each to minimize casualties, were all knocked out. There was not a single survivor below the rank of Major.

Unfortunately all these tanks were knocked out within easy sight of the road. The shortage of men made it quite impossible to bury the dead, and for days these tanks remained where they were knocked out – a fearful sight for every soldier who marched up this main road into action. As a result everyone was convinced that the tanks were simply death traps.

The six tanks were formed into a composite company, and we started back. But we did not go back via the Amiens–Roye road. We suddenly turned northward. I asked where we were going, and Cook replied laconically, 'Another action, old son.' I cursed hard, for I had had enough, and so had everybody else. It was not long before everybody spotted what we were up to (see Figure 42).

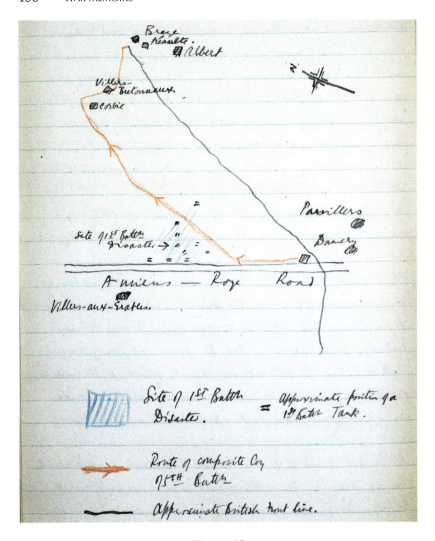

Figure 42
Movements after Aug. 10th battle.

Briefly, our job was this. We were leaving the point of the salient we had created and were moving northward to attack at the flank of the salient. Our actual place of attack was not yet known, but it was not very far from Villers-Bretonneux. We stopped for the night at a small wood. The next day we pushed on as fast as we could to a place called Corbie. Here we came across the Australians who had been the attacking troops in this sector. We reached our destination, just outside the village, at about 2 p.m. It was a pleasant and peaceful spot near a lake. The rest of the day was spent in cleaning up our very dud tanks and doing all we could to put them into fighting trim.

The composite 'company' was put under Aitches' command. But it was decided that the six tanks should be employed as a section. That is to say, they should operate simply as if they were an isolated section of one company and should be commanded in action by one section commander. This was obviously the right thing to do, as it was useless to have two or three captains commanding such a small force.

Finally they decided that I was to command this section in the coming action. I wasn't keen on the job, but I couldn't complain, as I hadn't done very much up to date. They made one more alteration before the action. They took two tanks out of my command – a supply tank and a wireless tank. These two were put under Hauser's command. Neither of them went in the first line but knocked about some 800 yards behind, where they were quite as useless as they would have been further up. The wireless tank was more or less in the nature of a sop to the Higher Command. No one regarded it seriously, and I haven't heard of an occasion when one succeeded in sending a message. The supply tank simply carted petrol and stuff about, and sometimes they were quite useful. Hauser was rather indignant as being saddled with these two but treated it as a joke.

The next day I awoke with a fever. I had caught the 'flu. I lay on the ground the whole day and let someone else superintend the various jobs that had to be done. But the rest was not very long. At 6 p.m. that evening our six tanks moved off – the four fighting tanks in front. We trailed through Villers-Bretonneux very slowly as there was a lot of traffic and, of course, lots of engine trouble. Fortunately Reynolds, the battalion workshops officer, was with us. He was an extraordinarily good engineer, and he usually put things right in less than no time. For my part, I was feeling very ill and neither knew nor cared very much what was happening. I was violently sick every half-mile or so.

They shoved operation orders into me as we went. We were to do an attack at the flank of the salient simply to prevent the enemy from retiring peacefully. It was now the 20th; on the 21st there was to be a big attack on our old front, where we were with the Guards Division.

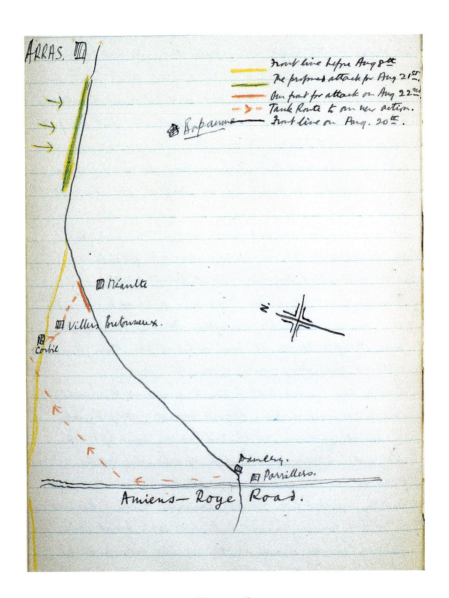

Figure 43
Movements before Aug. 22 battle.

Our own attack was to be on the 22nd, and our objective was our old Christmas Camp at Méaulte (see Figure 43).

The country looked quite good, as, of course, it was little shelled – all the fighting had been of a swift, surprise character, and so the shelling had not been great. While it lasted, it was as intense here as elsewhere, but owing to rapid advances you no longer had the awful devastation of a place like Ypres or the Somme.

Before long the moon came up. It was a cold and beautiful night. Buchanan, my runner, walked with me and helped me along. I will not trouble to describe this trip, as it resembled most of the others except for the fact that I was so violently sick that I really didn't mind much what happened. I remember leaning up against one of my tanks and staring at the moon while the crew sweated away inside trying to make it go. Such little things hardly worried now – one either helped or did not help, and it did not seem to matter very much which. After a time the thing would be sure to go on. Or it would not, and that would mean another crew safe and happy.

At about 1.30 my section of tanks got into trouble. One of my tanks tried to help another that was stuck in some mud and had a defective gear so it could not get out. We swore and cursed and sweated for about an hour and finally got the brute out.

At 3.30 we were within a mile of camp and on top of a ridge overlooking the enemy lines. We travelled along this ridge – parallel to the enemy lines and about five miles from them. At last we reached our destination, and after our usual preparations turned in to sleep. It was about 6.30, and the great Bapaume attack up north of us would have been just beginning.

We had about four hours' sleep, and then the crews prepared tanks for action, and I messed about reading maps and so on. I must have been a queer sight sitting on the ground taking occasional nips of champagne and reading large maps, which lay spread round me. At midday it was decided that I had better go forward with Carter and reconnoitre our route. As there would not be time for us to do a full reconnaissance and get back, it was decided that we should see the place and then wait, at an appointed place near the road, till the tanks were brought up by Hauser.

So Carter and Buchanan and I set out. Buchanan carted some champagne for me to keep me going as I still was in the throes of 'flu.

It was a blazing hot day and I felt absolutely beaten. I was limping with a sore foot and I was hot, feverish and sick. Carter could only keep me going by swearing at me and cursing me up hill and down. I kept on wanting to sit down and rest. He must have been sick of me by the time he'd done!

Well, I remember very little of all this. My impressions are mixed and are something like this: a tank route, which I wasn't to forget, whatever happened; terrific heat and a grey desolate landscape with white chalk diggings and old trenches shining in the sun; a few shells bursting very near; a lot of dead horses and a few men, all very decayed and reeking; some shell-shattered woods; a burning tongue and a very sore heel; finally, lying in the long grass waiting for the tanks to come.

The attack was due to start at dawn – about 6 a.m., I think it was. Aitches was supposed to lead the tanks to where Carter and I were, and then we would lead them to the starting-point. Aitches would then give the order for us to go into action, and after that I should take over the command of the section – it was the ordinary procedure for action.

At about 10.30 the tanks arrived. All seemed to be going on all right. Aitches, however, was not there. Carter and I made enquiries but could not find him.

We went to the front of the column of tanks and led them slowly on through the long grass behind the wood till we reached **B** (Figure 44). Here we stopped our engines and waited till Aitches or someone should come along. The crews all got out of the tanks and lay on the ground beside them. It was now about midnight, as, of course, we had been forced to travel very slowly for fear of making a noise. Carter and I had a discussion together on the question of Aitches' absence, as the matter was becoming serious. If he did not turn up, it meant that we should have to take the responsibility of commencing the tank action on ourselves. If anything went wrong, our position would be far from enviable. After some discussion we both found it useless to hide what was at the back of our minds, and Carter said bluntly that he thought Aitches was shirking the action through funk – it was quite easy to find an excuse for losing the way or remaining in a dugout. We decided that if he didn't turn up, we would put him under arrest – a very dangerous step for junior officers.

At this stage our deliberations were interrupted. First a salvo of shells came over and burst within about 100 yards. This was quickly

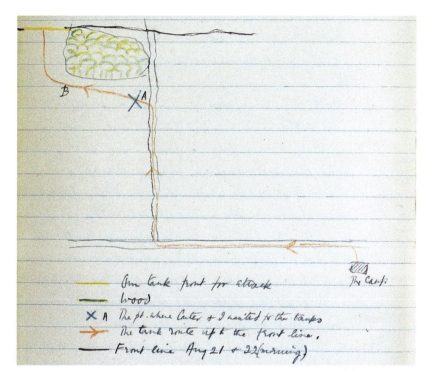

Figure 44

followed by more shells, and in less than no time a regular barrage had fallen all along our line. Had the enemy discovered we were to attack? It certainly looked as if this was a harassing barrage intended to destroy any preparation for an attack on our part.

There was nothing for us to do. We ordered the crews into the tanks and lay on the ground ourselves. The enemy were using their 'contact' shrapnel shells (Figure 45), and the pieces were moaning through the air and striking sparks off the sides of the tanks while we lay by them. We didn't altogether fancy standing up in those circumstances!

We spoke very little but just clenched our teeth and fretted beneath this roar of shell bursts and the whining of the splinters. At about half an hour before zero, the bombardment suddenly increased. It was quite clear now that they had got wind of our plans. His artillery were no longer doing harassing fire – this was the real bombardment.

Figure 45
This shell was a rather poor imitation of the British '106 fuse. It was designed to burst immediately it touched the surface of the ground. As a result the splinters would fly out sideways at a height of about three feet from the ground. The crater made would be small, but the effect of such a shell, bursting amongst infantry, would be very great.

There was still no sign whatever of Aitches. At last I shouted to Carter that I thought we had better start without orders. He agreed, and we both ordered the crews to start their engines. I ordered all tanks to follow the first one and ordered the first one to follow me. Carter's job was now over, and I took it for granted that he would go back. I envied him thoroughly. Here I had to walk in front of these brutes for about 400 yards in shell-fire that was much too heavy for my liking, whereas he could either go back or stay where he was till things improved and then clear out. But I found him walking into action with me. 'What are you doing?' I shouted at him. He calmly replied that he thought he 'might as well come along'! I know that if I am really fit I can usually go into an action somehow if I *have* to – but I could certainly never have taken his choice on that occasion. Under circumstances like those the chance of safety would be overpowering, to me at any rate.

The whole place seemed to rock and sway beneath us. I looked at my watch and saw it was a minute to zero. We were practically on the front line so that the 'timing' had been all right.

Here let me give our orders as they finally stood: it was expected that after the attack on the Guards front on the 21st had taken place, the enemy would retire on our front. Our attack was intended to harass their retreat. A few tanks from D Battalion (4th Battalion) were to attack the old Christmas camp at Méaulte – we were to attack further to the right. Our objective was the line beyond a row of trees (see diagram, Figure 46). Danger spots were the road that passed Méaulte camp and the valley known as Happy Valley – a singularly ironical title. At Ypres, in 1917, it had been the enemy policy to shell the tops of hills and high ground generally. But now they concentrated fire on the valleys. So that if we took the valley as intended, it was extremely unlikely that the troops in it would describe it as 'happy'.

The British artillery were to use a little smoke – especially over Happy Valley. The rest of the barrage was to be 'one-third thermite'. This meant that one third of the barrage were to be incendiary shells. The 'thermite' shell burst on contact and burnt anything near it, so it was quite effective against troops lying on the ground. I never really discovered if it actually did any great damage – it certainly must have done if it fell among troops in mass.

After the 'green' line (Figure 46) had been consolidated, we were to find out if the infantry wanted us any longer. If they did not, we were to rally our tanks and go back to camp. We all hoped the enemy *had* retired. But it was quite clear now that his guns, at any rate, had not retired. Their shells were falling fast, and all hopes of a walk-over were dispelled. I signalled to the leading tank that they were not on the line of attack, and Carter and I lay down in a shell-hole and watched the four go past and disappear into the smoke.

Carter then left me, and I went on in the hopes of seeing something of what the tanks did. I was very sick and groggy and didn't mind much what happened to me or my tanks.

I am really rather at a loss to describe the rest of the action. I only remember incidents and cannot remember how I got from one place to another. I think the best thing I can do is simply to give you a series of incidents in the order in which they came (as far as I know). The dotted line on the sketch map (Figure 46) gives you *some* idea of my wanderings, but I am afraid it is very inaccurate. It merely represents the best-connected idea I can give of an action that was blurred and indistinct to me even while it was on.

My first impression was coming up with the infantry, who were holding a line of very broken trenches. As far as I remember, I stayed some time watching and waiting for something to happen. The sun was bright, and it was already getting hot. Most of the gun-smoke had blown away, and you could see the landscape quite clearly, as I had seen it the previous day on reconnaissance. The men were lying up against the remains of the forward slope of the trench and watching for an enemy counter-attack. The flies were very troublesome and especially worrying a young boy in front of me. He was, however,

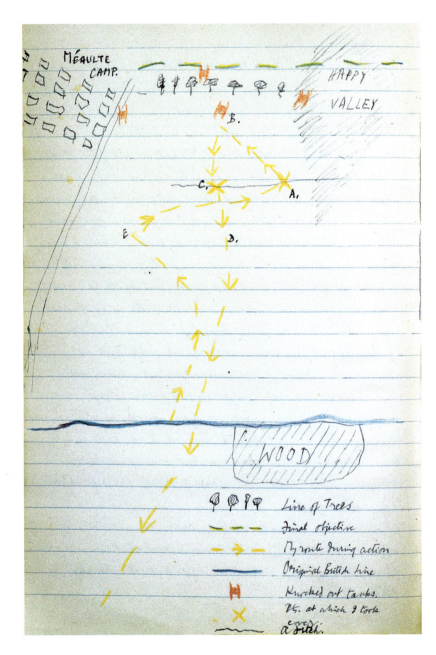

Figure 46

almost past caring, as he had a bad wound in his stomach. There was nothing to be done for him, as he was beyond hope. I remember feeling half fascinated by it all: the heat, the flies, the ominous lull in the battle and the poor boy with his face deathly white and half-shut eyes. I could see nothing of my tanks. Later, when the infantry had advanced again, I went rather to the left of our front – towards **E** (Figure 46).

The ground here was low-lying and rose gradually towards the enemy. The trees were on the high part of the ridge, and the 'green' line was on the downward slope again.

As I approached, I saw that the enemy were concentrating fire on a spot of ground in front of me (**E**, Figure 46). The lull was still on, but one gun seemed to have a particular dislike for this place. Every 20 seconds or so you would see a great red cloud burst up from the ground and roll out sideways, like some huge flower unfolding. It must have been an old house once, for you only get red like that when brick dust is going into the air. I approached the place to see if a tank was there, but found nothing. I lay on the ground for some time and watched the performance It was curiously monotonous – the same roar, the explosion and hissing of the splinters, and then the 'flower'.

The next thing I remember was tottering off towards the right. The ground was very scrubby – short furze bushes, thistles and dried-up grass or baked mud. The artillery fire was growing fiercer again.

It was now that the extent of our losses became apparent. Every here and there men were lying about wounded. The wounds were practically all shell wounds. Time and again I heard someone shouting and went over to find a man lying crumpled up. They all wanted help and wanted to be taken back. I, of course, lied and said I would send help soon and that they were all right. But I could always see they knew it was nonsense.

I found myself lying in a kind of small ditch grown over with thistles and scrub. There were three or four infantrymen with a Lewis gun by me. We had to keep our heads down as odd bullets kept coming over and sometimes you heard the unpleasant 'flick' of a near one.

It seemed fairly clear at this stage that the battle was over. Most objectives seemed to be reached, artillery fire was not very heavy, and everyone seemed to be waiting for something to happen.

Our wait was enlivened by some enemy aeroplanes. We heard droning and saw four or five aeroplanes come towards us flying very

low. Amongst the others there was one painted bright red – the colour usually believed to be affected by Richthofen [celebrated German pilot, nicknamed the Red Baron]. They saw us and blazed off some rounds of machine-gun at us, dropped a couple of bombs and cleared off. None of their efforts met with any success.

After some time I walked forward to **B**. This was a tank I saw when I was at the ditch. It had made no movement, so I presumed it had been knocked out. When I reached it, I found a hole in the side and the name ANCRE written on it. It was an old tank that had been used in the Somme battle of 1916. I had hardly time to see it when a shell came over. The enemy was determined to keep people away from it.

From here I just saw one tank on my right and in front of me. It was going up in flames and was in front of the British front line.

I got into touch with the infantry battalion H.Q. and found out that our objectives had been reached but with heavy casualties. The enemy infantry seemed to have been withdrawn, but their guns had done great damage. They had practically withdrawn all Howitzers, and short-range weapons generally, and pounded us with guns.

I decided to go back further left to see if I could find anything out about my other two tanks. I had reached the ditch again (**C**, Figure 46) when I saw a tank coming back. I went towards it and found it was a 4th Battalion tank. He told me he had seen four tanks going up in flames on his right and that he thought they were all 5th Battalion tanks. I assumed he had seen my three going up. I asked him if he had had any orders or knew anything. He told me all objectives were reached and that all 4th Battalion tanks had been told to go home.

I then decided I ought to go back to the front line. There seemed nothing to do when I got there but – if anything went wrong and questions were asked, it would be safer to be discovered looking for lost tanks in the front line than three miles behind it.

Figure 47

The attack, Aug. 22nd. Tanks are out of sight in a hollow on the left front. The enemy are counter-attacking, and British reinforcements are going up. The shell-bursts don't appear distinctly, but with care you can pick them out. Of course at this stage of the battle the fire was distinctly slacker than it had been earlier.

Just at this moment one of my runners arrived to say that all my tanks had been knocked out but we had lost *no* men. He said the crews had been given permission to leave (by the respective infantry battalion commanders), and, as they were useless without tanks, they had done so and rallied at the pre-arranged point. Carter had sent the runner off to tell me.

I thanked my stars and told the 4th Battalion officer, 'Home John', and off we went. As we trundled along, we were hailed by numbers of wounded who called to be carried back. The position was a difficult one. Tanks were expressly forbidden to take back wounded if limbs were broken. In a previous action they had been ordered, on coming out of action, to carry back all they could. The result was a tragedy. At the end of half an hour's ride, after an otherwise perfect performance, every wounded man that had been picked up with broken bones was found to be dead. Now all the wounded here were men with broken bones. The shelling had simply smashed legs or arms in nearly every case. A bullet usually made a clean wound, but a shell almost invariably makes a mess. The result was we were forced to refuse these people our help. It was an incredible business. They of course saw a tank as their great chance of safety. They saw us happily going home and clutched desperately at this sudden vision of hope, only to hear us refuse help. I repeated the stale formula, 'Full up, but will send a stretcher bearer', and we went on – probably cursed by men who had never before known one soldier refuse another soldier his help.

At **D** (Figure 46) we passed a whole group of badly hit men. We bound them up as best we could but no more. They were in a helpless and dreadful state and looked at us queerly when we went on without them.

When we reached the original British line, I told some very weary and overworked stretcher-bearers the positions of these men. They looked helplessly at me and said they would fetch them – when they could.

That was the end of the action as far as I was concerned. As soon as I got to camp, a leave warrant was handed to me, and I was told to meet a box-body Ford at a cross-roads just about 400 yards behind the front line from which the morning battle had started. I was very surprised and pleased, as I had not expected leave till very much later – for two or three months, at least.

I dashed off down to the rendezvous and was surprised to find myself going down a road that was being quite heavily shelled. Imagine it if you can – a man with harassed nerves, a touch of flu, a leave warrant in his pocket and a beastly strife on a road he has to take. The leave warrant was the most demoralizing part of it. It makes you so careful when you feel you are so near safety as that.

I reached the rendezvous – a broken church – and waited. The car was late, of course. It was due at 6 p.m., and at 6.05 the enemy started to shell the village. What were they up to? Was it a counter-attack? And what was that fool of a driver doing? Of course they would shell the church. I'd put that fool of a man under arrest as soon as he appeared. At 6.10 I decided it would save unnecessary ceremony if I shot him off-hand. At 6.15 the church started going up, and I edged into the street and bit my nails and cursed the A.S.C. [Army Service Corps] and their works. Why couldn't they be punctual? A minute later there was a whirl of dust, a terrific screech of brakes – and there stood a dear little Ford box-body with a most impertinent look on its face. I shot into it like a rocket and bawled out, 'Boulogne – and drive like hell.' He did.

We raced down the roads like demons, and slowly desolation changed to green fields and daylight to dusk. By midnight we were still careering madly on; but now the moon was up, and it was a peaceful and glorious night. At 4 a.m. we raced into Boulogne, and I got a stuffy little bed in a stuffy little room and was only prevented from thinking I was dreaming it all by the only too obvious fact that I wasn't asleep. Only those who know what central heating in a French hotel in August means can appreciate the fug I endured for those few hours.

At 8.30 I was on board ship, and at 4.30 p.m. I was lying in the Hamman Baths in Jermyn Street, reading about a battle there had been on the West Front. British troops had attacked near Méaulte and had taken a place called Happy Valley, it appeared. At 5 p.m. the enemy had counter-attacked and driven back our advance troops in some places. The enemy's losses were heavy. A man leant across to me – 'Nice little show that, eh, what?' he said. 'Oh, very!' I replied.

That evening I went to see 'The Boy'. I had found out there was no train to Lustleigh where Mother was until 10 a.m. next morning, and I thought this would be a good way of clearing the war out of my mind. W. H. Berry was the chief man, and very inane and silly the whole show was. There were lots of lights, brilliant scenes, nice banging music, loud-voiced and shrieking actors and, in short, everything to make for an unintelligent and expensive evening without any undue effort on my part. I sat back and watched the show and wondered at it all. Ridiculous old men sat about and laughed at silly jokes. Electric light and noise – that was all there was, as far as London was concerned. But I was too fresh from France, and the whole time I saw, in place of the scenes and silly fools, Happy Valley, and men asking to be carried back. It was not a successful show for me. The contrast of wartime London with 'out there' was too great. That London show was a nightmare, and France was a nightmare – but the latter was positively healthy in comparison. The next morning London was behind me, and at about 3.30 p.m. I was at Lustleigh.

The remains of 'flu and a touch of poison gas kept me rather seedy. A doctor gave me some stuff that seemed to do me good and visited me frequently. He refused all payment for he was an ex-army doctor and wouldn't hear of being paid by a soldier. It was just a little ordinary friendly help, he explained. I have since found out that it was a point of honour with all doctors who had been in the army to give medical help freely to service men.

I will not say anything of leave. On September 6th I went back to France. I was in a very cheerful frame of mind. The *last* time I had gone on leave I seemed to be going back to an army faced with overwhelming disaster. This time we seemed to be winning. The Drocourt–Quéant battle was a success, and the 'impenetrable wall of the West Front' seemed to be crumbling at last. One didn't quite like to think about peace; but, at any rate, a Great British Victory generally seemed to be followed by a slight German retreat – a feature that had been absent in most of our victories since 1914. Also, there seemed to be a fair chance that the Allies really would definitely win the war someday.

I got back to the battalion to find things in a queer state. They were all peacefully ensconced at Blangy, and people were up to their usual tricks – some wondering why they hadn't got D.S.O.s, others wondering why they hadn't got majorities. It was fairly amusing so long as you felt there was no chance of being put under command of an absolute fool. B Company remained calm, as any change in a commander could only be for the better.

There was one disquieting feature – a persistent rumour that the battalion was going into action again.

I arrived in the Company Mess at about 2.30 p.m. to find a disconsolate-looking individual endeavouring to deaden the bitterness of army lime juice with copious additions of ration sugar. He gave me the news.

Colonel O'Kelly was going or had gone. His place was taken by an old R.H.G. [Royal Horse Guards] officer who had been O.C. A Company. A Company were commanded by Major Huntlatch, a decent, easy-going old soul who had no intention of taking the war too seriously. C Company were still commanded by Gatehouse, who had got rid of Capt. Homfray (or rather hoped to do so – by pushing him for promotion to Company Commander, major). Our company was in a queer position. It was still commanded by Aitches, but he was moving heaven and earth to get to England to join the cadre of a new battalion that was to be formed. Cook hoped soon to get to England as a Company Commander in this same battalion. Capt. Nixon, who had been a major in the 4th Battalion, was now second in command to our company. He had been reduced to his temporary rank (he had been 'acting' major) as a result of an injudicious quarrel in the 4th Battalion. He was somewhat sore and disgruntled as a result. I had met him at Merlimont when I was there as instructor at the beginning of the year. He had then seemed very efficient but somewhat overbearing.

Carter and Hauser gave me much the same news and also told me about the last action. As a result of that show, the battalion had finished off all its remaining tanks. Nearly all were worn out before the show and so had developed engine trouble before getting out. The crews had formed 'strong points' round them, and in any case the tanks had been destroyed a little later by direct hits. Once they were stationary, they had presented too easy a target to be missed. As a result we only had one casualty, although all six remaining tanks had been destroyed by direct hits. Carter had reported Aitches for his performance and had added that I could substantiate his evidence. The brigadier had advised him to say no more and not carry the thing through, as he saw means for getting Aitches out of the way without any fuss – presumably by sending him home to England. The 5th Battalion was now a very famous battalion – it had been praised openly to the rest of the Corps by Sir Douglas Haig, and they thought it better for the reputation and morale of the battalion to get rid of duds quietly. I agreed with Carter that this seemed the wisest plan. The main thing was to clear out Aitches, and this seemed to be assured in the near future.

On about September 20th the battalion drew fresh tanks, and up the line we went. C Company, under Major Gatehouse, had been to Paris after August 8th to give demonstrations to various staff officers of the French and British armies. They had had a very good time and were in anticipation of good things still to come. Gatehouse, who would have given his soul for a D.S.O., had put practically his entire company in for something or other. Colonel O'Kelly had as good as told him he was in for a D.S.O. for his handling of the company on August 8th, and all looked merry and bright. Indeed, the whole battalion consoled themselves somewhat by the hope of pretty ribbons in the near future. In the meantime, however, this action business was certainly a bit of a bore.

We detrained at Roisel (which had been in enemy hands about ten days before), some ten miles behind the line, with the calmness and dignity of true soldiers. In actual point of fact that railhead was not quite the innocent spot it looked; while we peacefully trundled off our tanks, an ingenious little arrangement of wires, acid, etc. did its work equally peacefully some 20 feet underground. For the moment *we* were the important personages at Roisel; but our little friend had his turn later, and on October 28th or thereabouts, 30 soldiers, an ammunition train, two tank trains and Roisel railway station, all disappeared into the blue. That was a long-suffering and patient mine – but it had its reward.

We put up in a wood near the station. We spent the next day in tinkering about once more – the old routine – and in the evening we pushed forward again. We were now within five miles of the front line, and it was the night 26/27th September. As dawn broke, the earth suddenly began to tremble, and the air was filled with the thunder of our guns; on a front of thirty miles the British artillery had opened up hurricane fire. The last great battle for the Hindenburg Line had commenced.

As the grey morning light filtered through the trees, I stood and wondered wearily how long the accursed business would last. I could almost see the poor devils in the 'line' – earth and filth flying everywhere and chaos unutterable. The future could give no consolation.

The Germans were in the last ditch, and there could be nothing but the bitterest opposition. It was true that the war-correspondents had noticed a slackening in the German spirit – their morale, they said, was gone. But most of the fighting men I have spoken to had not remarked this. Perhaps the unfortunate Boche found it easier to face a British Tommy than a British war-correspondent.

I regretted heartily my refusal to go back to England and join a new battalion. There was one thing that was becoming very clear – I had lost my nerve. Everything I did was difficult; in action I had to force myself to do my mere job. I became more or less paralysed at the thought of action, and my brain would *not* work. There always had been the traces of this trouble – after the breakthrough of November 30th 1917, at Meteren in April '18, and on August 8th '18 – on all these occasions I seemed unable to shake off a kind of sluggishness and terror that threatened to crush all life out of me. I had reached the stage that many had reached before me – the B.E.F. [British Expeditionary Force] man who was 'not as good as he had been'.

My rather unpleasant thoughts were interrupted by Nixon's approach. I asked him if the troops were attacking that morning. He told me they were not. The British hurricane bombardment – 1/3 thermite and chlorine – was to continue for 48 hours. 'We've joined the right army *this* time' he said, and I heartily agreed.

An hour later a message came through to say that our battalion was reserved to follow through and not for the first assault. That, at any rate, gave us *one* more day, even if it meant that when we did go in our orders would be scrappy, incomplete and chaotic.

The day was spent in preparation for action. The usual nervous dejection and misery was enlightened by two events – one, the departure of some officers and men to form new battalions in England. Among others, Harrison and Cook went, and Buchanan, my runner, a jolly good fellow I was sorry to lose. The other event caused flutterings in the dovecote even at this juncture – decorations and promotions had come through! I had been awarded the Legion d'Honneur!

This decoration needs explaining. It was given, ostensibly, for gallantry in action on August 8th. In actual point of fact it was practically arranged before that action that I should get something out of the lucky bag. The Brigadier had said that a D.S.O. alone looked lonely and miserable – a touch of colour by its side would improve things no end, he declared. The Colonel said that I needed an extra to make up for missing a V.C. One or two company officers said that I deserved it for having served under Aitches so long. The men were past being surprised at anything.

This decoration was put into the shade by many others. The O.C. A Company got an M.C. for gallantry in leading his company into action over a heavily shelled bridge on August 8th. The company swore bitterly he had been nowhere near the place and that a Capt. Llewellyn had done the job. To do him justice, the O.C. A Company agreed with them!

Major Gatehouse had won an M.C.! – for magnificent handling of his company on August 8th and subsequently. The comments on this were many and diverse. A Company were inclined to be ironic and wondered why he hadn't made it a V.C. while he was at it. C Company kept their thoughts to themselves, and B Company said he thoroughly deserved it – for handling his company so well that he got them into Paris. Gatehouse confided his opinion to me. With amazement I heard him say, 'Infernal scandal, these decorations!' Had I misjudged him? Was he really modest and retiring after all? – and then he continued – 'The old devil swore he'd put me in for a D.S.O.! I and here I am with this dirty little M.C.! You can't trust these – – – Irishmen an inch! I'll get even with the old swine yet!' But, alas, O'Kelly was out of reach. He had suffered much from Gatehouse (and confided as much to Cook). He had promised a D.S.O., but as he would be safe in England with a new battalion by the time honours came out – one can only guess the rest! Poor old Gatehouse! There he stood, with a crowd of eager young faces round him – all his beloved officers – pressing near to congratulate their O.C., and not one of the blockheads seemed to realize how miserably unappreciated his services had been!

The O.C. B Company – Major Aitches, to wit – had not passed unnoticed. He was awarded the M.C. for magnificent reconnaissance work before August 8th, and for his gallantry in leading the company tanks over a perilous bridge and so into action beneath a storm of shells.

This we could not swallow. All officers decided *not* to congratulate him or, indeed, to notice the thing. Aitches was a born fool. He was as pleased as punch and raked up from goodness knows where a piece of M.C. ribbon. He turned up at our simple evening repast with a half-inch-broad ribbon sewn to his tunic and with a ready smile prepared to receive homage. Poor chap! He was genuinely proud of the rotten thing, and I don't believe he ever understood why none of his officers said a word.

There is one other decoration and promotion that I will mention now, as it happened to concern me later. A young boy named Windle, who had a certain charm of manner and was popular with Gatehouse, was awarded an M.C. and made a captain to command a section. His M.C. was for an alleged brilliant piece of work (on August 8th), which I knew had not taken place (as I happened to be there). Gatehouse had him promoted for this same thing and *then* proposed that he should go to B Company as a section commander. As soon as I heard this, I dashed off to Nixon and Aitches and advised them on no account to take him. I argued that Windle was a bad officer. I had seen him at Millekruisse at the beginning of the year and had taken over trenches from him. He was then useless and ridiculous as an officer. I had been on the spot on August 8th when Windle had been alleged to do his great show. He had not done it. I declared that he had merely been promoted and petted by Gatehouse, and that if Gatehouse promoted him, he ought to keep him. *He* thought him good enough for a section; *we* did not – therefore Gatehouse should have him. I said a bad section commander in our company meant more work for the other section commanders and a bad section to boot.

For the present my arguments prevailed, and Nixon assured me he would keep Aitches up to scratch. You will see later how true my words were.

The 27th and 28th passed without further interest, and we simply smoked, talked and did odd jobs while the guns thundered in the distance.

On the morning of September 29th the entire battalion moved forward. The final assault on the Hindenburg line had commenced that same morning. We trekked slowly on. Only the Colonel and a few officers knew where we were going. No one knew yet what we should be called upon to do. The morning mist was cold and wrapped us round until the leading tanks looked quite ghostly in the distance. The air was filled with the drone of our engines and the thunder of the battle which was raging away in front of us.

We ate our bully beef and biscuits for lunch as we went. I ordered my section to tie petrol cans filled with water onto the exhaust pipes on the roof – so that we should later have boiling water for tea.

The drive seemed almost interminable. At 6.30 a halt was called, and I ordered tea at once for my section. We just sat round our tanks and swilled hot tea and ate more biscuit. Nixon came along, and I asked him for news. He could tell me little. He didn't know whether we should be needed next morning or where we were going; he only knew that the opening stages of the attack had been fairly successful.

At 7.30, just as we were beginning to despair of orders, we were suddenly told to go on, and the weary trek began again. It was now getting dark, and I remember we seemed to be passing rather weird country. We were travelling along the bed of a valley, and the noise of our engines and the occasional back-fires set up a kind of muttering echo that sounded like a ghostly battle.

At last night fell, and still we went on. But our journey became less smooth. Every now and then the tanks in front would come to a standstill, and we would wait patiently while the weary minutes slipped by. At last we would start forward again, but only to stop in the same way a little later. Messages kept passing up and down the line for certain officers to go to the head of the column, or for information about the tail company. If we had been sufficiently interested, we might have wondered where we were going.

At 10 p.m. we found ourselves on a road. Not far in front we could see Very lights and the red glow of bursting shells. There was a lull in the battle.

At 10.30 p.m. we reached a fork road and a crucifix. I asked Nixon where we were, and he told me we were now on the Bellenglise road. He told me the enemy had been driven out of Bellenglise that morning and that his position was uncertain. Instead of going on down the Bellenglise road, we turned up the fork road and after travelling

---

Figure 48
Moving forward for action. A photo of the 5th Battalion tanks moving forward in the mist of the morning of Sept. 29th. Note the officer and man following the tank. Whenever it was just a case of follow my leader this was the inevitable procedure. You only put enough men to work the tank inside, and the rest would follow with hands thrust deep into pockets and slouching tread. It was curious to watch the little ribs of the tank track-plates continually climbing up and up the back of the tank.

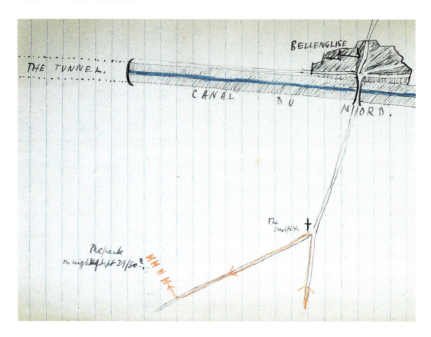

Figure 49
The park on night of Sept. 29th/30th.

about a mile we parked up just off the road under the shelter of some trees (see Figure 49). The men were very tired indeed, and most of us were nervy. The trek had been very long and just a repetition of the old story – halts, engine trouble, uncertainty – until we were all thoroughly worn out with it all.

I told my people to hurry up and get camouflaged and turn in as fast as possible, and it certainly did not take them very long. I looked at my watch and found it was midnight. Whatever the next day held in store for us, it at least looked as if we were to get some sleep that night. I was just congratulating myself on this when I heard someone calling for 'Captain Bion'. 'Yes', I shouted at him. A runner promptly appeared. 'You're wanted by the Colonel at once, please, sir', he said.

I left the tanks and went up the side track onto the road. Here I saw the Colonel's car standing by the ditch. I went up to it and found the Colonel waiting for me by the door. 'I want you to take a section of tanks into action, Bion', he said. I asked him when. To my surprise he said zero hour was at 5.45 that morning – it was now about 12.30. I asked him where, and he pointed out a spot about three miles away. I told him it was quite impossible. It would take quite three hours, with our men as tired as they were, to get our tanks there – quite apart from arranging the action. But at this he had a novel suggestion. At first he seemed somewhat embarrassed, and then after some hesitation he told me he did not want me to take my tanks into action. No – there was already a section of tanks ready to do the job, and they were only about two miles – rather less – from the starting-point.

This seemed suspicious. I was very tired, didn't want the show, and, for the first time, I said so. I asked if there wasn't some other man who could do it if the proper section commander was unfit. 'Oh no; the *real* section commander *isn't* unfit. You see, we'd willingly get another – but this show is very unexpected, and we want a really experienced man to do it. There's nothing in it, but as it's so hurried you must have a man who can be relied on. If the plans were all cut-and-dried, of course anyone could do it, but as it is . . . well, it's far too difficult. It needs a *really good* man.'

The compliment was no doubt very gratifying; but it was lost on me. 'Who is the section commander?' I asked; and as I did so I half expected the answer I got. 'Oh' replied the Colonel, 'It's Captain Windle – C Company. '

I was furious about it. I won't detail my feelings about this now – but I did then. It was the best possible example that could have been given to bear out the argument I brought forward before Aitches and Nixon previously. I asked the Colonel why he had been promoted, and I told him I thought the whole thing disgraceful. The Colonel was a weak man, or he would never have allowed me to talk like that. Instead of putting me under arrest, he apologized and flattered profusely.

I asked him for orders. I was to go to infantry brigade H.Q. The brigade was, I think, in the 3rd Regular Division – I was to find out from the brigadier what the infantry operations were and then simply to use my tanks on my own initiative. There was no time for detailed co-operation.

I was then presented with a guide who had come from this brigade H.Q. It was his job to lead me to the General.

We set out at once, and after going down the road towards the crucifix we suddenly turned sharp to our right. We were now on high ground, and, as far as I could judge in the dark, we were on a kind of plateau. It was a pitch-black night, and there were no signs of life anywhere.

Now, it doesn't matter how intelligent a man may be, but if ever you make him into a 'guide', he loses all sense, initiative and resource and falls into the groove common to all 'guides' that have been since the world began. Every 'guide' who prides himself on being a member of the fraternity behaves in the same way. He sets out with tremendous confidence and sets a pace that makes it impossible for any troops who may be following to keep touch. After a mile he begins to falter but assures you, with the confidence of a born actor, that he knows the place like the 'palm of me 'and, sir'. After about half an hour of this he is still full of confidence, but his conversation is based on the assumption that he has previously admitted himself lost – e.g. 'Shan't be long now, sir; this looks like our path. Know where I *am* now', etc. etc. If you are wise you'll shoot him on the spot, before he can do more harm, and try to disentangle the mess yourself. If not, another half-hour will bring the admission, 'Please, sir, I'm lost' – this last uttered in the tone of a man who has been the unwitting victim of sorcery.

My guide was no exception to the rule; we were lost – and it was already very late when we started.

Fortunately, after a little casting about, we picked up some telephone wires and followed them up till we came to an R.E. [Royal Engineers] dugout, which was the 'exchange'. We asked them for our brigade H.Q., and they put us onto the wire leading to it. We groped along the ground feeling for this wire, and at last we saw a chink of light coming up from a trap-door affair at our feet. We opened it and went down some steps to a dugout about 60 feet below the surface.

Headquarters presented the usual sight at such a time. The air was stale, and smoke from a fire hung about the roof. Men were lying about the floor rolled up in their blankets. In the middle of the dugout stood a table around which there were seated various officers who were poring over a map and trying to make out details by the dingy light of a smoky oil lamp that hung above them. I reported to the General, and he gave me a seat by his side. He then explained the action.

The Germans were holding out on our side of the canal on a hill called Tara Hill (see Figure 50). As far as could be seen, there were not many of them. It was intended to make a one-brigade attack (three battalions) *encircling* the hill. The tanks were to render any assistance

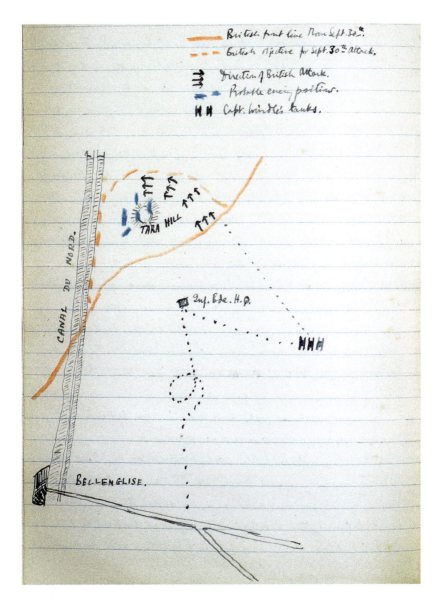

Figure 50

that might be necessary. The brigadier then yawned, stroked his two days' growth of beard, and asked if I had any suggestions to make. I looked at my watch and saw the time was 3 a.m. I had not realized how late it was. I told the Brigadier there was not time to carry out any suggestions and that I was afraid that, as it was, we should be late. 'Oh, that's all right', he said, 'I don't expect there will be any opposition – only just to encourage the troops, you know', and with that I went. At the top of the dugout I met Peter Barr – the company reconnaissance officer. He had been sent to meet me there and take me to Windle's tanks. He had been given maps for us both and had studied out a route for the tanks very carefully in the time he had. The cold night air struck us sharply after the thick atmosphere of the dugout, and we stepped out smartly. At 3.30 we reached the tanks. They were not quite ready for action, and we seemed to delay an age.

At last we set out. The tanks ran very badly, and we had endless trouble. Finally one gave out altogether, and we left the crew to shift for themselves. We had no time to spare, and if we couldn't have three tanks, we had to do with two. As we went, I studied the map. The route the infantry were due to follow was along a spur that ran out from the high ground forming the present British position. The spur ended in a blob known as Tara Hill – the place we expected most resistance. After studying the map, I decided that the best plan would be to go for the right-hand slope of the spur. I did this as it seemed to me the tanks would then be protected from German gunfire. The spur would shelter them from the Canal du Nord side. I anticipated no trouble from the right, as no guns could be so near the British front line as to attack us on that flank. Our main danger seemed to me to be from the left and front.

We pressed on as fast as we could, climbing steadily towards the British front line. Engine trouble held us up the whole time; the tanks seemed to be in fearful condition. At last it began to grow light; it was certain now that we should be late for the action. Barr and I were about thirty yards ahead and were steering straight across country by compass. I looked at my watch and saw it was 5.45 a.m. At the same moment a few guns opened up a desultory kind of fire. 'The action', said Barr, 'appears to have commenced'.

About twenty minutes later we arrived on the front line and found ourselves approximately where we wanted to be. The trenches of our front line were deep and crumbling. Owing to this and to thoroughly bad driving, both tanks at once became hopelessly ditched. This was too much. I fetched those crews out and made them dig as they had never dug before. In twenty minutes we practically levelled those trenches out, but I was taking no chances. I made them fix the unditching gear and . . . out came both tanks. The unditching gear was replaced, and we went on. Forty minutes late.

In the meantime there seemed to be no signs of the action. The guns had ceased fire, and the infantry appeared to be very well concealed. It looked as if the British Army had reached the Rhine while we had been fooling about.

We pressed on as fast as we could, and at last we got to Tara Hill. Here we found the infantry. They were sitting on various tree stumps, smoking their pipes, and cleaning their rifles. I found an officer and asked for news. 'Was there to be a battle here this morning?' I asked, 'or was it only a rumour?' 'Yes', he told me, 'there *was* to be an action; only our staff made a mess of it. They forgot to warn Hindenburg, and as a result there weren't any Germans left here to fight us. The dear old Boche had gone off to the Vaterland years before we arrived.'

I ordered the tank commander to drive home. No sooner had they started than one fool got stuck. I pulled out my pipe, sat on a stump and smoked peacefully while the crew wandered aimlessly round. They were thoroughly incompetent, and I discovered they were only a scratch lot got together anyhow. Windle was *not* responsible for *their* idiocy anyway.

Suddenly the engine back-fired. There was a moment's silence, and a sheet of flame shot out of the conning tower. The driver was the only man inside when it happened, and he came out of the tank in less than no time. He was slightly scorched. We squirted pyrene at the tank, but it was no use. It burnt like a torch, and the ammunition was soon blowing out all over the place. We all sat round and watched. One less tank to take back, thank Heaven!

I won't trouble you with details of the rest of this show. I got back and reported the action. Windle was left to collect his scattered section. This was not difficult. The burnt tank was so completely wrecked as to be useless and was handed over to the Salvage Department. The tank that had survived the 'action' reached the park without mishap, and the third tank, the one we left behind before going in, was put straight and rejoined the same day! For myself, I had lost a night's rest, cost the Government £10,000 by loss of a tank and accomplished precisely nothing. I was ordered to report to battalion 'details' for 'rest'. I got there at about 5 p.m. and went to sleep till goodness knows when next day. I then cleared out and rejoined the company, who were still where I left them originally.

Our time was now spent in cleaning up tanks and going through the usual tests. It didn't matter how much we had done this previously – we had since then travelled many miles, and the whole work was to be done again. No man in his right senses ever took any risks with his tank. All did their best to have the thing in first-rate running order.

I spent one day in wandering about with Barr. There seemed to be no immediate prospect of action, but we decided to get our bearings and look about the place. We wandered down to Bellenglise, and here we saw the Royal Engineers feverishly building a bridge over the Canal du Nord. The Germans had, of course, blown up the original bridge.

We wandered past Bellenglise and still kept to the canal bank. At last we reached the territory we had 'captured' in the last show. We went on some way and at last came to what seemed a regular battle. A screen of gas and H.E. [high explosive] shells were falling about 100 yards in front of us, and it looked as if we had gone far enough. We were not going to have a private battle if we could help it, and we turned back.

It had really been very careless of us to come so far, and we were reminded of our foolishness as we walked back along the high bank of the canal. A H.E. shell fell some 60 yards away, and we did not, of course, dodge for it. But it must have hit something very hard and burst on the surface, for the next moment there was a scream, a mass of sparks up from the metalled path and a very big piece of shell flashed into the undergrowth. I turned to Barr and found his hand bleeding from a slight wound and that was all. But it was quite enough.

We reached camp without mishap and found there was still no news. A and C Companies had gone up to the line, and there was a chance that B Company would follow the next morning.

The next morning found the rumour confirmed. B Company had to move forward. The orders came through at 9 a.m., and by 10 we had broken up camp (except for a kind of H.Q. which was left to deal with documents, rations etc.) and were moving forward. A fairly heavy mist hung over the ground, and it was difficult to see very far ahead. The usual drone of our engines filled the air as the line of tanks moved along. We were travelling towards the Canal du Nord, and, of course, the country was littered with signs of the battle that had passed over it. Everywhere there were abandoned German guns. These had become so common now that regiments did not bother to claim them as captured by themselves. Instead, we saw facetious inscriptions averring that they were taken by the A.S.C. or the R.A.M.C. or the W.A.A.C.s.

At last we reached the Canal du Nord at the point where it went underground. This had been the scene of hard fighting, and that for many seasons. First and foremost, the whole canal had been feared as a most formidable obstacle. This tunnel was the only crossing that the enemy really couldn't blow up. But he had done his best. The British had poured over this gap (about a mile wide) and swept round to the right in an encircling movement that was to take the canal in the rear and thus assist the troops who were making a frontal attack (24th Division). This gap had been mined and put in as fine a defensive state as possible. The landscape was littered with knocked-out tanks. But the greatest number of casualties seem to have been German. If you look at the photos (Figure 54), you will gain some idea of the obstacle the canal formed. These photos were taken at one of the steeper places on the banks of the canal and show the troops that took it. As a matter of fact, the capture was not as difficult as they expected, for reasons I will come to later.

When you consider the depth and steepness of the canal banks and then look at the photo (Figure 55) and see the way the banks were honeycombed with dugouts and galleries, you will get an idea of how much anxiety was aroused by the contemplation of an attack on it.

There was yet another difficulty. The tunnel itself was known to be occupied by German troops. There was consequently great fear of being taken in the rear. Actually all went well on the day of the attack. The photo (Figure 56) shows you the entrance to the tunnel. Troops were sent down it, and they bombed and hacked their way through. It cannot have been very pleasant. The electric lights were switched out (or went out) quite early in the battle, and this unearthly fighting had to go on in pitch darkness.

Figure 52
The Canal du Nord. This is a photo of the part along which Barr and I walked. There is, as you see, water in this piece, and the banks are not very steep.

Figure 51
The bridge at Bellenglise. The photo shows R.E.s beginning work on the bridge and artillery limbers crossing the canal by driving through it – an ordinary artillery limber would go up or across anything if only you had something to pull it. This sort of thing was a common sight along the Canal banks until the Engineers had built fresh bridges.

I said the capture had been made more easily than was expected. That was the result of the artillery bombardment. For 48 hours the German positions had been shelled, and many prisoners said no food had reached them in that time. The effects of the bombardment were still visible when we arrived, and they were ghastly enough then. The chlorine had turned the leaves of the shrubs on the canal banks quite yellow. The tangled undergrowth held some grim surprises. The Germans had placed many machine-gun posts amongst the shrubs. It would have been a difficult thing to find these men and a difficult thing to advance in face of a withering fire that came from no one knew where. But that fire was never opened, and the pale leaves hid many a ghastly sight from our eyes until at last health demanded a systematic search over those terrible banks.

I felt glad we had missed the first day's fighting at any rate. Our trek was uneventful. There was little engine trouble, and our only obstacles were the trenches of the Hindenburg line. These were all crossed without much difficulty. At about 5 p.m. the tanks were stopped in a sunk road by a wood. Here they were camouflaged and parked up. We had no idea when we should be wanted or where.

It was while we were here that I was sent back to the camp we had just left. I was told I should not be needed in the next action, that Nixon had to go forward in case Aitches was knocked out and he had to take his place, and that I was to act as second in command to the

---

Figure 53
Tanks moving forward for attack. This photo shows the 8th Tank Battalion moving forward for attack. They were on our left, and the photo gives you a good idea of our situation the same morning – the infantry watching rather interestedly, the leading tanks enveloped in mist, and the new kind of steel and beam 'facine' which we now carried instead of the clumsy affair we had in the Nov. 20th, '17, battle at Cambrai. The tanks on the left are supply tanks. The troops in the photo are Australians (9th Army Corps). Note the field telephone wires on the ground. The R. Engineers used to curse tanks bitterly, as we almost invariably destroyed their lines (and that of course just before battle – which was very serious). So long as we drove straight across all was well, but if we turned while we were actually on the wires, of course we snapped them.

Figure 54

The banks of the Canal du Nord. These two photos will give you some idea of the depth and steepness of the canal banks. The left gives some idea of depth and the right of its steepness. Yet tanks went down these and up the other side: The troops are the 73rd Infantry Brigade (who took this piece).

company while he was absent. I had got past the stage of inquiring too deeply into the mercies of the day. There had been a time when I felt the world had gone wrong when I was left out of an action. On this occasion I collected my batman and left the company before anyone had time to change his mind.

Life at Company H.Q. was placid. Rations arrived, were examined and sent forward. I was a kind of glorified grocer and eyed potatoes with suspicion and bully beef tins with the air of an expert. At night, bombing aeroplanes came over, but as we were near an anti-aircraft battery we considered ourselves safe. Not because the anti-aircraft would fetch them down – oh dear, no! – but simply because it was considered good luck to have an A.A. battery near. This, of course, was a delicate way of saying that you thought the A.A. the safest job in the war. You never *told* people you thought they'd hit on a good thing. That was bad form. You simply hinted it – as unmistakably as possible.

We slept and lived (much the same thing at that time) in a bell tent. One night my rest was broken by some fool who appeared to be trying to trip over as many ropes as possible. I listened with interest as his hands groped over the surface of the tent. At last he found the opening, the flap was thrown back and . . . 'Is Captain Bion here?' said a hoarse voice. I felt my heart sinking. What did the man want at this time of night? I pretended I was asleep.

It was no good. The voice grew louder and hoarser, and I gave in. 'What do you want?' I asked him wearily. 'You're wanted up the "line" at once, sir' came the answer.

I hadn't the heart to swear. There was no chance of snatching another delicious two minutes in bed – another two minutes of the luxury I had been taking so lightly – for all the joy had gone out of life, and even bed could have no enchantment under such circumstances. I pulled myself out of my flea-bag and reached for my clothes. How *stale* they felt! There seemed to be something very dirty about putting on these clothes I had just taken off. And then I wasn't going to wash. Everything was in a mess. The two spare officers who were in the tent with me were lying there without showing any sympathy. How well I knew what they felt! To them bed had suddenly become more precious as they realized what might have happened to *them*.

As I dressed by the light of a guttering candle, I could hear the runner's teeth chattering as he stood outside the tent and waited for me. I was soon ready and found myself standing outside the tent gazing up at a bright starlight night. I yawned and looked at my watch. It was 1.30 a.m.

We went up to the 'line' by a different route from the one taken by the company tanks. We crossed over the canal by Bellenglise and then struck across country at right angles to the canal. I asked the runner what it was all about and why I had been so urgently sent for. He said he didn't know but thought it was for an action. We trudged on in silence. We were both bored and tired. We reached Company H.Q. and the tanks at 3 a.m. or thereabouts. Nobody seemed to be very interested in our arrival, so I got down and went to sleep on a bench.

At 10. a.m. orders were explained. B Company were wanted for an attack on the last remains of the Hindenburg line. C Company were going into action on our left, and together we were to attack the Fonsomme line, as it was called. This system of defences was only half completed. It consisted of half-dug trenches and a little wire – they were in practically the same condition as our trenches were, five miles behind the line, on March 21st. If we could clear them from this line, all the defences of the famous Hindenburg Line would have been passed. As far as was known, there were no more trenches between this and the Rhine.

The immediate objective of B Company was the village of Sequehart (see Figure 58). This village had been taken by the British two or three times just previously. But the Fonsomme line (of which Sequehart was a part) was of such importance that the fighting was bitter and the Germans had won the place back each time. It was for this reason that they had decided to use tanks. It was most important

---

Figure 55
The Canal banks near the tunnel entrance. Note how they are honeycombed with dug-outs and underground galleries. 'Mopping up' meant clearing these nests of enemy troops who might come out and cut off the front-line troops when they had passed. This is not the steepest part but will give a good idea of the average depth and appearance of the shrub-covered sides.

that the army should get through before the enemy had time to dig more defences.

B Company were to be used as two sections – one under Hauser and the other under myself. Carter had reconnoitred the B Company position and said it was easy to see everything. Of course I knew Carter well or I shouldn't have believed a word of it. But he assured me that, from the point of view of direction and so on, there was no difficulty – Sequehart stood on a hill and could not be mistaken. Peter Barr, as company reconnaissance officer, had the job of leading us to the place where we were to start from – the usual 'starting-point'. The company only consisted of six tanks, so Hauser and I each had three under us.

The tanks moved off at about 7.30 p.m. We left the road and drove across undulating grass country. The tanks were running very well, and we seemed to have nothing to do but bowl along merrily into action. Actually the light was too good, and we had to make several stops.

At about 11 p.m. we reached a wood and were ordered to park up our tanks by its side. As soon as this was done, the men lay down by their tanks and tried to seize a few hours' sleep. The officers collected together to hear a few final instructions and then rejoined their crews. It was a fine evening, but the stars were hidden by thin cloud. For my part I spent the time before action in my usual way. It was impossible to shake off the feverish anxiety to have the battle over and done with. The quietness of the whole front only added to one's uneasiness. At about 2 a.m. the silence was broken by desultory shell-fire from the enemy. He commenced shelling our wood with light 'contact' shrapnel, and the rest of our stay was made even more miserable by the irregular shell bursts and their accompaniment of moaning shell splinters that often ended their flight by a vicious 'flick' against the side of the tanks.

The attack was timed to start at 6.30, and at 4.45 our tanks moved forward. Before we left, Hauser and I were told there was no need to

Figure 56
The entrance to the tunnel. Fighting went on down this tunnel.

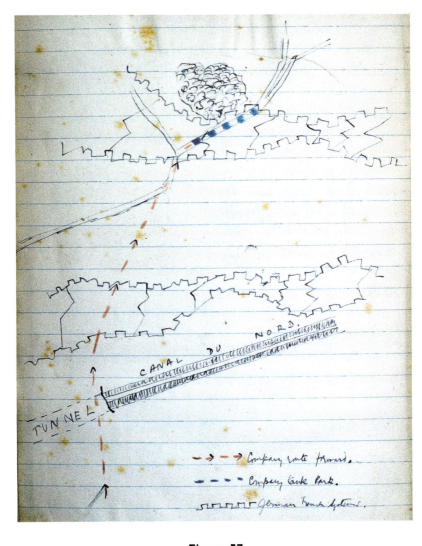

Figure 57

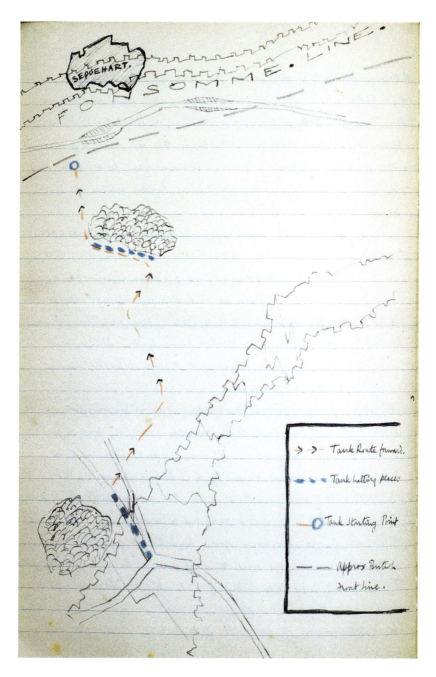

Figure 58

do any more after we left our tanks at the starting-point; we were only to keep a look-out and send back information of the battle. This, of course, had a very unnerving effect. What *were* we to do? Of course, we didn't want to get killed, and if we could stay at the starting-point we should be safer. On the other hand, these orders were clearly contrary to the spirit of our job. Hauser and I decided to carry on as if they had not been given.

The starting-point was about a mile in front of us; the ground was level and sloped down gently towards the valley in front of Sequehart. The front line lay in this valley.

At 6 a.m. we reached our starting-point. It was just growing grey in the east, and before long we could distinguish each others' faces in the pale light. We ordered our crews into the tanks – now drawn up in line – and waited.

As the light grew, we could make out various features of the landscape. The ridge on which Sequehart stood had already been visible some time; we could now distinguish the outlines of the village itself. Hauser and I stood and picked out as much of the place as we could. The whole field of operation was easily taken in from where we were, and this in spite of the fact that our only light was a grey uncertain dawn. In the distance a machine-gun opened up a slow tat–tat–tat and a moment later we heard the shrill flight of bullets high overhead. Almost as if in answer, the British barrage came down and the darkness of the village was suddenly stabbed by the red bursts of our shells. Our tanks started forward to the attack.

With the dawn there came a breeze, which blew softly into our faces and set the long grasses waving about our feet. For a moment the relief that came with the start of the battle and the end of our anxious waiting seemed to fill one with a curious feeling of peace. But it was not long before this was shattered; the pleasant morning haze, which had been so refreshing but a moment before, now brought with it the acrid smell of bursting shells.

For a moment Hauser and I hesitated; the information that we 'need not' go forward had a peculiar force just then. I managed to screw up a grin and pointed towards the village. Hauser grinned back, and we pushed off after our tanks. As he pointed out, we should probably be safer further forward, as the enemy's practice at this time was to shell valleys very heavily. As we walked forward, the sun came up behind Sequehart. It was a magnificent sight and one I shall not forget. The miserable greys of dawn were suddenly shot with gold. The sun's beams were an angry blood-red, and its rising behind the village gave the whole scene an unrealistic appearance. The village, with its tall-spired church in the centre, stood out clear-cut and black, like a cardboard model. Every now and then the outline would be broken as some part of the village was whirled into a cloud of sun-shot dust. The church spire remained untouched as if by a miracle, and not only now, but throughout the action, it stood immovable and stark, pointing resolutely to the skies as if it wished to distract attention from the agony of bursting shells and crumbling masonry that surrounded it.

As we went forward, the enemy barrage opened. It seemed to be half H.E. and half blue-cross gas shell. We had to suck air through our gas masks at times, but for the most part we were not troubled by it. As usual, the heaviest bombardment was in the valley, and we made haste to climb the slope of Sequehart.

In the valley, at the foot of the slope, there was a road that was partly sunken in places. Our front line was put out of action here. The tank was commanded by a 2nd Lieut. Reid of my section, and just as it reached the road and was climbing out, a shell struck it and ricocheted off to bury itself in the slope down which we had travelled earlier that morning. It was a dud; but it had done its work. We saw the tank had stopped, and when we approached we found the left side had been torn in two at the 'nose' of the tank and flung back. So we had one useless tank right at the start. Fortunately none of the crew was hurt. They were placed in front of the tank about 40 yards in advance of the road, and there they had to stop with their guns to form a strong point.

Hauser and I wandered aimlessly about the bottom slope of the ridge. The battle was not going well. We were not faced by any crack German troops – in fact, there were hardly any infantry there. But we *were* faced by the German machine-gunners, and their demoralization was not quite so apparent to us during the action as it was to the newspaper gentlemen after it. The fighting in Sequehart was very bitter. One of my tanks I saw disappear, well ahead of the infantry, over the top of the ridge. It did good work and ran out of ammunition finally. But I saw little or nothing of it, and so I will dismiss it now with a few words. It crossed the ridge to the south of Sequehart and there spent a very hot time well in front of our infantry, doing much the same thing as I had done before my tank was knocked out at Cambrai. He had no infantry support, for although they could see him, they could not reach him. He did a lot, but the place was honeycombed with machine-guns, and it was really too much for one tank. In the end, however, the infantry got up to him, but his ammunition was finished and he had to withdraw – the crew were thoroughly exhausted and probably could not have done much more, even if they had had the ammunition.

While this was going on, the third tank in my section met with disaster. As it was climbing the slope with the infantry, it was hit by a gas shell that exploded inside. Now a gas shell has only enough explosive in it, as a rule, to crack the shell and allow the gas to escape. This was of that kind. Consequently none of the crew was wounded, but, as they had very little time before the tank was completely filled with gas, they were most of them slightly gassed before they had their helmets [gas masks] on. Hauser had left me by this time to go further north to see if he could get any news of one of his tanks. As soon as I had seen this tank of mine stop, I approached alone. As I drew near, I saw smoke oozing from the joints and guessed what had happened. I put on my gas helmet ready to get in when the door opened and out tumbled one of the crew. I got in and helped out the remainder. We opened up the tank well to get the gas cleared out. The officer and driver had escaped most of the ill effects, but the rest of the crew were bad. I had hoped that it would be possible to start the tank again and run it into action with a depleted crew. But a few minutes showed me that this was impossible. There were only three of us fit for anything, and it was doubtful if the other two could stand an action. We tried to turn over the starting crank to restart the engine. This usually took three or four pretty strong men. But as it was, the gas had got into the cylinder and made the oil sticky like glue. We could no more turn the crank than if the engine had been completely seized up. I gave it up as hopeless and ordered the officer and driver to join Reid's crew. Here I thought they might be some use, for it was obvious that they could not by themselves do any good where they were.

I got out of the tank and rather dreamily watched the crew rolling about outside – some coughing, some groaning and one man lying almost still enough to be dead. I felt rather numbed and couldn't think properly. The infantry were now on the crest on which Sequehart stood, and we were not under fire where we were. One of my tanks was useless on the sunk road, the other had gone goodness knew where, and now the third had lost its crew. I wished I could leave the rotten thing there and go back – either that or else that the infantry would gain ground so fast as to leave us safe behind. Should I put the most conscious men in charge and go off in search of the other tank? That really seemed the best thing to do. But first I decided to do what I could to make the crew happier. I smashed the small ammonia capsules and held them under the noses of the worse cases. Those who could swallow I dosed with dilute doses of ammonia. In the meantime our artillery bombardment died down somewhat. But the enemy barrage was still concentrated fiercely in the valley and along its road not far behind us. It was that awkward stage in the battle where a temporary pause allowed one's nerves to relax. I remember, for the first time that action, feeling acutely conscious of personal danger. The sky was overcast, and the landscape wore that desolate grey colour that had preceded the dawn. I was hungry and chewed some bully and biscuits as I went round dosing one after the other of the men. After a time even the enemy barrage began to die down. It was now possible to hear the crack of rifle and machine-gun on the top of the crest. The lull in the battle was as complete as any I experienced; the front might have been in its normal peacetime state. I looked at my watch and saw it was only 9.20 a.m. What an age it seemed!

The worst case in the crew was a Corporal Short. He was quite a young boy and normally inclined to be lazy. But he had great pluck and endurance and was a serious loss. I spent most of my time kneeling over him and dosing him.

Suddenly a change came over the battle. The enemy barrage opened with a new and violent intensity onto the valley road. The chatter of machine-guns and rifles was drowned in the thunder that echoed and re-echoed down the valley. I looked back to see the cause, as I imagined the enemy had possibly put the barrage down to stop the advance of reinforcements. But I could see nothing.

My nervousness increased as I could get no information. The British guns did not seem to be firing. Sequehart was left in peace, and this seemed to indicate that both sides were in the village. I watched the crest in front anxiously for any signs of life. I had not to watch long. After a few seconds I saw three or four figures silhouetted against the sky and then lie down on our side of the crest. A moment later another batch of men – quite a large one this time – came helter-skelter over the ridge and lay down. They were British troops retiring.

I collected the crew under the lee of the tank and continued to dose them with ammonia. As I was bending over Short, I heard a shout. Two Tommies were lying behind a fold of ground and shouting, 'Tanks! Tanks! Tanks!' I yelled back. They shouted again, 'We want you! We want you! Counter-attack! Counter-attack!'

This was hopeless. I got up and started to go over and explain. As I stepped from behind the tank, the drums of my ears seemed to be shattered by crack! after crack! of a machine-gun. I was down on my stomach quicker than can be imagined. Even so the hst! hst! of very close bullets seemed to have missed me by inches. I knew that loud crack! very well. When a gun or rifle is pointing more or less at you, the crack of its shot sounds incredibly close. You may locate its direction but never its distance. It was quite clear that these shots were coming from the direction of Sequehart (at this time rather on our left front). So the enemy were back there once more.

I crawled to the men and yelled at them, 'Crew out of action! Can't do anything!' and they went back. I then wormed my way back and once more had the pleasure of hearing the bullets flick round. It seemed a particularly dirty trick. After all, I wasn't trying to hurt him.

I stood up under the lee of the tank and pulled at my pipe trying to think what to do. I felt very bored with the whole business but not really frightened. Whatever I decided on would probably be not much use. Of course, one thing was clear. If I was really the fire-eating, war-loving animal I should have been, my job was to get a few Tommies to help me start the engine and then run the tank into action myself and do something to stop the rot. In actual point of fact this *might* have been done – but not by a man who had seen any fighting. The idea occurred to me, but by this time the two infantrymen had rejoined their unit in front.

I waited what seemed an age to see how things would go in front. An increase of rifle and machine-gun fire on the tank made up my mind. It was useless staying here with the men, and I decided to get them out of harm's way. But first I took precautions in case the tank fell into enemy hands. I climbed into the tank and removed the plug of the magneto and the contact breaker. I then went to the Hotchkiss guns and took out all the firing pieces. This just disabled the tank from a fighting point of view, and I had time for no more if I was to get the crew away alive. The machine-gun fire had increased in intensity and was spattering the side of the tank.

I got out and went over to the three men who were fittest. I shouted to them (for the noise had now grown terrific) to get back as best they could. I then stowed away all the parts I had removed from the tank in various pockets and took charge of the two remaining men. One could nearly walk, so I got him to put his arm round my neck and I clasped him round the waist. Corporal Short I practically had to carry. And so we left the shelter of our tank.

We staggered back to our road; my impression is that we were not much fired at – at any rate, the three of us all escaped without being hit. We got back some 100 yards, and here I stopped to rest and take stock of things. The machine-gun had ceased fire, and the desultory sniping was so inaccurate as to be hardly noticeable. The worst passage lay before us.

I have already mentioned the enemy barrage along the bottom of the valley; as we looked towards it, we could no longer see the opposite slope clearly. Clouds of swirling dust and smoke arose from the barrage area. I almost gave up hope of getting through when there was a perceptible decrease in fire. Having regained breath, we pushed on.

Although the barrage seemed less intense, it was regular. I decided to risk it, for it seemed absurd to leave the men so near the front line in their condition. In a moment or two the shells were falling round us. As we approached the road, they fell more thickly. It was clear that the barrage line lay on the road itself. All appeared to be going well when the earth seemed to open up almost at our feet. I found myself lying on the ground still clutching Corporal Short, but the other fellow I could not see for a moment. 'Are you hurt?' I yelled to Short. To my surprise he gasped out a 'no'. Almost at the same time I saw the other fellow lying by my side. He too was unhurt. How we all three escaped I don't know.

It was quite clear that the quicker we got away from the road the better. For a while I crawled along the ground more or less dragging the other two with me. We were crossing rough ground, and I think that helped to protect us. It was only afterwards that I discovered we were also crawling through nettles!

We crossed the road safely and then had to stop. The exertion had been rather too much for the two men, so I got them into a shell-hole, and we spent some time there while I dosed them well with ammonia.

As soon as they had recovered enough we pushed on – the shell-hole was not exactly healthy. A few more minutes, and the fire decreased. We were nearly out of the barrage area. We could see the slope in front quite clearly and it was not long before we were well the other side of the barrage.

The exertion had had a bad effect again, and I made the two men lie down quietly. Occasionally I gave them another sniff of ammonia.

When they had sufficiently recovered to look after themselves, I went off to see how Reid was getting on. The barrage had now died down, and the shelling was merely desultory. I found him and his crew all right but very bored. They wanted to know when they could go. I decided there was nothing they could do, and as far as I could see they might as well go home. So I went off to get some information from the infantry. All was quiet at Sequehart, and I soon discovered that the troops had retaken Sequehart and gained all objectives. It was now 1 p.m., and the last of the Hindenburg defences had fallen.

I told Reid he could go back but that he must leave a guard of one man and an N.C.O. till others could be sent from the camp to relieve them.

We returned together and picked up the gassed men on the way. Corporal Short had to be carried back.

When we got back, I went to sleep under a tarpaulin. I was tired and nervy and also very dissatisfied. It had been an unsatisfactory show from my point of view – a section commander seemed more useless than ever in an action. If one was supposed to *fight* – then the task was almost impossible. If one was merely to control – then the work simply became one of shouldering the inglorious responsibility for ordering retreat from action. Perhaps I should have felt happier if I had known that my last action was over. My share of the Great War was finished.

The next day a party was sent off to see what could be done for the disabled tanks. Reid's was handed over to salvage, and, after some haggling, the same was done for the tank that was hit by a gas shell. The enemy were by then some miles away from Sequehart, and the British were pushing on slowly.

I had some trouble over the gassed tank: A C Company officer – Dawson – had seen it on the way back from his show (on our left). He could see nothing wrong with it and accordingly reported that he found a B Company tank, apparently in good order, deserted. Consequently Aitches wanted to see me and told me the situation was very serious as, of course, I had deserted a tank in the face of the enemy. I told him not to be a fool and explained the situation. He tried to look serious as he obviously wanted to impress me with the importance of the occasion. I told him he had better order a court of inquiry if he wasn't satisfied, and the affair fizzled out.

We stayed in the battle area for some time to give help if needed. While we waited, Aitches, Hauser and other officers left for England to take up new posts. So Aitches at last had achieved his heart's desire and prided himself, let's hope, on the success of his efforts. But England was not very safe after all. Three days after his arrival he was dead.

Poor Aitches! He got 'flu on arrival; he fast grew worse, and it was all over before anyone realized his illness. It seems queer now, but at the time I think there were few of us who weren't amused openly at his death. We made allowances for no one, and I don't think anyone could now appreciate the 'funny' side of what we then regarded as a really amusing joke. In the same way, any impartial man reading this would say I had been grossly unfair to Aitches, and, of course, I have, for my judgements and the judgements of others were ill-informed and harsh. But I put them down to show our attitude of mind. And if you think my criticisms of him are unjust, now I agree – but will add that if I had seen these criticisms during the war, when much might depend on the quality of the company commander, I should have said they were not harsh enough. It is one thing to talk academically of not judging one's fellows – another to put the principles into practice when your life and the lives of others depend on a weak and cowardly man. After all, his nerve had been shattered by the war, and he suffered as many before him had suffered. The fault may not have been his, but we could not trouble about 'trifles' like that then.

After a day or two's wait we went forward so as to be within distance of action if wanted. The entry of our troops into Bohain was a curious business. Peter Barr and I went forward to make arrangements for our company's movement forward and saw the place soon after its capture. The village lay beyond the Fonsomme line, and we skirted Sequehart in our reconnaissance. The village was badly battered and full of dead. The road to Bohain was good as it had been little shelled – the advance had been far too rapid for that.

As we drew near the village, we saw many dead horses that looked just skin and bone. Here and there they had been cut up as meat for the French inhabitants. One such horse had been completely stripped of all flesh except at the head. This one lay in the entry to Bohain and had apparently been the food for the village.

When we entered Bohain, the village had just been taken by our troops, and we could hear odd crashes of rifle fire from the other side. A few minutes after our arrival a British band arrived and played the Marseillaise. A few people, who had till then been hidden in cellars, appeared and looked on in a dazed way. But no signs of joy seemed to light up their faces. I don't think they quite believed they heard aright. Later I was told that whenever the band played, the enthusiasm was terrific.

Barr and I stood and watched for some time. The people looked careworn and miserable and very old. They had, it appeared, suffered many restrictions which people in larger towns escaped. I think they imagined the enemy would retake the place; they could not believe they were free.

As Barr and I watched, our attention was suddenly attracted by a young girl who came out of a house and crept across the street. We were both horrified; for although she was clearly about 16, terror seemed stamped on her face. I had never seen, and never want to see again, such misery and horror disfigure any face. She walked half-way across the street, looked fearfully at us, and then dragged herself into a doorway opposite. We stared after her and then walked away quickly. We had both seen terrible things before, but there had always been some relieving feature – fearful mutilations at least meant escape from war, and death was no hardship. But from *her* misery there seemed to be no release. Some days after this she gave birth to a German baby, but what happened to her I don't know. I can't see that the suffering written on her face can be accounted for by any system of ethics. I only hope she died, for I can't imagine the possibility of her regaining life or happiness.

The tanks were brought up to a place just outside Bohain, and Barr and I did our last reconnaissance. We stood on a slight rise of ground some two miles beyond Bohain and there looked over the country over which we should have to attack the next day. Actually when we got back we found orders saying the attack was off and that the battalion was to go back to rest. But we did not know this then.

It was evening, and in front of us lay flat, unenclosed land covered with green grass. About a mile in front of these meadowlands was the edge of the great forest before Valenciennes. The landscape looked curiously peaceful and lovely. We were not used to the fresh green of the trees and grass. There were no troops to be seen. Our men lay out in the meadows in front of the forest, but we did not know where the Germans were. As we finished our examination of the land, a few guns opened fire, and red splashes appeared over the dark green mass of the woods. A few stars appeared in the sky, and the cold night wind blew gently in our faces. There was another burst of gun fire; and as the reverberations rolled over the flat meadows, we turned our backs on the front line. We had seen our last shells fired.

On our return we heard the good news that we were to go back to rest areas to get new tanks and refit. A few days later we were at Beaumetz – the former railhead for Wailly. And so we entered on our usual routine – training reinforcements, drawing new tanks and so on.

I am coming to the end of the diary now and will not dwell long on the rest. Our arrival at Beaumetz was heralded by armistice talk – rumours that the Germans would accept *any* terms and so on. These were immediately contradicted by Army Orders as G.H.Q. did not want the troops to be weakened by premature hope of peace. The general policy of officers and men, as far as I could judge, was simply that the time was ripe for a just peace – a peace that would make war impossible. There was no feeling or desire of any kind for revenge. Wilson's 14 Points seemed just and reasonable and promised the kind of settlement that would give Christian idealism a place in international affairs.

Towards the end of the month the battalion began to prepare for action. One company was to go up to the front – a composite company from the whole battalion. Gatehouse was in command of it, and four tanks from my company were to join it. The company was to entrain on the 11th November.

On the evening of November 9th wireless messages came through saying that the German courier was lost, or had not reached German

H.Q. at any rate. On Sunday, late in the evening, we picked up wireless saying the Germans had signed the terms. I don't think we really believed this. It certainly made very little impression.

At 10.30 next morning as I sat in the company office – I was now commanding B Company and had done since Aitches' departure – a wire arrived. I opened it and found it was a general wire to all troops of the British armies. All troops were to stand fast in their positions and cease fire at 11 a.m. that morning. So the war was over.

The news did not create much of a sensation. I don't know why. I suppose we were all too numbed to appreciate it. Drill went on as usual, and no one seemed to know quite what to do. In the evening the officers messed as usual, and a few of us speculated pleasantly on the prospect of sleeping in beds for ever and ever and never getting up to see 'dawn' again. The men – mostly reinforcements – didn't realize their luck. One or two hardy spirits were under the impression that they were now free from the hated necessity of revering their officers any longer, and spent the weary night watches in the Guard Room. These men were all new to the battalion and didn't find themselves at all popular in the company.

Life after the armistice consisted chiefly in drill and games. There was a good deal of discontent as everyone wanted to get demobilized at once and the food was bad – three or four potatoes to an entire company was a frequent occurrence. But when it was pointed out that the food they did not get was being given to the population of the liberated areas, grousing died down a lot. Some companies had serious trouble – there was almost a mutiny in C Company, but we had no trouble.

As time wore on, we became more accustomed to the idea of no more war. Christmas seemed to mark the thawing-point with us all. We now had a new Company Commander. I reverted to my position of second in command, and a Major Craig took over. He was a first-class fellow. In very little time he was immensely popular with officers, N.C.O.s and men. He made our Christmas and New Year a really good show, and I shan't forget either in a hurry. I never saw anyone really drunk the whole time. But I think any outsider would have thought us all either drunk or mad.

On January 3rd Carter, now demobilization officer, told me I was to leave for demobilization the next day. A few men from the battalion were going as well, and at 2 p.m. on the 4th, after we had said our farewells, we mounted our lorry and drove off. It was a cold winter afternoon, and as we drove off through the mist I could hardly believe it was all over.

As we drove out, Corporal Short and another man chased us and clambered onto the front of the lorry. They wanted to say goodbye to me and mumbled out thanks for my having pulled them out of the last action when they were gassed. They jumped off, and the company camp was soon lost to sight in the winter mists.

I will miss out the journey to England. It was uncomfortable and miserable. Arrangements were bad, and food was bad. The staff who had to see to the demobilization were inexperienced and discontented because they were not being demobilized themselves. On the morning of January 11th we sailed from Dunkirk in a rough sea. Everyone was too pleased to be sea-sick. We landed at Folkestone and here found the arrangements excellent. We were each, officers and men, provided with biscuits and a large cup of tea. We then marched up to Shorncliffe camp. I think to some extent we were depressed by the lack of welcome. No one took any notice of us, no one seemed to know we had been fighting and were glad to be back. We simply trailed up to camp – about 1,000 of us from all parts of the British Front and from every conceivable unit – and no one even deigned to look at us!

There was one exception. And the sensation it caused showed, I think, that the men had missed a welcome. As we marched up the steep road to the camp, an old lady came out of her door and, waving a small Union Jack, said 'Welcome home, boys, welcome home', in a quavering deep voice. Of course she looked rather ridiculous – but no one minded that then, and as the troop marched past they cheered and blew her kisses! Poor old soul! She looked very pleased – and indeed she had done more to thank us than the great British Government ever did.

By 6 p.m. we were free men – free to do what we liked and go where we would. The special train left the camp station for London at 6.30 p.m. and we were to journey up as civilians. We had got our release – but it might have been the sack, as far as the Government was concerned. The last scene on the station was curious. Two trains were at the platform – one a civilian express to town and the other our special. The civilian train was lit up properly, but ours – through some official carelessness – was in darkness. The men greatly resented it, and one Boer War man, who wore the D.C.M. for this war, got on a carriage roof and aired his feelings. These were his words: 'We were b_____ heroes in the Boer War and so much dirt when it was finished. In this war we were b_____ heroes again – till it's all over. Nothing too good for the dear boys while it lasted – but *now* – well, we're so much dirt again. Thank you, kind ladies and gentlemen, for your patient hearing.' With this he took off his cap, bowed elaborately to the assembled crowd of ex-Tommies and civilians, and clambered off the roof to the platform. The station staff then bustled round and, after some delay, lit up the train. An hour or so later we steamed into London to separate and disappear again into that obscurity from which the world's most astonishing armies had emerged.

COMMENTARY

In the early 1970s I decided to make a typescript of Bion's diary to facilitate any future reading of it and as an insurance against any possible loss of the original – somewhat late in the day, its having already survived many house removals in the '20s and '30s, London bombing raids in the '40s, further house removals in the '50s and '60s, and a voyage of six thousand miles to California in 1968. That typescript tempted Bion to read the account for the first time since he wrote it fifty years earlier and to make some revealing comments on his reactions. As he rightly observes, 'I am amazed to find I wrote like an illiterate when I had already been accepted at Queen's'.

The Commentary is written in the form he used in *A Memoir of the Future*, although here the conversation is between two characters only: Bion, the inexperienced young man of twenty-one, and Myself, the wise old man of seventy-five. Memories come flooding back, reinforcing his dislike of his personality and poor opinion of his performance as a soldier. He says, '. . . I never recovered from the survival of the Battle of Amiens. Most of what I do not like about you [myself] seemed to start then'. Fortunately this lack of self-esteem was offset by his pride in his family and his work as a psychoanalyst – the two areas of his life that were of greater importance to him than any other.

Francesca Bion

1972

Lying beneath the stars, wrapped warmly in our blankets, my friend and I discussed the wonderful news. 'I really feel almost sorry for the Germans. They haven't a chance with France and ourselves against them. They have really gone too far this time.'

It was August 1914. The diary was written in 1919 at The Queen's College, Oxford. Since I wrote it I have not referred to it again till now, sixty-three years later. I write this under Californian skies.

* * *

I have changed some names as a way of avoiding hurting those who might recognize someone loved and no longer able to defend themselves. Nevertheless, I know that very little effort would be required to link the battles, the units engaged and the people who took part. I rely on the inertia of those who might make cruel use of what I say, to protect myself and others from unnecessary pain. There is no criticism that I make of others which could not with equal justice be applied to me.

There is one spirit from the 'vastie deepe' [Shakespeare, *Henry IV*] that I can conjure up. Here he is: powerfully built, inclined to fat but otherwise, superficially at least, physically fit; somewhat surly, though rarely given to outbursts of laughter; it is noticeable that he does not smile. His best friend at The Queen's College once told him, with shrewd and kindly acuteness, 'You do rather retire from the college and sulk.' His name is BION.

Myself [today]:   Let's look at your 'diary' now. Having read it, I feel it is interesting and worth publishing as it stands. Do you mind if I cut out the 'verys' and superlatives? You had a 'very' bad attack of the 'verys', verily very virulently. They make it difficult to read.

Bion [age 21]:   No, of course not. But I don't want it to appear that I was better educated than I was. I find it salutary to be reminded of these disconcerting facts that I had forgotten.

MYSELF: Well, then – out with the 'verys' and superlatives, but otherwise the unvarnished 'Bion'. After all, it has to be 'Myself' unvarnished.

BION: But apart from that?

MYSELF: Alter nothing.

BION: I am glad you found it good enough . . .

MYSELF: Oh, no: interesting enough, but certainly not good.

Bion (*abashed*): Oh. Then may I ask why you think it worth publishing? What's wrong with it?

MYSELF: That is difficult to answer. I think the best thing would be to go through it together, and I will tell you more precisely and in detail my appreciation (positive or negative).

BION: Looking at it again, I am amazed to find I wrote like an illiterate when I had already been accepted at Queen's.

MYSELF: You had in fact been accepted before your war service, and had had no education from that time on. It is a surprise – though it makes me fear I am no more advanced now.

BION: Why is that? What have you been up to?

MYSELF: That is a long and interesting story. I think it would depress you. Let's leave it for the present. How did you get to Tanks?

BION: I don't remember. I was extremely anxious to see these newly invented things, and joining seemed the only way of seeing them. But I cannot remember how I worked it. I was becoming less of a greenhorn by that time. On the way up to the camp from Wool station, there at last my ambition was achieved – there was a TANK!

MYSELF: Let's look at your 'diary' again. Why are you so down on the officers?

BION: I fear I was a narrow-minded prig. I often think my fellows must have had a good deal to put up with.

MYSELF: From what I remember, that is true. Indeed, from what

I have learned since, I and my closest friends did not stand up to the rigours of war very well.

BION: Of course we did not know that, though I was always afraid I would not. I think even the diary shows that as it goes on, though at Oxford I was still too ashamed to admit it. And very glad of the opportunity that Oxford gave me to be seduced into a more self-satisfied state of mind. But I never quite got rid of the sense that all was *not* well.

MYSELF: That ultimately drove me into psycho-analysis.

BION: So, that is what you have been up to. Do you find it interesting?

MYSELF: Yes, finally I did – after many years of hating it. But let's get on with your war; later I may tell you what I have done to us both since. You were explaining your priggish superiority.

BION: It was not that only, but also ignorance of the strain to which combatants had been exposed in previous fighting.

MYSELF: I thought your comment that they had gone into Tanks to avoid fighting [p. 8] was quite breath-taking in its disparaging insolence. Do you still mean it?

BION: Let it stand, like my lack of culture, as a monument to my effrontery. I am ashamed and would like to cross it out.

MYSELF: As long as it serves as a reminder of what we are really like, and not as a slur on 'them'.

BION: I fear that much of the diary will appear, on this reading, to be an exercise in sheltering my complacency from the chilling blast of truth.

MYSELF: It does read like that. Your reference to the boy as 'street-bred' [p. 6] and a 'grouser' makes me wonder if the war and Oxford had gone to your head. I hope not, but then it is disconcerting to think such 'street-bred' superiority is a basic quality. Maybe at twenty-one you had not grown past adolescence. That poor boy later showed what I learned to call 'schizophrenic-type reaction'.

BION: You remind me of my senior officers, though I don't know much about your competence. I was aware that *I* was not competent, particularly as I was so scared and that did not seem to fit in with being a soldier. I could not even be sure of what I was frightened. Death? No. Being terribly mutilated? Perhaps; I knew a bit more about the possibilities later. Going mad? No. Whatever I thought of, it didn't seem to be right. Anyhow, I was right about our senior officers.

MYSELF: I don't think you were, although there were certain plausible, superficial qualities that were reprehensible. Your failure to write home was reprehensible and not superficial.

BION: I could not. I agree – I knew – it was reprehensible. But I could not do it. I wrote once, after Cambrai.

* * *

BION: The Sunday before we were to leave Bovington [p. 8], the padre preached a sermon to the whole battalion. His text was, 'Soldiers, be content with your wages'. I don't remember what he said, but he remarked smoothly that some of us might think his choice peculiar.

MYSELF: You obviously did, but how odd that it is the only part you remember.

BION: I was probably hoping I would not run away. I know I feared it before I knew what action was. I was not awake to much of the next day; we must have marched down to a stirring military tune whose name I forget.

MYSELF: 'Bollocks, Bollocks – and the same to you.'

BION: That was *not* what it was called. 'Marche Militaire', perhaps. I say, it's a bit odd your remembering words like that after all these years and an Oxford education, isn't it?

MYSELF: One's early priggishness wears off. Or perhaps it simply becomes socialized as pornography.

BION: I hated the band playing 'Auld Acquaintance' and 'Home, Sweet Home'. My mother stayed in her cottage in Wool, or I would have hated her too.

MYSELF: I had forgotten the Brigadier shook hands with all the officers; I suppose you were right?

BION: Oh yes. It was a bit embarrassing – 'manly gesture' and all that, you know. I wonder if that was what made them so rude to Henry V before Agincourt. It was a bloody night on the *Australind*.

MYSELF: All I remember about Le Havre [p. 9] is the astonishment of a waitress on being asked by Greene, in his best French, to bring some teacake *'avec la vitesse de l'antelope'*.

BION: I didn't think it worth mentioning. I was fond of Greene, an officer in A Company – always cheerful and amusing. A barrister and wit. As we marched through Le Havre the band played the 'Marseillaise', and the people seemed surprised to see such a large body of large men. I heard one or two say, as they saw our regimental badges, *'Mitrailleurs'*, as we had Machine-Gun Corps insignia in those days – 'Heavy Machine-Guns' was the term, to avoid advertising 'Tanks'.

MYSELF: I suppose it sounds cynical to say that the Germans must have been amongst the most interested and informed part of the audience. If not, why not? One of the great armies of the world cannot surely have omitted to keep a capable body of spies at such key places as the ports.

BION: I don't think we believed it in spite of all the *'Taisez vous: Mefiez vous'* in the world, though we had a profound belief in our own Secret Service.

MYSELF: With some reason, I think. Unfortunately we also had some reason later for bitter army gibes about the RN as the 'Silent Service'. We didn't see the positive side – that nothing had interfered with our own crossing.

* * *

BION: These clichés [p. 10] do nothing to convey an impression to anyone who had not had the experience, but to me – sixty years later – their very banality recalls that immensely emotional experience. The behaviour, facial expression, and poverty of conversation could give an impression of depression and even fear at the prospect of battle. Fear there certainly was; fear of fear was, I think, common to all – officers and men. The inability to admit it to anyone, as there was no one to admit it to without being guilty of spreading alarm and despondency, produced a curious sense of being entirely alone in company with a crowd of mindless robots – machines devoid of humanity. The loneliness was intense; I can still feel my skin drawn over the bones of my face as if it were the mask of a cadaver. The occasional words exchanged echoed like a conversation heard from afar. 'Wipers', 'Yes, the Salient.' 'Guns sound a bit frisky.' 'Awful – but cheer up – you'll soon be dead.' 'You've said it.'

* * *

MYSELF: I had forgotten these details [p. 51]. I remembered the episode as a recommendation from the Company Commander. I had been correspondingly uncomforted – having added to my disillusions the fear that I must have grossly misrepresented my youthful escapade.

BION: I was anxious at the time, and troubled at my good fortune in coming out unscathed where Cohen, Stokes and, to a lesser extent, Quainton had suffered disaster. I did not know how badly Quainton had suffered till long after.

MYSELF: I remember meeting him, quite by accident, years later in Oxford. He was changed from a cheerful, frank fellow whom I had envied for his easy capacity for deep friendliness, into a timid, cautious and scared apology for a man. I could not penetrate his reserve, and he would say nothing of what had happened to him in the war, or since he left the Maudesley.

BION: Of course, I did not know that the Quainton I knew was only surviving as a physical representation of himself.

MYSELF: Now you have reminded me of it, I think his story of using whisky to topple the tank into safety is probably a fabrication of an already disordered personality. Incidentally, I think the VC could have toppled *you* into a 'breakdown'. You were lucky not to get it.

BION: Most people got killed trying to deserve the award later. I only knew one, and he seemed to be insensitive to an ordinary conversation. Of course, he may have been like that before.

MYSELF: Who knows? I suppose awards for valour do stimulate the impulse to be valorous. I think professional soldiers may be able to survive them unharmed better than people with fewer years of discipline. And yet . . . those brave rows of ribbons: I often wonder what they portend. I see you mention that you were all very nervy, which I had forgotten.

BION: I felt embarrassed to meet my crew. It seemed so ridiculous that I should be singled out. I was able to recommend Richardson for a Military Medal, which he obtained. I indulged in a shuffling apology; they knew I had been recommended for something – mercifully, they did not know for what.

* * *

MYSELF: Our senior officers were *not* inefficient [p. 20], but we could not know that our world had reached its Niagara. We were bits that betrayed the accelerating speed of the flood.

BION: The only flood we knew came down in sheets from the grey, shell-shattered skies and up from the sodden, glistening mud. I did not know of any officer or man who did not admire our staff and preferred them to Lloyd George, Asquith or Curzon, and sundry very important snoopers who came out to have a cosy shudder of patriotism. You forget that we could see for ourselves what our immediate seniors were. I knew only too well that if I relaxed my grim, determined jaw, my teeth would chatter.

MYSELF: Don't you think your immediate seniors had fears that likewise had to be masked? They too had seniors in rank and time.

BION: They died; we were killed.

MYSELF: Somehow, I am not sympathetic. Perhaps I am too comfortable and too forgetful; your self-pity does not leaven; it is flatulent.

BION: At Oxford, when I wrote the account, we were not so critical. I don't think it was because it was against orders, but because it was less awful to think all was well than to believe our bigger enemy was what you later called . . .

MYSELF: . . . the Establishment. Certain gross words would have been – still are – more appropriate.

* * *

MYSELF: 'The rain continued practically without stopping . . .' (p. 20). I remember this as peculiarly horrible. We used to go for apparently aimless route marches, but I suppose they were intended to keep us physically fit. I remember one that ended up in darkness – dank, steamy, wet. On the way back we heard a raid – and saw it – lighting up the sky. Our guns made the sky a white, bright backcloth against which the 'hills' of the salient were silhouetted. The light was continuous but pulsed. It was punctuated by spots of red fire; these were the enemy shells bursting in reply. I suppose we must have initiated the raid – they were only replying. I heard a man mutter, 'struth' as we stared at this terrifying spectacle. It seemed the only comment possible as the sight struck chill in one's heart. How the infantry stood it I cannot even now imagine – and they would have to lie in the mud and wet all night.

BION: I remember. Of course, I did not know then what I knew later about straying from No. 5 Infantry Track.

MYSELF: Could any amateur army like ours have survived? Surely that, and the Somme before it, must have killed the heart of our soldiers, our initiative.

* * *

BION: How well we were prepared [p. 51]! We had not been prepared for the victory; we had not been prepared to take seriously the information our intelligence services had given us.

MYSELF: This is in no way different today – or ever was. The success of the First World War was thrown away, the good fortune of our survival at the end of the Second was likewise frittered away.

BION: Are you not blaming the Staff and the Establishment, as you call it? It sounds as if you are grousing as much as you say I am.

MYSELF: It does; but I do not blame the Establishment. It is us I blame – all of us. Victory seems to be regarded by us as desirable because it leads to an opportunity to sink into slumber again.

* * *

MYSELF: The part I remember, that impressed me most [p. 52], was the sight of the Guards Division advancing in open order and in formation so perfect it might have been a parade-ground exercise. They took Gouzeaucourt and swept on to Ribécourt.

BION: Yes, now you remind me. I forgot it as soon as I saw it because we who were left without arms to 'stand to' had to march back in the afternoon. The Guards set up a 'prisoner-of-war' cage into which they shepherded the fleeing remnants of the infantry division. This was done by their camp details while the main body continued their advance. I hated the machine-gunning from the air, though it didn't seem to do any harm.

MYSELF: I seem to remember that though we had Lewis guns, we did the planes no harm either.

BION: Well, they came so fast and so suddenly.

MYSELF: You could hardly expect them to walk, or give you notice. You were on the open road, and a battle had been raging for about fifteen hours.

BION: They didn't come back, so we hadn't a second chance.

MYSELF: Second chances are rare; second, even third, thoughts are possible, but choice of which thought to transform into action has to be instant and not dependent on second chances.

BION: I certainly felt demoralized; so much so that I do not remember bothering about my threatened decoration. I loathed having to go back and take over the tanks we had left in charge of Quainton and others.

MYSELF: I had hardly any memory of going back to Moult and the return till you reminded me.

BION: I am not surprised. I forgot it as fast as I could. At Oxford, when I was writing the diary, I used to have a recurrent dream of clinging to the slimy bank of a torrent that rushed by some twenty feet below. As I was slipping, I tried to dig my fingernails into the mud. But as I became tired I moved to ease myself – and this meant a further slither. This vast raging torrent waiting for me below was the Steenbeck. I have described the trickle of dirty water that was the geographical fact.

MYSELF: Your 'dream', as you call it, sounds a better description of the 'facts' than the facts. The crossing of the Steenbeck swallowed up many an English soldier – for what?

BION: I remember the corpse in the shell-hole that sheltered us both – his bluey-green skin stretched tight over the bones of his face, his mouth pulled open by the contraction of death.

MYSELF: I renewed the acquaintance in the dissecting room.

BION: We held Ypres.

MYSELF: No. Peace broke out with its customary virulence. With heavy industry idle, workers rotting for lack of work, we 'prepared' to fight another war without arms, without training, without spirit. We did NOT 'keep on' holding Ypres. And now we slither to our Niagara. This time it is not a dream.

BION: It was no dream at Méaulte. We went back after one stint with the supporting troops. Merry Christmas to you all. Quainton had a marvellous fur coat, which, he declared proudly, excited the Colonel's envious eyes – as well it might. But the future was hidden from both: no comfort could keep out the chilly blast of the future.

* * *

MYSELF: Your description of Méaulte [p. 63], which was admittedly a horrible camp, a horrible Christmas, and a period of low morale in the troops, is certainly evocative, but I am disagreeably impressed by your sanctimonious priggishness – not only in the army, but at Oxford where you wrote your account. I cannot believe that your army friends were as bad. If so, it was not surprising that Cook, Homfray, and Clifford disliked you as much as you did them.

BION: I think the 'diary' is a fair enough reflection of me.

MYSELF: It must have been your athletic skills that saved you at Oxford.

BION: I could *not* work, and though I swam and played rugger, I did not know what enjoying games meant. Very occasionally a friend took me round to the rooms of another Queen's man who played the piano and sang to us. He was charming and unpretentious; sometimes I secretly wished I could be released from my athletic prowess. But I could not – it was too important a lifebelt for me to be able to let go my hold of it.

MYSELF: Like your DSO?

BION: I suppose so, but in fact I did not find that compelling. I forgot it, and remember one occasion at least when it was quite a shock to be reminded of it by a friend.

MYSELF: I remember that.

BION: Then perhaps you will not be surprised that I would have been shocked had I known what I should become if I survived the war.

MYSELF: What upsets you most?

BION: Your success, I think. I hesitate to say it, because it sounds ungrateful. I cannot imagine what was wrong, but I never recovered from the survival of the Battle of Amiens. Most of what I do not like about you seemed to start then.

MYSELF: As you had not realized it then, I am surprised that you say so little about events that in retrospect seem utterly horrible.

BION: I should have thought that there was nothing material excluded.

MYSELF: Possibly. It may not have struck you as dramatic enough to mention the time, long before Ypres, when you were asleep on the stone floor of a farmhouse that had been levelled in previous fighting. That sickly, sweet stench of corpses which . . .

BION: . . . we couldn't locate. I remember perfectly. What about it?

MYSELF: Nothing: that was what was so awful. You were not even frightened. By the time you got to Oxford, you had 'forgotten' it. *I* don't remember it, but my gut does. I was and am still scared. What about? I don't know – just scared. No, not even 'just' scared. Scared.

BION: That 'sweet smell of the dead' I remember. It was pervasive. Where was that? I know it was before we had tanks.

MYSELF: And how could you have been such a damned fool as to let that Boche drag you to the dug-out where his dead pal was? On August 8th it was.

BION: I remember. Asser was about to die – refusing to surrender. He could have been fighting for something of which I could not be aware. But his death killed me. At least, it made me feel I could never be a man with such intensity that I would knowingly embrace certain death.

MYSELF: Years after, many years after, I learned that I could hardly claim to love a woman because the woman's love included her love of the father of her children. I do not know. I can only aspire to such love and suffer the uncertainty that it is only an aspiration of which I fall short.

BION: I had no doubt – do not ask my why, but I repeat *no* doubt – that Asser, nearly a year younger than I, was such a man. I do not feel that about you, who I have survived to become.

MYSELF: I certainly do not claim it. I am still 'becoming', though. It depends if death forestalls my growth. I can hardly claim more time as of a right.

BION: What else surprises you?

MYSELF: Your enthusiasm to go into battle and the fact that it seemed to endure.

BION: I recognize a quality that you might mistake for endurance, but I do not remember any behaviour I would call enthusiasm. Once, perhaps twice, I felt enthusiasm when I saw the guns in the field near school, and when I saw the North Midland Division marching.

MYSELF: Before you went to war, you had what I think of as a morbid change-and-decay-in-all-around-I-see religiosity.

BION: That was shared by all my contemporaries; it was indistinguishable from the Headmaster's sexual pi-jaws [pious talk; public school slang]. I had a vague sense of impending ill-defined DOOM mixed up with 'poison in the food' – another of his solemn and terrifying ploys. I also had a vague feeling that I would be killed for a pleasurable sin – probably masturbation.

MYSELF: I do not remember your ever feeling that abstinence would confer immunity.

BION: No, I could hardly achieve that degree of stupidity. Facts of action could not fail to penetrate. After Cambrai it was obvious – not a single one of my personal friends was in existence.

MYSELF: Except Cohen and Quainton.

BION: Both were recognizable only in the way that an insect's chitinous sheath could be recognized as something from which the pupa had emerged.

MYSELF: What about Hauser?

BION: He did not become a friend, but a fellow officer for whom I developed an immense and enduring respect.

MYSELF: His comment on your stolid and unhurried loading of your revolver after Mont Kemmel had fallen impressed you.

BION: It must have done, but I did not realize it at the time. I was only aware of a sense of utter emptiness. I thought the infantry officers who saw me walking to my machine-gun crews regarded me as some sort of pathological case.

MYSELF: I think they were right. After all, you had not the background of training and discipline of a real soldier.

BION: I don't suppose they had either; we were all amateurs without an amatory tie with a warlike profession. The Guards Division at Hazebrouck, at Cambrai – *they* could stand up to any troops in the world.

MYSELF: I still feel the admiration that was born then.

AMIENS

As Bion writes in the Prelude to this unfinished narrative, memories were aroused by our train journey in France on August 3rd 1958. I remember his being visibly moved as he talked of his painful recollections; I became heavy-hearted, thinking of the lost generation of young men and those who were left to carry with them the burden of bitterness and disillusionment throughout their lives.

He writes in the third person and becomes the story-teller, attributing some of his own actions and experiences to other characters. It is a solemn chronicle of tired men grown cynical after years of futile losses and dashed hopes, unable to feel any enthusiasm now that the tide has turned in their favour and an end to fighting is at last a possibility. The only relief from the atmosphere of anxiety and fear is in the wry, ironic picture he draws of Major de Freine, although at the time, as he told me, he (transposed to Cook) found it impossible to see the 'funny side' of that living caricature of a cavalry officer of the 'old school'.

The account ends in mid-sentence – other more pressing commitments intervened. He was working on *Learning from Experience* at the time (1960), followed by four more books published by 1970. I know he did not read my typescript, which was filed and half forgotten by me over the ensuing thirty years until recently, when publication of the diary became a possibility. I have edited it, as I did many of his writings, in the way of which he approved. The titles, Prelude and Fugue, are my choice, the latter meaning 'loss of one's identity, often coupled with disappearance from one's usual environment' (*OED*).

Francesca Bion

Prelude

[August 3rd 1958]

The train was now travelling at speed. The sideways gentle oscillation of the coaches blended rhythmically with the thundering forward surge of the train itself. It was hot. The men working in the fields were bare to the waist. We could see them toiling over the vast rolling expanses of cornland that the train was now passing through.

Francesca sat opposite to me, looking as usual cool, neat, beautifully turned out, with her sweetly smiling face. She studied the menu, and in a moment or two the waiter came up to us, and we ordered our cocktails, which arrived in glasses already frosted with the contrast of their contents and the warm, humid air of this hot summer's day.

The fields disappeared as we approached the outskirts of a town, and soon we were threading our way through the network of rails and points that made up Amiens station. Amiens – so that explained it. Some twenty minutes earlier we had passed a peculiar configuration of the ground about which Francesca had questioned me. I had recognized at once the signs of shell-holes overgrown with weed. They pock-marked the ground round about some marshy pools, where the willow trees hung green and graceful in the bright sunlight. Still they seemed to be ineradicable, to be very little older than the shell-holes had been in the war, where one marvelled at the speed with which they were covered up with weed and willowherb in the period of the war itself. What surprised now was that so little further disguise had taken place.

As the train sped through the complex of lines, I said to Francesca that it seemed strange that it was almost forty years ago to the day when I had last been here, and in such very different circumstances. It was a dream for her to be sitting opposite to me – a girl so beautiful, so loving, so near to a dream that I had always thought could never, never come to pass for me.

The train, freed of the marshalling yards, had settled down into the steady rhythm of its speedy rush towards the sea. Was it not Julian Grenfell who wrote, 'The naked earth is warm with spring"? I think it was in that poem that he spoke of the man 'who dies fighting has increase' ['Into Battle', published in *The Times*, 27 May 1915].

I wonder. But what an army it was. Can there ever be collected together again so many men of splendid minds and splendid physique? And is it possible that, if they were collected together again, they could be suffused with so fantastic a devotion to war, so mystical and overwhelming a belief that it was the cure for all the ills of the world – 'as swimmers into cleanness leaping', as Rupert Brooke had it ['Peace', 1914], speaking of his entry into the war? The wonderful experiences of peacetime were really nothing; or rather had in them the seeds of some kind of disease that would be purged away by the actual process of war itself.

There were not many of those left by 1918, and yet there were some. I remember Asser – Asser, who was only nineteen and who joined our battalion with all the freshness, enthusiasm and youthful belief that he was joining in some wonderful and glorious adventure. He did not grow old, 'as we who are left grow old' [Laurence Binyon, 'For the Fallen'].

Fugue

1

In the early evening of August 7th, 1918, Captain Bion, DSO, had been ordered to rest before the battle, since he had been at work from early dawn after several days of prolonged preparation of his tanks for action. He lay down on a rug on the grass of a high plateau overlooking the valley of the River Luce. Before him was a screen of trees of the wood in which the tanks of his battalion were concealed from enemy observation. The green leaves hung heavily in the hot evening air, their colour touched with bronze in the rays of the declining sun. He was twenty years old, and he commanded a section of the 3rd Company of the 5th Tank Battalion. Sharing the rug with him was 2nd Lieutenant Asser, aged eighteen, just newly joined with the battalion. The time was approximately 14.00 hours. The battalion was due to take up its positions for action, commencing the march-to-battle positions at 18.00 hours. The 3rd Company was to lead the battalion, and Bion's section was the last one in the order of route. He and his companion composed themselves for sleep.

The move to the forward area had commenced four days previously, when the battalion, lying some twenty miles behind the front line already prepared, had been ordered forward to entrain and then proceed to Amiens where they were to start the forward move in their vehicles. The journey, which had to be performed in the utmost secrecy, had been extremely arduous. The first stages of the approach to the entraining-point had been over untouched country, which was therefore particularly likely to take the imprint of the tank tracks. So it had been necessary, in addition to the usual ardours of an approach march, for parties with brooms to cover up the tracks, so that they would not be visible to the enemy aerial photographers. This burdensome task had employed at least half of each tank crew. Every forward move, including the journeys by train, had to be performed after night had fallen. The days were accordingly spent in greasing the tanks, oiling, filling with petrol, and general maintenance duties. In this way it had been possible for few to obtain any rest at all, nor had there been any time for speculation as to what the new move might portend. It was, however, vaguely known that the impending battle was to be extremely important for the fate of the whole Western Front. Some details were known to the company commanders, but below that rank the information did not go. Even company commanders and higher officers were still kept in the dark regarding the actual location of the coming battle.

The battalion arrived at railhead before dawn on August 6th; the tanks were detrained with the greatest possible rapidity and driven into a neighbouring copse for shelter. Then before light came the tracks were again obliterated by the same laborious process as before. It was then that Bion had the idea of attaching a large hurdle to the back of his tank and, telling the men whose duty it was to obscure the tracks to stand on this hurdle, dragged it behind the tank and so saved a great deal of unnecessary labour.

For this Bion was commended by his Company Commander. Such commendation was for him not unusual; as his ribbon of the DSO showed, he had the reputation of being a courageous officer in battle in spite of his extreme youth.

His second in command, Asser, had only been appointed to that position on Bion's representations to the Company Commander on the day on which the forward move had been inaugurated. He had displaced an officer some two years older than Bion, named Cartwright, on the grounds that he was not a suitable officer for that position. In Bion's view he was lacking in courage and initiative and was too much disposed to mix on over-familiar terms with the men of his crew; furthermore, he showed a great lack of discretion in his attitude and manner when addressing his subordinates and was disposed to behave as if he found their company more congenial that that of his fellow officers. Bion considered Asser, although only newly arrived from England, far more suitable for the post, qualified both by his natural disposition – one of a cheerful cast of mind – and by his general grasp and aptitude for the duties he had to fulfil. He had taken his promotion, which involved no official recognition in the army lists, with modest assurance and pleasure but without any undue elation. Cartwright, on the other hand, as might have been expected, became still further disgruntled and even more disposed to speak and behave in a manner that was considered to be unworthy of an officer. It was assumed, however, that his crew, a good one, would not come to much harm from this behaviour except that which arises through not being able to have a great deal of confidence in the officer in whose hands they were placed.

When all the tanks of the battalion had been safely moved into the positions pre-ordained by the advance party in the wood, they were further camouflaged for additional precaution, although they would seem to be amply hidden by the leaves of the trees. When this was completed, the officers tried to tidy themselves, to shave and carry out such ablutions as were possible with hot water they obtained through strapping water-filled petrol cans onto the sides of the exhaust vents of the tanks. Men and officers then had their early morning meal. Since no fires were permitted, this consisted of cold water, bully beef and ration biscuits. After the meal the men set about their routine tasks of tank maintenance, but the officers, down to the most junior taking part in the battle, were summoned to a conference to be held in a tent pitched in the wood. This conference was to brief them on their orders and to explain to them the nature of the approaching operation.

On arrival at the tent, Bion and his officers, Asser, Cartwright, Broom and Hauser, all tank commanders, were issued with their maps. Bion, as section commander, had no tank but proceeded into action on foot in the front ranks of the leading infantry. On opening their maps, they discovered that they had been allocated a sector, a front of advance lying to the right of a straight road, which ran from Amiens to Roye. Amidst excited but subdued talk and the rustling of the maps being unfolded, there entered the Corps Commander with the GSO1 and his brigadiers. The noise was hushed as all the officers stood to attention. The Corps Commander and his staff motioned to them to sit down, and they took their seats at an improvised dais.

'Christ, this looks like the big stuff', said Broom, whispering to Hauser, who sat there, short-sighted, almost bat-like, disgruntled, famous with officers and men alike for his unique perversity of disposition.

Hauser, who spoke with a habitual snuffle, looked caustically towards the exalted officers on the dais and replied in not too soft a whisper, 'With all these big guns here, they should be able to produce a bigger balls-up.'

Broom was shocked. His excited eyes seemed to protrude from the pink moon of his face. 'You don't mean that', he said.

'You watch', hissed Hauser briefly, for the Corps Commander was already speaking.

His speech at least belied Hauser's gloomy prognostications. He was precise, he was accurate; he appeared to know minutely the orders he wished to communicate. He hardly ever referred to notes except in matters of minor detail, and then only to confirm what he had said, never to make a correction. He began by explaining that for reasons of security he proposed only to deal with the immediate front, which concerned the battalion and its neighbours on either flank. He said that the battle was to be a major one and would probably decide the fate of the war.

Hauser, reduced to silence by the importance of the occasion, thought that he had heard this before, like the last battle, and the one before that, and the one before that, and the one before that . . . he reflected bitterly.

The Corps Commander continued: up to the present there was no sign that the enemy was aware of what was going on on his front. Secrecy had apparently been entirely successful; the latest reports from our agents indicated that there were no extra troop movements on his front. Nevertheless, he emphasized, the enemy were in great strength because it was their intention to launch an attack within the next few days that was designed to capture Amiens and so break an important hinge on the front of the allies. This front was the point at which the French and British armies joined. Our attack was intended not only to forestall the enemy move, but to be a major contribution to his total defeat.

Bion's heart sank. 'Why the hell', he thought to himself, 'do we always have to choose the point at which the enemy is most powerful?'

The attack was to be carried out, the Corps Commander continued, by two divisions of the British army, by the Canadian Army Corps, by the Australian and New Zealand Army Corps and by the First French Army. Some of the battalion's tanks would be operating with troops of the First French Army. He showed on a map a line that marked the respective fronts of the right flank of the attacking British, and of the left flank of the First French Army. At some 3,000 metres from the front line this limiting line joined the Amiens–Roye road, which, from that point onward, would provide the frontier separating the British Armies, the Fourth Army and the First French Army. After he had spoken in fairly general terms, he sat down and handed over to his CSO1, who then gave detailed instructions to the companies and sections that were to operate.

In tense silence all the officers followed the instructions with the aid of their maps. Bion and his officers became tense when they heard the orders that affected them as a section. It appeared that they were to be on the extreme right of the British Army, that they would start operating with troops of the Canadian Army Corps, and then, when the Amiens–Roye road was reached, they would be taking over the protection of the French Nancy Division. This division would consist of the Foreign Legion, the Chasseurs Alpines and –

'It's the French Iron Division', whispered Hauser, momentarily dropping his attitude of disillusionment.

The staff officer went on to say that the utmost precaution must be taken to preserve secrecy; there must be no risks taken whatsoever. Up to the present, he said, there had only been one aeroplane over our lines, and that had been shot down. There were some ironical murmurs at this point as ground troops had very little faith in the marksmanship of the anti-aircraft batteries. He explained that, since the enemy were not anxious to spring a surprise upon us, it was quite likely that they would not risk sending out any reconnaissance planes more than they could help for fear of arousing our suspicions. One of the difficult problems, he continued, was how to keep the enemy from being suspicious when our tanks moved forward into battle position. It had therefore been arranged that flights of Handley Page bombers would take place over the front lines at the time when our tanks started forward before the battle. It was hoped that the noise of the aeroplane engines would mask the sound of the tanks, and that the sound of the tank engines would be explained to the listening enemy as being made by the Handley Page bombers, which they themselves could see.

Detail followed detail for something over an hour; then came the questions, terse and tensely delivered. As a matter of course, nobody less exalted than a company commander could ask the questions. Then the Corps Commander rose, indicated that the conference was at an end, and with his fellow staff officers left the tent. The officers of the battalion broke up into small groups, discussing the information they had been given. Bion's officers kept together.

'This means Croix de Guerre for all of us', said Broom. 'You can never go into action within ten miles of the French without being showered with the things.'

'If the Boche are so stupid that they can't tell the difference between a tank and a Handley Page bomber, I wonder why we have to fight them at all', said Hauser.

'It will be too late by then, anyway', said Bion.

'Oh no, it won't', said Hauser. 'What about that German major fellow at Cambrai? He chewed us up pretty thoroughly then if you remember. You've only got to give these chaps a little bit of notice, and they sit there with their guns nicely trained waiting for us to show our snouts over the top.'

'Don't be such a wet blanket', said Bion somewhat uneasily. 'You know very well that we will have a very heavy barrage put down on him.'

Asser, who had been silent all this time, absorbed with thoughts of excitement about his first battle and the thrill of seeing so many important officers whose names were legends to him, now broke in. 'I think there should be far too big a barrage for it to be possible for any German major to be firing over open sights at our tanks. After all, you have heard what they said about Greenwood Copse: he said the Boche had sixteen machine-guns in there, and they were turning five 9.5 Howitzers on to it for that part alone. That ought to finish them off if anything should.'

'Rubbish', said Hauser acidly, 'you know perfectly well that whenever one of those idiotic guns fires, all that happens is that the Boche is presented with a huge crater. He simply shoves a little bit of barbed wire round the top, puts a few machine-guns in it, and there you are – a perfectly good strong point – and he hasn't even had to bat an eyelid digging one single spadeful of earth out of this mucky soil.'

'I see you're in very good form, Hauser', said Bion. After many months of fighting, he knew Hauser was one of the stoutest-hearted officers in the battalion. He covered up whatever feelings he might have by a perpetual flow of acid comment about the world in which he was living. It was not unamusing, although it sometimes had a very irritating effect, both on his colleagues and on his men. His men, however, in between intervals of hating him, really worshipped him, because they knew he was utterly reliable, that there was no chance of his ever failing them in battle, or neglecting any detail at all that could make for their comfort and care.

The Battalion Intelligence Officer, Captain Carter, approached the group. 'Tell Captain Bion that he is wanted by Major Hotblack.'

Major Hotblack was standing some few yards away, and when Bion approached him, he said that he would be glad to take him up to the front to have a look at the River Luce. 'We might as well have a look round if you feel like it first thing tomorrow morning, I think. Perhaps have a peep into no-man's land.'

Bion did not much relish the prospect at all, although he was not able to say so, for Hotblack was a man with a legendary reputation for his actions both in battle and in the Secret Service, where he was reputed to have carried out some extraordinary feats behind the German lines. There was nothing to do but to agree with him. 'But', said Bion, 'I have to be back in time to go to the H.Q. of the Iron Division.'

'Yes, I know', said Hotblack, 'but I think we shall have plenty of time before then just to have a little look at our friend over the way.'

They arranged to meet at the bridge over the River Luce just before dawn on the following day.

2

It was after this reconnaissance and the conference at French Divisional H.Q. that Bion had now had his first chance of a rest. Something about the morning's work had clearly upset him. He appeared to be nervous and anxious, rather pale and not by any means the self-assured person that one would have expected from somebody with as good a reputation as his. However, he and Asser were now at last able to lie down and snatch a few hours of sleep before the battle – if they could. For Asser the main obstacle to sleep was undoubtedly his excitement and pleasure at the thought of his first battle. Mixed with it, of course, there were also fears and anxieties, as might well be supposed. Yet for Bion the state of affairs was different and much more complex: he had been frightened; he did not like being on this reconnaissance, and he did not like being in company with a person whose courage was so outstanding that he would find it easy to detect in Bion signs of the fear, the deterioration as a soldier that Bion felt he was only too well aware of himself but did not wish to communicate to others. Something had happened on the reconnaissance, yet from a certain point of view nothing could have been more peaceful.

The two of them had met at the appointed time at the small bridge over the River Luce and had then gone forward without any difficulty, on a glorious morning, towards the front-line positions. There they had finally decided, under a burst of machine-gun fire and with the advice of the infantry on whose front they were, to proceed more cautiously, going into a stooping position and finally crawling forward as best they could, making use of any cover they could find in order to advance towards the enemy without being detected or running, as Hotblack said, 'any undue risks'. Nevertheless Bion had felt extremely frightened. Whether he was more frightened of the enemy or of Major Hotblack it would be difficult to say, but the upshot of it was that at one point he had become so extremely panicky that he had had to resort to taking a whole series of compass bearings of the position that he said he had to occupy with his tanks that evening. Hotblack seemed to be somewhat amused at this, but at the same time he did not raise any objections; he did not appear even to be unduly impatient about it. Yet to Bion his whole attitude was sinister; it seemed incredible that anybody with Hotblack's experiences could fail to observe the trembling of his hand, the tenseness of his expression and manner, his inability to converse clearly. Furthermore, there seemed to be absolutely no excuse for taking the compass bearings. 'Just to be on the safe side', he had said. But the safe side of what? Hotblack did not visualize there would be any need for these bearings at all; the landmarks were clear, the position was easy, there was nothing whatever to suggest that when the time came in the evening to lay down the tapes for the tanks to be led into position, there would be any difficulty. No, there was no doubt about it – it must be obvious to Hotblack that the compass bearings had very little indeed to do with the impending action but a great deal to do with Bion's need for camouflage to hide his true feelings.

As Bion had hoped, Hotblack finally said that he was going forward a little bit, as there was something that he found attractive and interesting, and that he would rejoin Bion when his observations were complete. This gave Bion the much-needed respite he was seeking; it was with great relief that he continued to observe, to take bearings, to scribble in his notebook, trying more and more to feel that what he was doing was justified by the military needs of the situation and that his manner in doing it showed nothing but that of the calm, collected, wise and prudent officer. By the time Hotblack had returned, he felt that he had thoroughly restored the situation. Nevertheless he was uneasy. He fancied that Hotblack looked at him queerly as if he suspected something.

The pair were back again now at the Luce bridge from which they had started. Hotblack said he would walk with Bion some of the way towards the Divisional H.Q. because it lay on his path, and then he would go on his way while Bion went by himself to the Division.

'What do you think of the new officers you recently had out from England as reinforcements?' asked Hotblack.

'They seem to me to be quite first-class', said Bion.

'Sincerely, though, do you really think they are up to the old standard?'

'Yes', said Bion, 'Indeed, I think that one I have just had in my section is perhaps one of the most efficient officers I have come across. He had all the keenness and enthusiasm we used to have at the beginning of the war – at least, perhaps I should say at the time I first came into the army myself.'

'Well, that's very good news', said Hotblack, 'but you know, I'm not sure that this experience of yours is altogether typical. I know the Brigadier is very worried about some of the reports he has had. Of course, you can't expect the country to be producing the same number of first-class officers now as they could in the old days when we had the pick of the public schools. Some of the people who have been promoted from the ranks cause us a great deal of trouble and distress.'

'You mean', said Bion, 'that you feel they lack a good deal of polish and so forth?'

'Oh no, not at all', said Hotblack, 'that would be a minor matter. I don't think anybody minds very much about that. What is much more serious is if their lack of manners – or 'polish', as you call it – really shows the vulgarity or indifference of their minds. Too often, it seems to me that these people have any amount of personal ambition and drive, but very little idea that they may have obligations to fulfil when they reach positions of importance.'

'Yes, I see what you mean', said Bion, 'but I don't think officers have been lacking in the past who had just the same defects and indeed some that were even worse. I remember one man we had who, I think, got his commission because the head of his firm had a certain amount of pull; why he should have been commissioned as an officer otherwise I cannot possibly imagine. He had neither manners nor polish nor any sort of courage.'

At this point Bion became somewhat anxious and troubled. He was not feeling that he was a very good officer himself, nor was he at all sure that if he spoke too loudly and too clearly in his criticism of others, expressing thereby his belief in his own worth, he might not invite criticism, silent though it might be, from Hotblack. Indeed, he had begun to feel that Hotblack would realize he was just exactly one of these undesirable officers about whom he had so many misgivings.

At last they had reached the point at which Hotblack had to get back to Corps H.Q., and Bion went on by himself. 'You'll find them quite a nice lot', said Hotblack in parting. 'They are a very fine division – they've had a good deal of battling.'

Bion's mood was not helpful to him when he at last found himself at Divisional H.Q. He was introduced to the senior officers there, particularly the Battalion Commanders whose troops his tanks were to cover. When they found that he was unable to speak French – typical of the British, the French seemed to think – they lost all interest in him, and though this gave him an opportunity to stand rather to one side and watch the strange spectacle of French H.Q. at work, it intensified his feelings of being basically an outsider and one who would be recognized as such if his true worth were known, as opposed to the appearance he managed to project of himself and which in some respects he felt was projected onto him.

It was a large dugout. There seemed to be a general air of confusion, of telephones. Seated at a table was a senior officer, certainly not the Divisional Commander, but probably the equivalent of the GSO1; at another table there were three junior officers, and at still another there were drawn up a few chairs where the Colonels were studying their maps and were to hear from Bion an account of his proposals. These orders he then attempted to explain in English. The French officers listened for a while, then wearily laid aside their maps and gave up any pretence to be understanding what was said. It seemed to be understood that his tanks would he there, and the French commanders did not expect to receive any valuable help beyond possibly harbouring the hope that Bion's tanks would not open fire on the French troops.

A one-armed officer came up and offered Bion a drink, which he took more because he could think of nothing else to do than for any other reason. This officer wore the ribbon of the Legion d'Honneur and the Croix de Guerre; he was pale and seemed to be an extremely sick man. Bion could not help wondering whether he had completely recovered from his wound.

There was an atmosphere of starkness, of bitterness, one might say, alien to the somewhat schoolboyish, football-playing enthusiasm of the British armies, and even alien to the rather irresponsible inconsequent cheerfulness of the French troops such as Bion had seen on the retreat from Mont Kemmel, when they had relieved his own battalion.

As soon as he conveniently could, he escaped from the H.Q. and worked his way back again to his own company lines, feeling very much worse for his whole morning's work, and in particular a prey now to the feelings of anxiety and dread lest his deterioration, as he felt certain it was, should show itself in some spectacular manner in the oncoming battle. Indeed, in some respects he felt a fear that it would not be anything spectacular but simply the sort of terrible decline that he had so often seen in others. He remembered with what astonishment he had heard the news of Captain Yates.

Yates was a man he had not liked, a man who, when he arrived at the battalion as a newly joined subaltern just commissioned, seemed to occupy a great position because he had been present at the Gallipoli landings. Even then he appeared to be drinking too much, to be hectically over-cheerful, ostentatiously bawdy and somewhat assertive. On one occasion somebody had joked to him about his wearing the holes in his rank tabs for far senior rank to that which he held at the time. To this he had replied that he had already held that rank, but his manner was disgruntled and assertive, as if he felt he should still hold the rank. Nevertheless he passed as a man of experience far superior to the youthful subalterns; yet when it had come to the first action of the battalion, news had rapidly spread that when he had been ordered to go forward to a reconnaissance, he had at a certain point broken down, taken shelter in a ditch by the side of the road although there were no sounds of gunfire and although they were many miles from the front line, and had refused to go forward any more. He had burst into tears and remained huddled up in the ditch, with the unfortunate subaltern by his side trying to encourage him to continue with their task. Bion was then too young to sympathize with Yates, but he had been able to take in what seemed to him the horrible disgrace of this situation – a situation in which an officer to whom had been attributed so much courage and bravery, who had had such a distinguished war service, should suddenly be reduced to a point where it was obvious that he was far less use than the most inexperienced and recently joined subaltern. It is clear that the spirit of man cannot contend with years of inanimate flying steel and bullets; sooner or later the morale goes; that was the thought that was haunting Bion at this time. He himself was by this time a veteran of some eighteen months of warfare – no mean life for an officer in a tank regiment.

He composed himself to rest, pulling over him a grey service blanket. It is nice of the army, he thought, to provide these without any further charge for the burial of the dead; extraordinarily generous of the British nation to allow a man who dies in battle to be buried in his service blanket as his winding sheet, no charge made against the relatives for the expenses incurred in the loss of the blanket.

In the meanwhile work was proceeding at Battalion H.Q. in a manner that seemed to be both desultory and feverish. The Colonel was not present, but the Battalion Intelligence Officer, Captain Carter, was. He had much to do and was engaged in conversation with various company reconnaissance officers who had the task of laying down the tapes that were to lead the tanks into position. None of this could be done until after dark, lest the enemy should send over a plane that would be able to detect the tapes on the ground and thereby deduce that something was afoot. The clerks were busily engaged in various minutiae of administration, filling up forms and so forth. Every now and then a new officer would come in to raise some point that seemed to have been neglected or, it was feared, had not been properly attended to already. Major Cook was also present there.

The Colonel came in for a few minutes. He seemed to be abstracted and to be at a loss to know what it was he wished to find. 'Is Major Morgan about?' he said at last. Morgan was called for, and the Colonel then discussed with him some points about the operation on the left flank, where the battalion would be contacting the Australian and New Zealand Army Corps.

'What about Captain Bion?', he asked 'Has he been to see the Divisional H.Q.?' Nobody seemed to know. Then a Lieutenant Greene, a newly joined officer, spoke up and said that he thought Captain Bion had been out with Major Hotblack but that they had returned. One of the orderlies said that he felt quite sure that Captain Bion had been to the French Divisional H.Q., but by this time the Colonel's attention seemed to have wandered, and he once more spoke to Major Morgan about some detail of the 1st Company's dispositions.

Such were the comings and goings throughout the course of the afternoon. 'We move off at 18.00 hours', said the Colonel unnecessarily, to nobody in particular.

'Yes, sir', said Carter, taking up the theme as if he felt that presumably it was he who was being addressed. 'I think everything is ready, sir. It ought to be a good show.'

'Quite', said the Colonel, 'Quite. I think it ought. I'm not very happy, though, about our right flank. I don't trust these French people a bit. I think they may not start at all. Has Captain Bion been told that the Corps Commander thinks it is quite likely that when zero hour comes, the French may not even move from their trenches? You know what the blackguards did at Mont Kemmel, don't you?'

'Yes, sir. I was talking to Captain Bion about this myself – we were discussing that event. He proposed to leave one tank behind to patrol on our right flank so as to form a defence against any possible counter-attack down the flanks from the enemy if the French don't move.'

'Good. Excellent idea. That's splendid. How is Captain Bion? Is he all right?'

'Oh yes, sir. I think he's quite all right.'

Greene then interposed to say that he had been talking to Captain Bion and that he felt that the whole question had been gone into very thoroughly.

'I am going to my tent now to get some rest', said the Colonel, turning to Carter. 'You know where to find me. If there is anything you want, send Mr Greene along with a message and I shall deal with it.'

He had hardly left when Greene observed to Carter that the Colonel was extremely jittery. He had no hesitation at all in making such an observation about his senior officer, although Carter, as one of the old school, would scarcely be likely to approve of such behaviour. However, he was perhaps more reconciled at this stage to the aberrations of the newly joined officers. Greene himself was an ex-ranker. 'I think at any rate that he's a very good colonel', said Carter.

'Well', said Greene, 'he needs to be. The last one, who didn't even know how many machine-guns a tank has got, seemed to me not quite up to the job of commanding officer of a tank battalion.'

'I don't think you should talk like that, Mr Greene', said Carter severely and left him in order to deal with some documents that an orderly had just brought to him for signature.

Quite unabashed, Greene moved away, and when Carter had finished his signatures, he found that Hauser had arrived to talk to him. A queer kind of sympathy existed between these two. Although Hauser was only about twenty-five years of age, he nevertheless had a certain rough, neurotic, obstinate maturity, which chimed in well with that of Carter, who was a man grizzled, vigorous, about forty years old, having spent most of his life in Malaya.

He gave Hauser a pleasant smile and said, 'Well, how are things going?'

'Oh, all right', said Hauser. 'I think it's pretty well complete when you consider all things. I think we've got them taped up this time, don't you?'

'Yes', said Carter, 'I think we have.'

'Nevertheless', said Hauser, 'I don't like this silence.' At that moment a battery of our guns opened fire.

'Bloody fools', muttered Carter. 'They have been told not to loose off anything at all – the orders are strictly that on the whole of this front there must be no registering of guns whatsoever, so that the enemy doesn't suspect anything's afoot.'

'Exactly the same as at Cambrai, I suppose', said Hauser.

'Yes, that's the idea. And now they do that.'

However, nothing further happened. There was no answering reply from the enemy, and the flurry of gunfire might have been just a routine duty round such as will shake the quiet of the most peaceful front.

'I don't like the way the Boche are so quiet', said Carter 'I wonder whether they smell a rat. You always know they are up to some mischief when they are as well behaved as they are now.'

'Just what I had been thinking myself', said Hauser. 'In the whole of the approach here we have been left singularly free from any kind of molestation at all. And what is more, when I was talking to some of the other reconnaissance officers at our conference yesterday, nobody seemed to have had any experience of any activity at all from the Boche. It's altogether too good to be true. What does the Colonel think about it?'

'He's in extremely good form', said Carter. 'He's quite convinced that this is IT, that we're going to break right through and end the war.'

'Ah, yes', said Hauser bitterly, 'this war, like the last war, is to be the war to end war; and the next war, like this war, will be a war to end war, and so on ad infinitum. And all the breakthroughs are the last possible breakthroughs which break through everything of course, naturally.'

'I see you are in very good form too – sarcastic as usual. Still, I sympathize with you. I can't honestly say that I believe that this is going to be the last war, and in fact I think it would be a damned bad thing if it was.'

Hauser snorted. 'You had better be careful how you say that kind of thing to the Christian contingent. I don't think I should be inclined to air your views too much to Bion and his pals if I were you.

'No', said Carter, 'I don't think I would. Still, they're not a bad lot in their way. The trouble about these damned Christians is, of course, that although they're so full of high ideals, and so packed with enthusiasm, and so determined that right will triumph, they fail to appreciate some of the more seamy sides of this business. Then when at last it does get through to them, they have a nasty way of cracking up – in my opinion. I remember one poor devil. We used to think the world of him, but he just went west when he discovered his colonel was trying to do a bit of graft on him and had thwarted his possibilities of promotion simply because the colonel himself was afraid that if he promoted such a promising officer, his own job would be jeopardized. He became unstuck, and the next thing he did was to have a kind of breakdown. This had the effect of proving that the Colonel was quite right, when in fact he was quite wrong. What's the time?'

'5.30', replied Greene, who had wandered back to the group again.

'In that case I'd better go and see what my lambs are up to', said Hauser, and off he went to visit his crew, whom he rarely left in peace for very long.

'What's the weather forecast, Greene', asked Carter.

'Set fair', said Greene, 'days and days of fine weather.'

'It's an absolute sitter', said Carter. 'The ground's as hard as a rock, none of that damned mud we had at Ypres. It's much more like Cambrai. There shouldn't be a tank stuck on the whole of the front, I should imagine – not unless it catches a packet from one of their field guns. Otherwise I can't see there's anything whatever to stop us. It's absolutely perfect, no dangers of any sort at all.'

'Ah, yes, nobody ever can', said Greene, 'but they'll be there all right. Very interesting to see what happens this evening; between now and tomorrow morning at dawn there is sure to be some almighty balls-up as usual. I've never known anything else in this ruddy army, have you?'

Carter remained silent. He did not like this kind of talk. It was not the sort of thing that was done in Malaya. He wishes to discourage Greene from his irreverent observation, but Greene was not so easily deterred.

He continued, 'We need a great many more professional officers. None of your peacetime officers, none of your public school boys. What you want is a few more men like me, we people who have had to learn how a machine-gun works, how to fire a rifle; also we people who know a thing or two about lying, detention barracks and thieving. We're not fighting Old Etonians on the opposite side. To be a jolly good officer, you need to be a jolly good liar, a scrimshanker, a man who keeps out of the way of any dirty job, the kind of man who unhesitatingly hits somebody else below the belt, yes, and stamps on his face when he's got him down.'

'Oh, for Christ's sake, shut up!' said Carter, and turned and walked away.

'All right', said Greene after him, 'but you'll see I'm right.' Deprived of his audience, Greene then turned to his corporal, who had come up to take a message from him, and let him have the benefit of the remainder of his observations. 'You see, Corporal, these fellows don't know what they're talking about. Even in peacetime the best of our regular army officers were fellows who had been taught at Sandhurst and elsewhere how to take absence without leave, how to go off up to town when they weren't supposed to. The best of them were always the ones who used to do a certain amount of work, a little bit of play and the rest of it cheating and lying in one form and another, I don't believe that these so-called gentlemen really exist. And anyhow, we don't want any gentlemen in the army. Good old fifth-form louts of the public school, some of those were some use; otherwise they are no good at all, none of them. I don't believe you want anything except a handful of officers who obey orders inside out – that's the business of the private soldier, not the officer. The problem for the officer is how to be insubordinate, how to be in a state of rebellion, and how not to be caught at it – that's what I say. Why, if some of our politicians had been like that instead of talking about standing up for bloody little Belgium and honour and right, we shouldn't be here, none of us; we should be sitting snug in England, letting the old Boche fight the French and anyone else he liked, keeping our navy and army intact. You can do almost anything with an army or a navy providing you don't use it, you know.'

'Yes, sir', said the corporal dutifully.

'You got a fag?' said Greene.

The corporal handed him one without further comment. 'Can you tell me, sir, what army we're in here?'

'Yes, 4th Army. Good God: Do you mean to tell me you didn't know that? You'll be saying you don't know who the army commander is next.'

'Well, sir, I don't know who the army commander is.'

'Rawlinson. Wherever were you brought up?'

'Rawlinson, sir? I never heard of him.'

'Never heard of him?' It was now Greene's turn to be scandalized. As an old ex-army ranker, he was quite familiar with the names of the senior officers – Plumer, Allenby, Byng, Home – they were all people of whom he had heard, albeit in junior rank. Much of this was, of course, exaggerated by him; he had every facility for giving the impression that he was quite familiar with the big names in the way described by Shakespeare in *Henry V* [IV. iii].

'Well, to tell you the truth, sir', said the corporal, 'I don't much mind what army we're in so long as it isn't the Third Army. I've got no use for an army in which the Q Staff are so bad that you can't get proper grub and rations. Give me all the grub and rations I want, and for all I care the army can be commanded by Jesus Christ himself.'

'You're being blasphemous, Corporal', said Greene, but not with any particular sincerity. 'Still, there is something in what you say. I can't say that I think your theology matters very much, but I think that from a military point of view your ideas are correct – if you give the troops the food they need, you needn't worry about anything else.'

'Women too?' asked the corporal emboldened by his officer's friendliness.

'No', said Greene, 'I don't know that I would agree with that. I think they're a bit of a nuisance sometimes; from all I've heard tell of the Peninsular War, they used to carry their women with them, but they got in the way as much as anything. Still, not that I'm averse to a bit of stuff myself if I can get a twenty-four hour . . .' He broke off as all the officers and men stood to attention at the entry of the Adjutant.

He was a clean-shaven, rather horsey-looking man of about thirty, sparely built; he was unkindly described by those who were not friendly disposed to him as having all the smartness of the jockey. Nevertheless he had the reputation amongst all ranks of the battalion of being efficient, courteous and agreeable, although there were many who were given the impression that he felt himself to be socially superior to them. He had had many years of experience in the editorship of a small paper in the provinces and prided himself on his erudition and education – a pride that was not altogether misplaced. He had withal a pleasing wit of which he made good use on occasions, such as mess nights, when he had composed some entertaining rhymes bringing in the names of various officers and hitting off their characteristics in a few simple and entertaining phrases.

'How are things getting on, Sergeant-Major?' he asked. 'No fresh messages? I suppose everything is all right? The battalion will have to be moving off within the next four or five minutes. I suppose everybody has their orders clear.'

'Oh, yes, I think so, sir', said the Sergeant-Major. 'We have had one or two queries here. There's one lot come in from B Section H.Q. Rear. They want to know about the return . . .'

'Oh never mind about all that stuff now, for heaven's sake. We've got something else to do. I don't know why it is that even when you've got a battle on your hands, you have to be cluttered up with heaven knows what rubbish from the rear.'

'Latrine stuff – bumph, sir', said Greene, deciding to be witty, but he was simply ignored for his pains.

'Better just send up the runners to company commanders, Sergeant-Major. There's not much point in it – they all know what to do – but just to make sure of the job. And see they all get started on time.'

'Very good, sir', said the Sergeant-Major.

'Overture and beginners', said the corporal who prided himself on his theatrical experience, having spent some weeks of his life in a small touring repertory company.

'You had better tell the batman to get the Colonel's and my kit moving too. From now on we shall be in the forward H.Q., as you know.'

'Yes, sir', said the sergeant-major, 'the orders have already been given, and the men have started moving things forward.'

3

Bion and Asser were moving uneasily in their sleep as the declining sun began to touch the tops of the trees. Finally Bion woke up with a start and woke his companion.

'Time we were getting moving, old boy. It's just about a quarter to six. Better see that all the tanks get started up, because we ought to be on the road. As you know, our section have to be the first over the bridge. I don't know about you', he added, 'but I can't say I feel I've had much of a rest. I always hate this sleep before action; one gets the most appalling dreams, and then when you wake up you don't know whether it wouldn't have been better to go on sleeping. The dreams are so much nicer than the actual reality we have to face now.'

'Just what I was thinking, sir' said Asser laughing. 'I had a most foul dream, but I must say I feel much happier awake than to go on sleeping with that. Blue trains – that's what I was dreaming about.'

'I can't see very much wrong with that', said Bion. 'From what you told me of your experiences on the continent before the war, Blue trains ought to mean something very pleasant to you.

'So they do, but Blue trains in dreams are a different proposition', said Asser. 'Anyhow, I suppose we had better get on with this stuff now.' He went off to the wood to his tanks.

Bion, after making one or two adjustments to his equipment – his batman having arrived with his harness, his revolver and ammunition – started off a few minutes later. His was not in an enviable state of mind: he still felt filled with his uneasy sleep and dreams, and he had woken to a consciousness of the unpleasant anxieties that he had had in his reconnaissance with Major Hotblack that morning. 'If only I could pray', he thought bitterly, 'but somehow I don't seem to get any consolation from religion now in the way I could when old Quainton was here.'

Quainton had been a good friend, a man who appeared to possess a placid and calm outlook, and a deep religious faith, which Bion had thought a solid foundation that could not possibly be shaken until Quainton had gone on leave to England and had then written back a letter that seemed, to Bion, to be entirely incredible; he had been driving a car, had had a sudden breakdown and had driven the car into a ditch. While he himself was uninjured, the doctors had seen him, pronounced him suffering from a nervous breakdown, and told him he could not return to the front. The worst of it was that he had written a similar letter to Broom, of all people, a man who could not possibly have been felt by Quainton to be a friend. Broom had made the most of it, not concealing in the least his belief that Quainton had worked the whole thing as a method of escaping from the war. He showed, in the most undisguised manner, his belief that Quainton was nothing more or less than a coward and, by implication, so were the other officers who were friends of his, such as Bion himself. As he buckled on his belt, walking slowly towards the copse in which the tanks were waiting, he suffered sensations of nausea and fear and was filled with feelings of impending disaster.

Carter caught up with him as he was going and wished him good luck. 'As far as I can see, old boy, it's a sitter. I don't think the Boche expects a thing. Everything is absolutely taped out, and I think we've got the most marvellous ground on which to operate. By the way, you ought to be able to get a Croix de Guerre out of this at the very least. I think even the Colonel expects he's going to get a medal for agriculture, or something of the sort, out of the French.'

'Well, let's hope it won't be for manuring the ground with our dead', said Bion gloomily.

'You're in an extremely cheerful state of mind, I must say', said Carter. 'I don't see why you think we should have any casualties at all. We've got the most terrific gun barrage, I don't mind telling you. You remember what the Corps Commander said, but I know for a fact that even then he wasn't telling you everything. It's the biggest concentration of gunfire I think we've ever had.'

'The gunfire at Cambrai didn't do us much good', said Bion.

'The gunfire at Cambrai was chicken-feed compared with this lot. That was just a trial run. I tell you, the Staff learnt something then. This time we've got ten guns to every one we had at that show, and you know it wasn't such a bad bombardment even so.'

'As long as the guns knock out the enemy and don't just fire short and get our tanks, or plough up the ground so much that we can't get through, I don't mind', said Bion.

Well, it isn't Ypres', said Carter. 'At Ypres they certainly made the place into a frightful mess; in fact, it was such a frightful mess before we ever started that no tank could possibly live in it, but this time we've got ground that's as hard as iron. Even if they went on with a bombardment for a fortnight, I don't think it would make a great deal of difference to the way our tanks go. Well, good-bye for the present – I shall see you down there before zero hour I expect, anyway', and Carter strode off.

By this time the air was electric with excitement. There was still every need for precautions; it had been impressed on the entire battalion that there must be no let-up whatsoever until the actual moment of zero hour. No fires, not even cigarettes were to be lit unless in some concealed spot so that the flame of the match could not be visible to the enemy, nor should there be any undue noise lest his listening posts should pick it up and interpret it as a sign of the impending attack. In spite of this suppression there could be felt the excitement in the men as they bustled to and fro, finding their tanks, manning the starting handles and checking up in the last few moments the various gauges that showed the petrol and oil supply. The shelter of the wood allowed for some relief from the restraint that everyone felt had been imposed upon them and which, in any case, the dread of battle imposes even without the orders for caution. The cool and bustle of the wood contrasted vividly with the heavy silence and heat outside the shelter of the leaves.

Although a certain uniformity had been imposed upon the battalion for its starting time since it was imperative that the order of march should be preserved on the restricted approach routes, it was not felt to be desirable that all tanks should start at the same moment as that would put too heavy a load upon the camouflage arrangements that had been made to disguise the noise of the tank engines. Therefore the various individual tanks would start freely in their own time, while ensuring only that they would get on to the mud tracks in their right order at approximately the right starting hour.

Bion's visit to the tanks was only short, as he was due to go down to the River Luce in order to repair the bridge that spanned it at the crossing-point for the tanks of his company. After a word or two with Cartwright and then with Asser, who looked at him with undisguised admiration, he went to collect his small party of troops with picks and shovels and then marched them down the slope from the high plateau to the River Luce in the valley below. For the sake of safety he told the corporal in charge to keep the men in single file and scattered, though they were not to lose touch with each other; also that it would be better if they avoided the dirt track, in case the enemy were making observations. It was imperative that nothing at all should be done to arouse suspicion, even the marching of a small body of men such as this was.

Bion went on ahead independently. The bridge was only a mile and a half from the copse in which the tanks were concealed. It was nothing much more than a small culvert across a stream that could hardly be called a stream. A dirty trickle of water went through the centre of the shell-holes, for this particular point was subject to much bombardment as the enemy were anxious to destroy the bridge and to deny its use to the British troops. The bridge itself was a ruin of stonework that had fallen into the bed of the virtually dry stream. It had been decided that it was unnecessary to make any attempt at rebuilding the bridge, but rather that the passage should be ensured by filling the stream with facines of wood. These were huge bundles of faggots, tied powerfully together with wire rope, that weighed anything up to about 15 cwt each. It was an arduous job trundling them into the stream from the dump where the lorry had placed them earlier in the day, and the task was not made any more pleasant because it was well known that about this time every evening the enemy would open fire on this spot as a routine matter, seeing to it that any repair work that had been done was efficiently demolished the same day. Bion, who had really nothing to do beyond the nominal supervision of what was essentially a task involving no brains at all, did not feel he was in a position to keep at a safe distance – which he would very much like to have done. He therefore, somewhat ostentatiously, sat upon the remains of some rubble on the actual site of the crossing and smoked.

Some of these jobs, he thought to himself, might just as well be done with a dummy stuffed with straw. I wish I was a dummy stuffed with straw now. Unfortunately, if I'm hit it hurts, and I hate being hurt. I don't think anybody knows how much I am afraid of physical pain. If I could be sure that I should be killed, I don't think I would mind, but the ghastly and terrible thing, the awful thought of one's shins crumbling up inside one's legs at the burst of a shell and the flying splinters, is more than I can stand. Why am I such a damned fool as to sit here and think about it then, I wonder.

Not for the first time, he felt that he had no morale left. He felt confident that there were many soldiers who regarded him as being a person of some consequence and courage, but he himself remembered only too vividly the earlier part of the year, when the enemy were attacking the Messines Ridge, when he had felt for some terrible hours, in a small tin shelter, the full force of passivity in the face of imminent death, when there seemed to be no courage, no resource, no reservoir of courage on which it was possible to draw. On that occasion he had thought, 'If the enemy come over, I know that I shall automatically put up my hands. I cannot fight. I want only to be removed from this ghastly hell of mud and shell-holes and corpses.' It was all very different now, but *he* didn't feel particularly different. The British armies were now on the offensive, the whole Western Front in flame ever since the French attack at Soissons earlier in the year. The allies were attacking, the enemy were finished, they were on the run – that was the official story. Yes, that might be true for armies as a whole; it might be true for the nations gathered together to administer the death blow to the German forces, but it was not true for the individuals. He felt that there was nothing in front of him except steady decline. There was no corresponding excitement or pleasure in him as he heard of further advances, of battles successfully fought in which the enemy was thrown back. It was no thrill to be told he was now participating in one of the major battles of the war. The optimism and cheerfulness were appropriate to members of the Staff, of those whose chances of death were minimal and then restricted to the few occasions when they were right up in the forward areas. As for him, he had been in battle after battle in which only two out of every three who took part in the tank war survived to tell the tale within twenty-four hours of the start of the action. This was not a matter, then, for any optimism; it was not even a matter of fighting; it seemed to be simply a question of statistics and the laws of chance.

The men sweated and grunted and swore, working sullenly, with depression and heaviness showing in every movement they made with the heavy, recalcitrant facines that would not roll, could not be lifted and could only be steered with the greatest difficulty and by the exercise of sheer brute force on the part of the tired men. Bion looked at his watch. Half an hour had passed. There were yet another two hours to go before the tanks would be starting the approach march, and at any moment the enemy shelling, their evening routine fire, would open. But it had not happened so far, and the enemy were reputed to be very regular here, as always. They should have opened fire half an hour before; Bion reflected uneasily that there was plenty of time yet because it would take at least until zero hour before the river could be effectually filled in. This operation had been timed to be completed before the first tank arrived; it had not been feasible earlier, because it was necessary to make it as late as possible in order not to arouse the enemy's suspicions. In any case, any repair that had been done before six o'clock would be likely to be demolished by the six o'clock strafe.

As time passed and no shells fell, the men began to be more cheerful. The corporal came up to Bion. 'It looks, sir, as if we're going to be lucky.' 'I hope so, sincerely', said Bion. The men's work became more animated; instead of the heavy, silent slogging, there were exchanges of comment, banal enough in all conscience, but still it was comment. It was nerve-racking work; there was nothing to be afraid of, there was nothing happening – just physical strain, and yet at any moment the whole operation might be thrown into complete chaos by the dropping of a few shells. After a time the very silence of the enemy batteries began to be a source of unease. Once again the thought obtruded itself – why were they so quiet? Why did they not fire? It was notorious that when they were most quiescent and most well-behaved, they were up to something. This was a commonly accepted part of the story throughout the British Army, and indeed seemed to have much substance in it.

Every train of thought Bion took up was soon dropped; it was impossible to pursue any to its logical conclusion. Just as one anxiety broke up, another took its place.

'That's about it, sir', said the corporal. Bion looked at the work, inspected it thoroughly and agreed that it seemed to be sturdy and ample for the task it had to fulfil, formidable though the crossing of such a stream was by a number of very heavy vehicles.

'Get the men away from the bridge as far as you can, then, Corporal. Over there, about four hundred yards back, will do. We don't need to go back, we can wait here for the first tanks to arrive.' He looked at his watch and saw ten minutes to nine. The crews would shortly be starting their engines.

He joined his men some four hundred yards from the bridge, and all lay down on the grass by the side of the track. It was a lovely evening, now turned dark so that there would be no risk of the tanks being seen by aerial observation. The air was calm and heavy, scented with the summer smells of the countryside – a most unusual experience for those who had been used to fighting in the mud of Ypres and other battlefields so fought over that trees were non-existent and the song of birds completely unknown.

'Good God!' exclaimed Gunner Harrison, 'hark at that!' It was the sound of a tank engine starting up.

At this distance, even a mile and a half away from the wood, the sound of the engine roaring into life seemed completely to shatter the peace of the entire front. How on earth, they thought as they listened to this infernal din, could anybody possibly fail to hear that row? At the same time the Handley Page bombers were heard droning overhead. The sound, to people expert in tank warfare, was absolutely unmistakable; there could be no confusion of the two noises. To Bion, Hauser's comment when the project of camouflaging the noise of the tanks by Handley Page bombers had first been raised, had been entirely apposite: it was inconceivable that anybody could be deceived by it. But whether it was that nerves were on edge or for what other reason, the starting of the other tank engines seemed hardly perceptible. The characteristic, rhythmic throb became merged in that of all the other engines and settled down to a dull, steady murmur, which was far more capable of camouflage than had been the sound of the single tank.

'I think, Corporal', said Bion, 'that we might just as well stroll back gently to meet them coming.'

And so the party got up and gradually and informally straggled along the pathway towards the wood.

4

The final check-up tended to be a somewhat desultory affair: throughout the whole of the approach march to the battle area, the tanks had been fully maintained. No matter what the fatigue of the crews, the orders were strict – before they went to attempt any rest whatever, the tanks were to be fully greased and oiled. In addition, the ammunition had been sized – that is to say, every round of small-arms ammunition carried by the tanks had been tested to see that its fit was perfect for the barrels of the machine-guns by dropping each single round into the breech and extracting it and replacing it in its clip. This arduous task had been made necessary because it was well known that there was much defective ammunition, in particular that supplied from the United States. This had now been withdrawn and was used only for practice purposes; it was useful for training in rectifying stoppages in machine-guns while they were firing. Nevertheless there were still anxieties that, by some chance, defective ammunition existed, and a stoppage of a machine-gun in battle was too serious a matter to be risked through any negligence in preparation.

As Asser saw over his tank and talked to his corporal, Corporal Smith, he noted the various items that had to be in order, and then passed on to have a word with other tank commanders, chatting to members of the crews and occasionally to the officers. He was at some pains to talk to Cartwright, who, he knew, must be very sore at having been displaced by him. It is doubtful whether a more experienced officer would have worried to do this, because it was quite clear that Cartwright was suffering not merely from chagrin at being displaced, but was already a seriously demoralized man. However, the desultory exchange of comment went on and then Asser moved over to talk to Hauser, who, as usual, was fussing around with his crew and complaining bitterly of supposed defects in their preparations.

'Are you looking for somebody?' Asser asked Carter, who came up at this moment.

'Yes. Where's Bion?'

'He's down at the bridge carrying out the repair, you know', said Asser.

'Oh, I had forgotten. I think it might be a good plan if I go down there to see how he is getting on. Is everything all right here?'

'Yes, I think so', said Asser.

'How's old Cartwright? He looked a bit blue about the gills', said Carter.

Asser laughed. 'Well, I think he's all right', he said somewhat sheepishly. 'He seems to have got his tank into very good order, and our other tanks are all ready to move off at any time now.'

'You've got another half-hour to go yet', said Carter, 'but I think I shall be moving off to see if I can find Bion down there.'

At last the time came to start. Asser collected his crew, and they swung the engine, which then roared into action. The whole 75 hp of these powerful machines filled the air with a throbbing pulsation. One by one they started, and then Asser's crew moved their tank out of the wood onto the dirt track. The orders were to proceed in top gear for the first mile. After that they were to drop into low gear and go on with the very minimum of power possible, so that there should be hardly any noise from the engines, which would then be within close reach of the forward listening posts of the German army.

Everything went smoothly, and Asser had just given the order for his tank to drop into low gear when they came upon Bion and his party. It was not usual for more than two men to remain in the tank when they were carrying out the approach march. Only the driver and one other to help him were in each tank, the remainder walking at ease behind the machines, ready for duty if they were called upon by the two inside.

Bion hailed Asser, asked him if all was well, and in turn reported on the bridge. 'Everything is perfectly all right. We've got it absolutely bunged as full of facines as it possibly could be. Even if you stray off the narrow path. it won't matter. We've got it broad enough to take two tanks abreast at least, I should think. Anyhow, there's no water in the stream worth talking about. It's just a little trickle and that's about all. I don't know really why we bothered to have a bridge, though of course the real trouble would be that we'd churn the whole lot into complete mud soup if we hadn't bothered but had driven straight through it.'

'It's a wonderfully clear evening', said Asser.

* * *

[Three pages missing here; the following extract has been inserted from *The Long Week-End* for continuity.]

No one had mentioned the fog. There could not be a fog; the river, the banks, the low ground, all were as dry as a bone. I myself had seen it. Why, oh why, had I not reported back from the reconnaissance that there was a danger of fog? I had cursed the fools who acted as if forty tons of steel could float on Ypres mud. Yet here was I. . . .

I could see the report: 'An experienced Tank Corps officer had been sent forward to examine and report on the suitability of the terrain for tanks. Unfortunately he thought of absolutely everything and even noticed that there was no water in the river bed, but still failed to see the obvious point that since the water had abandoned the river, it must have take to the air.' There it was – thick, solid, impenetrable.

'Now what?' said Carter. I heard my own voice talking. 'Let's go and have a look.' We walked down and came to the wall. The next step and we were trying to see our hands. At arm's length they were out of sight.

* * *

If I hadn't been in such a terrible funk, he thought, I might have done those compass bearings properly, and now would be the time to use them. I don't even know if they are any use at all. I was spending my time trying to do them simply so as to keep my hands from trembling and to prevent Hotblack from seeing my state of mind. He wondered whether he should tell Carter that he had got the compass bearings. It would be so much simpler to leave it unsaid. The responsibility, after all, was not his, and he had no reason at all to place any particular reliance on the bearings he had taken with such meticulous care since he felt that he had not really been concentrating on the work itself.

'I suppose', said Carter, 'you didn't by any chance take the directions when you were down there with Hotblack this morning.'

'Well', said Bion, his hand forced, 'as a matter of fact, I did, but I really don't know whether they are very much good. You know I'm not an awful lot of use at this kind of thing.'

'My dear chap, it doesn't matter a damn if you're much use at it or not. It's those compass bearings of yours or nothing. We shall never get any tapes down to lead these tanks into action unless we get the routes taped out and the tank positions for them. I've got my men all ready here; let's have a look at them. Can't you leave Asser in charge of the section?'

'Yes, that's easy enough', said Bion, 'I haven't any doubt that he will manage the job perfectly easily. Would you like me to come with you?'

'Indeed, I would', said Carter with great relief.

Since the pace of the tanks was so slow, there was ample time for Bion, and Carter with his men, to go forward to the bridge and to set about the task of putting out the tapes – or would have been ample time for them to do so if it were not for the fog, which was so intense. However, Bion and Carter hurried forward, and as they went the fog swirled up to meet them. In a moment or two everything was absolutely blotted out in pitch darkness, with the mist swirling through lungs and throats and blinding everyone's eyes.

'We'll have to start working by compass now before ever we get to the bridge', said Carter. 'You didn't by any chance take bearings from here?'

'Yes, I think so – I think I've got them. In any case, I know this bit well enough', said Bion.

By slow degrees they went forward and found the bridge easily and quickly. From that point on it was a matter of Bion studying his field service notebook and reading out the compass bearings to Carter, who passed on the instructions to his sergeant and men. There was nothing for it but tense, concentrated attention to the work in hand, and somehow or other the task was ultimately finished; the positions were taped.

By this time the leading tank, which was Asser's, had reached the fascine bridge and picked up the tapes that had been laid down. One after another the tanks crossed and swung left to form up behind the front line of the infantry, which at this point lay some 200 yards in advance. Bion and Carter worked their way back to the bridge by means of the tapes, exchanging words and passing on instructions to the tank commanders as they came up with their machines. At the point where the tanks swung left, they waited, for at this point they had a rendezvous with the Company Commanders and the Battalion Commander who had arranged beforehand that they should station themselves here. It was not Bion who should have been there, but in view of his compass bearings he remained with Carter, leaving the command of his section to Asser.

At the rendezvous, they waited. 'I'm jolly grateful to you, Bion', Carter said.

'You wait till you know the results of the bearings', said Bion. 'I wasn't bargaining for this, and with all these tanks about the place, goodness knows what sort of distortion the compass has. I *think* they're all right, but I really don't know.'

'Here's the Colonel. Good evening, sir.'

The Colonel shook hands with Carter whom he had not seen for some time. 'This is a pretty mess. I don't think I've ever seen a fog anything like it. Is your company in position all right?'

'Yes', said Major de Freine, who had come up at this moment, 'it is, sir. We've got the tanks out in their proper positions.'

'But A and B Companies are not out in theirs – they don't know where they are at all. There have been no compass bearings taken. Bion, I think you had better go and help them get it all sorted out. You've got the compass bearings, haven't you?'

'No, sir, I haven't', said Bion. 'I've only got those for my section. I had to extend them to get the whole company positions .'

'Yes, but surely to God, man, you can do better than that, can't you? Is there any difficulty at all about extending it as far as the end of the Canadian Divisional front?'

'No, sir – but I only did the bearings for my own section.'

The Colonel was now very angry indeed. 'Aren't you able to do a bit more than the barest minimum of your job? As a section commander I expect you to be able to take full command of the company if need arises, and here you are telling me that you don't know how to extend your compass bearings properly.'

'Excuse me, sir, I didn't say that. I said that I don't know whether I can extend them properly.'

'Well, dammit man, go and try' said the Colonel, absolutely furious by this time.

Bion's state of mind became angry and further depressed by this new burden thrust upon him.

'Hard luck, old boy', said Carter. 'After all, it's not your fault. If anybody is to blame for this, it is really myself as the battalion reconnaissance officer. The Colonel has got the wind up properly. I don't know that I blame him – after all is said and done, it is his battalion that is in action; it covers the whole of the Canadian Division, and we're responsible for the tanks of the French Division as well. So if he hasn't got the tanks properly positioned for the battle, he might well have the wind up. I can see myself getting a court martial out of all this. I'm not at all sure that the Colonel doesn't see himself getting one.'

'I think it's much more likely', said Bion, 'that he's thinking he is going to get a DSO out of it. I wish somebody would give it to him. These damned people always wanting to get a ruddy decoration are more than a pest when it comes to real battle.'

'Well, old boy, you ought to know', said Carter. 'You've got a DSO out of it, anyhow.'

'Yes', said Bion, 'but that was an accident.'

'Oh, don't be so banal – every damned fool who had got a decoration always talks rot like that. You know perfectly well that if anybody deserves a decoration in action you do. Not that I hold any brief for the things myself. I suppose we've got the right tape', he added in an undertone, groping on the ground to pick up the markings.

From that time on there was silence as they grunted and felt their way forward until at last they came to Asser's tank. From there Bion extended his researches still further to find the rest of the company, and from that point on he and Carter proceeded laboriously to work out further bearings for the remainder of the battalion beyond the Amiens–Roye road to the left of the divisional flank, where it joined up with the Australian and New Zealand Army Corps. Eventually, after Carter and Bion had put the remainder of the battalion into their battle positions, they found on rejoining Hauser that there were only a couple of hours left before zero hour.

'I gather', said Hauser, 'that you have done something to modify what appears to be a first-class balls-up. Funny thing', he continued happily, 'they always manage to get a balls-up somehow. Nobody seems to have heard of the River Luce producing a fog until tonight, and yet it must have done so every evening for years and years and years. Let me congratulate you. It takes some doing to stop the British Staff once they get into form.'

They spoke in whispers in the pitch darkness while the fog swirled round them.

'I really believe it's thicker than ever', said Carter.

'Yes', said Hauser, 'I wish I could see what I'm doing. It's damned serious not being able to see a thing you do.'

'Well, what *are* you doing?' asked Carter.

'I'm trying to shave, dammit', said Hauser. It appeared that he had ordered hot water to be prepared on the tank exhaust simply so that he should be able to do this. He was most meticulous that his appearance should be correct and precise before going into action.

'Do you mean to say', said Bion, 'that you make your poor devil of a batman undo your shaving kit at this time in the morning before you start off a battle?'

'Well, of course I do. You don't expect me to go about looking like a tramp all the time, do you?'

A runner came fumbling along the tapes. 'Is Captain Bion here?'

'Yes', replied Bion.

'Major Morgan wishes to see you, sir', said the orderly.

Bion then turned and found his way wearily to the extreme left flank of the battalion. I wonder what the devil he wants now, he thought. When he reached Morgan, he found that he was simply anxious to ask whether Bion was quite sure that the bearings were correct. Funny, thought Bion, fetching me all this distance at this time of day, as if I had nothing whatever to do with my own section, to ask me damned silly questions like that. He reassured Morgan, who seemed to be disposed to be chatty and wished to walk along the tapes checking up with his tanks and to have Bion with him. At last Bion managed to take his leave and find his way back to his own section on the grounds that he had urgent work to do with his own men.

As he worked his way along the line, he came across group after group of officers at various points along the tape, all talking in whispers exchanging views about the uncanny silence of the enemy. Nearly all the officers and men were alike disquieted by this phenomenon.

'It would be something of a lark if we found that the enemy attacked at the same time as we did. It would be a real mess-up, I'm bound to say', said one of the A Company section commanders.

'I think we've got a pretty fair mix-up already', said Morgan, who was accompanying Bion on his journey up to the end of his own company front. 'I don't think I have ever known such a fog as this. It's worse than anything we have ever come across. Even before we start, the place seems to be absolute chaos. You still can't see your hand in front of your face – look', and he held up his hand. 'I can't distinguish a single finger from this distance.'

'It certainly gives you a pretty rum feeling, sir', said one of his tank commanders. 'It makes you feel as if you were wrapped up in cotton wool . . .'

'. . . cotton wool of a very frightening kind', said Morgan. 'I don't like cotton wool with bullets concealed in it flying about the place.'

'I wish there were a few more, sir. I think a few pinging overhead adds a pleasant sensation of liveliness. But this is absolutely dead – you can't see anything, you can't hear anything, you're just wrapped in silence.'

'The more silence, the better', said Morgan. 'Put that light out', he roared as somebody lit a match trying to light a cigarette. 'You tell these damned men they mustn't show a light anywhere – oh, I beg your pardon, I didn't realise it was you, Carter.'

'Very sorry, sir, I forgot myself.'

Before long the wandering of senior officers ceased. They took up their positions in the H.Q., which they had arranged to occupy in the early stages of the battle so that all would know to what point messages were to be sent as soon as the action started – or before, should the enemy begin action first. From Villers Bretonneux on the left to the French First Army on the right, the tanks were all in their battle positions, or so it was hoped in so far as could be told, thanks to the all-pervading fog. Small groups of officers continued to chat with each other in the increasing anxiety and tension as the time for zero hour drew near. Above all there was the silence, occasionally broken by the chatter of a machine-gun in the distance. Sometimes there would be the Sherman gun, noticeable for its slow and heavy movement; then the answering chatter of the Lewis gun or the British Maxim.

Carter was passing methodically from each group of officers to the next in order to check with them the exact time; all watches had to be synchronized at the last moment. As he came to each group, he would count out the seconds, ten . . . nine . . . eight . . . seven . . . six . . . until at last everyone had precisely the same hour, which he himself had in turn obtained from the Brigade H.Q. The tank crews stood by the side of the doors of their tanks, getting the last breath of fresh air before they shut themselves in for they knew not how many hours of the stifling, carbon-monoxide-laden air of the tanks.

'Do you know – that short-arsed little runt wanted his shaving water again today. He always does it, he doesn't seem to mind if there's a battle or not. He's got to have it hot, or you catch it hot.'

'I don't care', another man was saying, 'whore or no whore, she done it for 'im free, and that's wot caused all the trouble.'

Now orders were being given to the tank crews to man their tanks and start their engines. The officers who would be in battle on foot instinctively turned back to look in the direction from which the tanks had come, back over the position where the River Luce ought to be, towards the heights of the plateau where the copses had been used to shelter the tanks from aerial observation.

'What wouldn't I give', said Harrison to his second in command, 'to be back there. Nothing so comfortable as those lovely woods, a sort of paradise compared with this hell – or the hell that's going to be here in another minute or two.'

The attack was timed to start at dawn, but the thick fog meant that all was still bathed in darkness, as if it were still night. The British guns massed for the bombardment were in positions sloping from the heights of the plateau down the gentle slope all the way to the front line itself, where the lighter 6-inch Howitzers were in position. Nothing of the plateau or its slopes could be seen from the valley because of the all-pervading fog, which had not lifted or abated to the least extent.

As the hands of their watches reached zero hour, the officers, staring back towards the top of the plateau from whence they had come, saw it suddenly stabbed with white flashes of light. The bombardment had started. For a moment or two it seemed as if there was some vast wall of fog illuminated from within by these ghostly explosions. It was a wall, however, in which the officers felt themselves embedded; at one and the same moment gun flashes seemed to be at a distance and yet to be up against their very eyes and faces.

At first all was a silent fiery curtain, and then came the sound, a rushing, pulsating sound which came in gusts against the skin of face and hands as well as ears. 'They looking back, all the eastern side beheld/ Of Paradise, so late their happy seat,/ Wav'd over by that flaming brand, the Gate/ With dreadful faces thronged and fiery arms' [Milton, *Paradise Lost*, Book xii].

Bion, who was in Asser's tank by his side, said, 'Let her go, and good luck to you', then tumbled out into the open to stand watching with others the wall of fire behind. For a time nothing happened. Why didn't the German guns reply? A minute passed, two minutes, three – and still nothing happened. Then suddenly the earth around rocked and swayed with the falling shells. Bion turned towards the front to walk slowly forwards trying to judge his pace so that he would keep at the distance of some thirty yards behind the line that his tanks were supposed to be following; with one hand he held his runner, Sweeting, by the belt to his side, as with the other he held his compass.

A large shape suddenly loomed in front. It was a tank, stopped. Bion went round to the front flap and shouted at the top of his voice through it to the tank commander inside. He could not hear the reply, but went round to the door, which was opened for him to enter while Sweeting lay down by the side of the tank sheltering from the shell-fire. Inside he found the tank was Cartwright's. What had happened? The petrol feed had gone, came the reply. The corporal driver, Stone, was already by the side of the feed apparatus, looking at it helplessly, stonily, while the tank wobbled in the blast of shell-fire.

What's the matter with it? Think, Corporal, think. Hear what comfortable words your sergeant instructor, Broomback, said. It is a hot summer's day at Bovington camp. The hut is silent but for the buzzing of a bluebottle, which drifts drowsily about, hypnotizing the hearers. Outside the windows can be seen, swimming in the heat, the rhododendrons flaming with fire. What is it? What is it? This feed pipe, says the instructor, is much superior to the old-fashioned pump. That was very efficient in some respects. . . . Oh, do get on with it man, get to the point. What do you do when you have an engine on your hands, when you have forty tons of steel immovable in a barrage, what do you do? The old-fashioned feed was one that had great merits in that it never broke down, but should the tank be hit by a shell, then at once the tendency was for flames to be fed by the sprays of petrol still under pressure. Yes, yes, that is so, but I want to get on to the point where you know what you should do when the feed fails. Listen to the bluebottle, keep awake, Corporal Stone, keep awake. Listen to it. Yes, it will be pleasant to go into Bournemouth this afternoon. But listen to what your instructor is saying. Don't stare helplessly at it. My God, are these tanks made of jelly? Why do these walls wobble so? Not bluebottles now, but Handley Page bombers. Not bluebottles, no, but crumps; great things that hurtle through the sky like express trains, as the soldiers always say. Ah, at last he is coming to it. Tap the sides of the container gently with the knuckle. Yes, gently with the knuckle, not with a 95 Howitzer shell. Gently, with the knuckle. Filter, gently, nothing happens. Swing her again. Nothing happens. Swing her again. Nothing happens. Filter. Now try her once more. Nothing happens. Filter. Ah, yes, that's right. Filter. Take out the filter. Good heavens, it looks as if the birds have been nesting in it. Ah, that's it, blow through it, that's right. The beautiful flaming rhododendron bushes in the hot sunlight. Listen, Corporal, listen. He put back the filter. Swing her again – this time the engine broke into a roar. Bion dropped out of the back door, lay flat while the tank moved forward.

Suddenly its sides seemed to open like a flower, a sheet of flame shot above it, and there lay the tank with its sides bulged open and its roof gone. The end of Sergeant O'Toole, yes, and the whole crew. In the reeking fumes Bion could see some bodies flung over the top of the now bulging walls from where the roof ought to have been. It looked like the guts of some fantastic animal hanging out of a vast gaping wound.

Sergeant O'Toole is dead, thought Bion glumly as he went steadily forward with his hand still gripping tightly onto Sweeting's belt. Suddenly he felt that the nature of the ground had altered. He stooped down and noticed that it seemed to be some sort of track, maybe metalled. He and Sweeting threw themselves into a shell-hole and sheltered, waiting, as they were in advance of their time. Bion felt sick. He wanted time to think. Sweeting pressed himself as hard as he could against Bion, who then realized how frightened the young boy was; certainly there was reason for fear. The shell bursts were incessant; there was no pause between one and another, and it was now impossible to distinguish the sound of any guns – it was lost in one colossal storm of sound.

He tried to think: there was this rendezvous . . . he had to get to Berle au Bois . . . he had got to get to the *estaminet* at Berle au Bois . . . he must be at Berle au Bois by 10.15 . . . there he was to meet Asser . . . Asser's tank . . . there he was to meet Asser's tank and to give further orders. He tried to think. He tried to keep up against the battering of thundering pressure of the wind of the explosions against his body. What was he doing here? Why should he be here? Surely, Captain Bion, you ought to know that a metalled road, if that is what it is, is not the place in which to rest. Surely you ought to know better than this. Have you not been told *never* to wait by a landmark, something on which the enemy guns can easily register. Do you not know that shell-fire is always most intense at a point that is well marked on a map? What are you waiting for? The shell-fire is too heavy, I can't move. It's better to wait here. If I try to go forward out of the shelter of this hole, then I shall be blown to bits. I can't move. What are those trees there? He was looking across the way he had come, and there in the distance it seemed, through the lifting fog, that there was this row of poplars, a long straight line of poplars. What could it possibly mean? This long straight line of trees? Obviously it could only be one road. Surely it must be a main road. It was the Amiens–Roye road. But what was it doing there? Why was it in this peculiar position then? The terrible truth came to him: he must have got his compass bearings wrong. He was sure then that some terrible blunder had occurred. If that was the case, this road would be leading straight into the enemy's lines, and he had launched the battalion tanks not towards the enemy, but across the British Front. He compelled Sweeting to look back and see the road. He asked him what it meant. Sweeting agreed that it must be the Amiens– Roye road. It could be nothing else. Nothing on earth could look so like a dead-straight heavy road, lined with these tall poplars as he knew the Amiens–Roye road to be. Pale with fear, Sweeting again buried himself as deep as he could into the shell-hole, clutching closely to Bion's side for further shelter.

Bion was aware that Sweeting was trying to talk to him. Above the sound of the barrage it was impossible to hear any ordinary speech. Bending his ear as close as he could to Sweeting's moving lips, he heard him say, 'Why can't I cough, why can't I cough, sir? What's the matter, sir? Something has happened.'

Bion turned round and looked at Sweeting's side, and there he saw gusts of steam coming from where his left side should be. A shell splinter had torn out the left wall of his chest. There was no lung left there. Leaning back in the shell-hole, Bion began to vomit unrestrainedly, helplessly. Then, somewhat recovered, he saw the boy's lips moving again. His face was deadly pale and beaded with sweat. Bion bent his head so that his ear came as near as possible to Sweeting's mouth.

'Mother, Mother, write to my mother, sir, won't you? You'll remember her address, sir, won't you? 22 Kimberly Avenue, Halifax. Write to my mother – 22 Kimberly Road, Halifax. Mother, Mother, Mother, Mother.'

'Oh, for Christ's sake shut up', shouted Bion, revolted and terrified.

'Write to my mother, sir, you will write to my mother, won't you?'

'Yes, for Christ's sake shut up.'

'Write to my mother, mother, mother. Why can't I cough, sir?' Gusts of steam kept billowing out from his broken side. 'Why can't I cough? You will write to her, sir?' His voice began to grow faint. 'You will write to her, Mother, Mother.'

He fell limply into Bion's arms, now no longer attempting to press himself into the hole. His face, ghastly white, turned up to the sky. The fog swirled as thickly as ever around them. Every moment they seemed to be bathed in showers of bright sparks of red-hot steel from the bursting shells.

Never have I known a bombardment like this, never, never – Mother, Mother, Mother – never have I known a bombardment like this, he thought. I wish he would shut up. I wish he would die. Why can't he die? Surely he can't go on living with a great hole torn in his side like that.

5

Asser elected to take over the driving of his tank himself. He let in the gears and opened up to full throttle, the engine responding with a tremendous roar as the tank moved forward. The enemy bombardment had not yet opened, and there was only the sound of British guns, formidable though that was. Filled with exultation, he drove as fast as he possibly could.

His driver said, 'This'll make 'em think there are tanks in action all right, sir.'

'Yes, I mean to make them think just that. I hope by the time I've finished with them they'll notice us', said Asser, laughing happily.

Within a few moments the opening German barrage began to hurl clods of earth against the side of the tank.

'This thing wobbles like a jelly', said Asser. 'I used to think tanks were pretty solid affairs till we began to rock about like this.'

By this time it was necessary to talk in shouts if there was to be any communication whatever. The driver caught the infection of excitement from his officer, and this in turn seemed to permeate the crew in a mysterious way, although they could not hear the conversation taking place in the front.

'I think we had better shut down the flaps slightly', said Asser. 'There seems to be just a bit too much stuff flying in here, and although I like to see where I'm going, since I can't see anyway we might just as well have a bit more safety.' The front flaps were pulled down, leaving only a slight slit.

'I think the light is coming through, don't you, sir?' said the driver.

'Where?' said Asser.

'Look, over there, that's the high ground in front, isn't it, sir? It seems to be quite bright above the horizon there.'

'You idiot!" said Asser. 'Don't you realize what that is?'

'No, sir.'

'That's the shining of the lights from behind. Switch them off.'

His driver responded, and at once the supposed dawn disappeared. It was only the reflection on the front flap of the lights of the tank itself.

After a while Asser said, 'I suppose we're going in the right direction. I know we are on the right compass bearing according to our compass, but I don' t suppose for a single moment the thing is all right by this time. Not that I care much where we are going, so long as we're going somewhere. I hope we see some Boche sooner or later.'

A hail of sparks came off the front of the tank. 'That's a bit better', said Asser, 'that's somebody firing at us, I think.'

'Yes, I hope it's the Boche and not our people though, sir.'

'Oh, I don't think it's likely to be our people, do you? I haven't seen any of them.'

'I haven't seen anything of anybody, sir, if it comes to that. I can't see a thing. It seems to me to be just pitch-black.'

At that moment a bullet came in through the front flap and splashed on the tank engine cover behind the driver.

'Pull down that flap a bit more', said Asser. 'I don't think you ought to go shoving your snout out just now.' A moment later, 'Hello, what's this? Tree trunks? Oh no, I see they're men. Must be ours. We've caught up with our front line, I do believe. I think it's all rot this business of our staying behind the infantry. I'm going to go right through them. We can always say they got held up and we had to go in front. After all, what is the good of tooling around here as if we were carrying drinks for the troops? I'm all for having a bit of a scrap if we can, aren't you?'

The driver assented though with not quite the same degree of enthusiasm. As it happened, there was no need for Asser to disobey orders. The men in front, who still seemed to be shadows, began to drop and then one of them waved agitatedly to the tank, pointing in a certain direction. Asser did not have time to notice that the fog must have lifted considerably for him to be able to see any men at all. He drove straight forward and then, turning the tank more or less in the direction the man had indicated, he soon found the machine-gun bullets again spattering off flakes of red-hot sparks from the front of his tank.

'Shut the flaps', he ordered. 'I think we can deal with this all right. All we have to do is to keep on driving so that the sparks keep coming off in front of you and me. Then we're bound to run down the sod sometime.'

'But he may shut up firing', said his driver, 'and then we would go over him and not know anything about it.'

'That's true – better open the flaps slightly. I'll open my flap and keep a look-out. After all, it would be a bit of a fluke if a bullet came through the flap.'

'I've known it happen though, sir', said the driver, and indeed he had.

'Anyhow, nobody can say we've got any damned infantry in front of us now', said Asser. Peering through the chink, the fog suddenly disappeared, and he found himself in bright sunlight. 'Good God, what's happened now? An absolute transformation scene', he said to his driver. 'You have a look.'

His driver cautiously opened his flap. There was no doubt about it – as far as either of them could see through this restricted slit, they were right out into the open country and on rolling grassland. In front there was a little scrabble of white stuff that looked like chalk.

'That's probably the chap', said Asser. 'It seems to me somebody has been digging something there. It can't just be rabbits.'

They drove hard at the spot and were rewarded by seeing a frightened-looking German machine-gunner putting up his hands, partly unable to stifle his curiosity at seeing a tank at such close range.

'Well, what do we do with him now? We can't stop and take him prisoner. I think we had better wait here just a moment covering him with our guns until the infantry come up.'

'Yes, sir, but all the same we had better keep on the move because they may have a field gun trained on us.'

'You think of everything', said Asser.

'Well sir, I've had plenty of chance to do it. I've been in action now for about a year one way and another. I know most of their little tricks. The only thing I don't know is driving a tank over this kind of country where tanks ought to be used. It's a novelty that unhinges me slightly, sir.'

They had arrived at a small strong point consisting of a few trenches in which there were probably two or three machine-guns, although the gunners were not visible to the members of the crew. Asser passed the word back that they were to keep their guns trained on this patch of torn earth and trenches, and that he was going to circle the tank round it until the infantry were able to come up. It was not many minutes before they saw an infantry sergeant who came with his men and took over the German prisoners who were getting out of their trenches, starting to work their way back with their hands above their heads.

'Now I think we can get on', said Asser. 'I hope this compass is right. I've got to get us onto our line again. We're miles before our time.'

'For God's sake, don't run into any field guns, sir. I had my bellyful of that at Cambrai. We came across that German major chap – you know, the fellow who knocked out so many tanks. He got our tank, but he only got it in the tail. Even so, we had to get out pretty quick before the flames spread.'

'Hello, what does this chap want?' said Asser.

An infantry lieutenant had appeared at the flap and was shouting through it. It was extremely difficult to make out what he was saying because of the din of the engine and the very heavy bombardment outside. As last Asser got the message.

'Can't you take your bloody tank away?' said the officer. 'They'll start shelling us to hell here if you don't.'

Asser felt extremely indignant and wanted to reply that this was his battle and he had just taken the position. Instead of that, he said, 'Anywhere else you want us to do some more jobs for you?'

'Yes, lots', said the officer, 'but do get away from here. You know perfectly well that the Boche start shelling anywhere they see a tank, and if they see you sitting here they will know that the position has been lost and they don't bother very much about shelling their own men once they have been taken prisoner. Get over there, about four hundred yards over to the left. I think you'll find there are some shrubs there that seem to be giving a lot of trouble. We're getting fire from that, and several of our chaps have been dropped.'

By this time it was a glorious day. The sun beat down brilliantly on an entire wide plateau that they had reached, a plateau standing over the valley of the Luce in the way that the plateau at the starting-point had done. A half-mile to the left of Asser's tank the Amiens–Roye road stretched out in a straight line, the poplars waving in a stiff breeze. Everywhere else the ground was grass-covered. Far away on the right front was a village marked by wire that stuck like a slender finger into the dark blue of the sky.

'My God, I believe we've got right through', said Asser. 'There's nothing between us and the Rhine, if you ask me.'

At that moment a heavy burst of machine-gun fire with bullets spattering through the louvres in front of Asser and the driver caused him to shut down hurriedly.

'It seems I'm a bit premature', he said. 'I think it must be this damned bit of scrub.'

With that he turned the tank so as to bring the flying sparks off the sides and opened up full throttle.

'Steady on, sir', said his driver. 'There are probably trenches there, and if you go like this you'll find yourself completely ditched in the middle of it.'

'It seems to me', said Asser, 'that you had better command this tank.'

'Sorry, sir.'

'Not at all, I'm afraid you really ought to be running it. You chaps have seen a great deal more action than I have.' Asser felt quite contrite.

He heard his sergeant shouting in his ear, 'There's something wrong with our right-hand gun, sir. I don't know what it is, but we can't get it to fire at all. It doesn't seem to be a normal stoppage.'

'There never is a normal stoppage', said Asser. 'Look through the rear port and see if you can see anything from outside.'

In a moment the sergeant was back again. 'It looks as if the cat has been at it, sir. It's all chewed to ribbons. I never saw anything like it.'

The driver broke in, 'I know what it is, sir. It's the machine-gun fire which has cut the gun off from outside. We had it like that at Cambrai in our tank. When they open up a heavy burst like that, it shears right through the gun cover and cuts it to ribbons.

There was a sudden crash, and Asser and his driver were both thrown violently against the front edge of the tank, receiving cuts on the foreheads which began to bleed profusely.

'Look out, sir', said the driver. Asser at once stopped the engine and reversed. 'Must be a wall or something.'

They opened the flap very cautiously and saw that they had indeed driven full tilt into what appeared to be a piece of masonry. 'Looks like a sort of pillbox to me', said Asser, 'only it's made of brick.'

At point-blank range the 6-pdr guns opened up on the building from which they had backed away a few yards. Before very long, enemy began to appear with their hands above their heads, running towards the advancing infantry to give themselves up.

Asser suddenly felt depressed and frightened. 'My God, I've forgotten the time – I've got to be in Berle au Bois for the rendezvous.' He looked at his watch. No, we are still on time, he thought with relief. 'We had better start off to get over to that church spire there – that's Berle au Bois, I'm absolutely certain.'

'Very easy to see now, sir', said his driver. 'It's not like that fog we've been having – it's not like any of the battles we've had so far. This time you can really see something on the ground that looks what it's supposed to look like on the map.'

By this time the first driblets of the infantry had arrived at the position, and as soon as Asser had satisfied himself that they did not need his help any longer and were firmly in possession of the trench system that lay hidden in the scrub, together with the low pillbox-like structures – into one of which he had just driven the tank – he turned half-right in order to face towards the direction of the church spire.

'I think we had better put in our spare guns here to take the place of those that have been shot away', he said.

'Yes, sir, if we can get them out of the hole. It's very difficult sometimes to withdraw these guns through the ports because of the spattering of the outer casing.'

'Well, anyway, we've got to do it', said Asser, 'because we're changing over into the French sector, and we don't even know if they have started. They were certainly making a hell of a row this morning with their star shells and the rest of it, and I think it's likely they got off the mark at the same time as we did, but we can't afford to take any risks. Better be careful, too, not to shoot down any of the French – they wouldn't like it a bit.'

On the even ground Asser was able to keep the tank in top gear with the engine at full throttle, which meant that it was making very good pace, presenting a frightening spectacle to any of the enemy – and perhaps some of their own troops – who might see its career.

Within a few minutes he passed the enemy gun position. 'My God, look at that!' he said. Scattered around the deep trench work in which the German field guns had been placed were men lying in many different and grotesque positions. Some of them even wore pyjamas, showing the completeness of the surprise that had overwhelmed them with the onset of the British bombardment.

'What do you think of that? It seems that our guns have got their range right from the very start. All the Boche guns are upside-down as far as I can see. None of these men seem to have had a chance.' Asser drove on, feeling somewhat sick in the pit of his stomach.

He was still driving across the advancing front and wondering what sign he should look for to show him when he had actually reached the line of demarcation between the British and French armies, when he suddenly saw groups of troops sitting about in bunches of two or three. The line seemed to stretch away far to the right, and he saw that they were wearing French uniforms.

'This looks like it', he said. 'You had better put out our signal flag.' This was pushed through the top port of the tank, a red and yellow flag, the pre-arranged signal with which to identify themselves.

The French troops showed a mild interest in the proceedings, and one of the officers walked over to the tank.

'Légion Étrangères, he said through the window.

'Armes Britannique', said Asser, airing his French without any particular embarrassment at the hazards of a foreign language, which he treated with the same cavalier spirit as he treated the enemy. 'Je vais abimer les Boches Berle au Bois', he said in an atrocious accent and pronunciation, but the Frenchman obviously understood the tone of the message and grinned broadly, waving Asser on in the direction of the spire, which rose out of a clump of trees some four hundred yards distant.

'The *estaminet* ought to be just opposite the church', said Asser. 'I wonder if we can get a drink there.'

'If it's anything like the places up at Ypres, sir, you won't even be able to find it.'

'Yes, but you can see the church there already. You're a bit fond of Ypres, aren't you?' said Asser, not without a hint of jealousy and envy in his tone of his driver's knowledge of warfare.

'If there's been any drink there in the last three years', said the driver, 'I bet the Boche will have had it, sir.'

Asser opened up the front flaps fully. The gunfire had died down completely; there was no enemy gunfire at all, nor was there any from the British guns.

'It must be our guns coming up now, sir. The first stage of the advance is over. There's usually a silence while they move to forward positions.'

'Yes, but what has happened to the Boche?'

'It seems to me, sir, that what's happened to the Boche is what we saw in that last gun pit we came to.'

'It looks a bit like it', said Asser.

At this moment a flurry of machine-gun fire came from the woods above the church, and one of the French officers came up to say that they were being harassed by gunfire from it. As far as he could tell there was no other opposition there. Asser therefore changed his direction, and instead of making for the street that entered the village he was to patrol, he went straight for the small copse surrounding the church. In a moment or two there came out a couple of German machine-gunners with their hands above their heads, and that seemed to be the end of the organized resistance.

Asser then turned and took his tank back to the outskirts of the village, where he found a small mud-track that entered into the main street. He trundled on until he came to the *estaminet*.

'Better keep on the move, I think', he said. 'We've got another five minutes to go before Captain Bion is due here, and then we shall get some orders from him.'

He kept the tank in the shelter of the houses and moved slowly up and down on the look-out for any sign of enemy fire, putting an occasional burst of machine-gun fire through the upper windows of the houses lest there should be snipers or machine-gunners lurking there. Within a short time the advance troops of the French started their forward move again and were penetrating into the outskirts of the village. Within a quarter of an hour the place was in their hands but for the mopping-up operation, in which the men were going through the houses with hand-grenades to see if there was any opposition, and to stifle it. A few grenades were trundled down the steps leading to the cellars below the houses just to make sure that there should be no trouble from that quarter. Asser told his driver to take over.

He and his sergeant then got out of the tank, leaving the driver in charge with a couple of men to man the guns in case of any accident. He gave him orders that he was to take over command of the tank in the event of anything happening to himself or to the sergeant. The two of them then entered the *estaminet* and, with their revolvers ready, decided to wait there for Bion's arrival.

'It hardly seems to be a battle at all, sir', said the driver. 'It looks to me like a complete walkover. I've never seen anything like this before, except possibly at Cambrai, and even then there were lots of Boche about the place who seemed to do a bit more fighting than this. We had a very sticky time up at the corner of Flesquières there. Then afterwards, of course, we had all that trouble at Bourlon Wood. I don't know if they've got any reserves over here, but I suppose they'll be putting in a counter-attack before long.'

Asser, probably through fatigue, was beginning to feel somewhat depressed and disillusioned. He did not at all like the way his first battle, which he thought had been extremely successful and exciting – and with reason – was to occupy such a very unimportant place. Everybody seemed to have had so much experience of real fighting and to be convinced that this was not the real thing.

'You fellows think about nothing but some terrible counter-attack. I don't know why you should think that the whole war was fought before we started this action, and that there's nothing more to be done after what you chaps have already done.'

'No, sir, it isn't like that. I was in the infantry at the Somme; I don't think the army is ever going to be the same after that business. It was terrible going over the top having taken a trench with lots of your pals dead and dying around you, and then to have to stay there night after night, day after day, with the enemy putting in everything he'd got to take you out of it, and as likely as not knocking you out of the trenches back again to the place where you started. In this, at least you get a decent meal and a shave away from the racket of war as soon as the battle has finished.

'Yes, but when do you think the battle finishes? I don't think we've finished with this, do you? Even now we shall have to go forward. I know, for my part, that I shall be very sorry to miss any more. I hope that when Bion comes he'll give us orders to go still further forward. I'm all in favour of our giving them no rest at all. Even if we have broken through, I think we ought to pursue them.'

'I don't think there's anything to pursue, sir', said the driver, not at all relishing the prospect of serving under an officer who seemed to be such a fire-eater.

'There's a frightful stink in this room, sergeant', said Asser after a pause. 'Look and see if you can tell what it is. I think it must be coming from that cupboard there.'

They opened what looked like a cupboard door and found it led into a passage. Inside was a German private, still alive, extremely frightened, with pale face and several days' growth of beard. In his terror he had passed motions into his uniform.

'Oh, my God', said Asser, 'chuck him out, for God's sake. Tell him to go to the Intelligence people. Where is the Intelligence Post?'

'I don't know, sir. I think it will have to be one of these French chaps. We can give him to one of the French privates to take off.'

'Yes, do, at all costs. We can't have this man smelling around the place like that. I was hoping to have my lunch in peace and quiet with a bit of decency about it.'

The abashed Boche was led off and handed over to the first French private the sergeant saw. 'I thought it was probably a dead one, sir', he said on returning.

'I think he is pretty dead. I wonder what has happened to Captain Bion. I hope he hasn't been killed. I can't say that I would like to have been in that barrage walking about outside. I felt the tank was dangerous enough, but at least we'd got some steel around us to keep off the worst of it. He's half an hour overdue already.' He looked impatiently and nervously at his watch. 'Funny thing', he added inconsequently, 'the way these Frenchmen go about with their overcoats on, all buttoned up to the neck on a boiling-hot day like this. You'd think they were at the North Pole. I wonder what has happened to the rest of our tanks. We shall hear, I suppose, when Captain Bion turns up. I wish to God he would buck up. I don't like this at all – we don't know what on earth we're supposed to do here. It's no use asking the French for orders, I can't understand their lingo properly anyway. If this goes on much longer, I shall work my way over to the Canadian Corps front again. I'd better find out from some French officer whether I have his permission to leave. We were supposed to patrol this place in case of any counter-attack, but I can't see a sign of any anywhere.'

The French troops began to move forward again. In front of the village on the enemy side there could be seen long-drawn-out lines in battle order slowly advancing at the rate that had been laid down originally when it was supposed that artillery support would be necessary. In fact, the German resistance was extremely feeble, although some heavy shells were bursting amongst the advancing troops, but since they were in extended order it did not seem that any particular harm was being done.

'Just as you say, sir', said the sergeant. 'It does seem a bit silly for us to be staying here with the froggies going ahead as they are. We shan't be a great deal of use to them.'

'No, but we aren't supposed to continue the advance with them beyond Chatigny, which is only the next village. After that the 1st Battalion should be coming through, but I've always understood from you old veterans that there never are any reserves. Isn't that right?'

'Well, sir', said the sergeant sheepishly, 'certainly we don't seem to have had very many up to the present time.'

'I'm fed up with this, anyway', said Asser. 'We're three quarters of an hour over our time – let's get in and get on with it. We'll go on to Chatigny.'

He assembled his crew again, in the tank this time, leaving the sergeant driver in the driving position, taking over the position of second driver himself. They went through the village and beyond to catch up the advancing line of French troops. His orders were to stay in close support, not to be in advance of them, so that he could go through the advancing lines whenever it seemed to be necessary because the troops were held up. He had almost caught up with them and was reconciled to the idea that the battle was virtually over, when there was a sudden flurry.

'My God, sir', said the driver pointing to a great stir of movement on the outskirts of the village of Chatigny. There was a great deal of gunfire and then, suddenly bursting from the houses of the village and from some supporting orchards, there came on the waves of a German attack.

'Here comes the counter-attack all right, sir. Another Bourlon Wood, perhaps.'

'Oh, shut up, sergeant, for Christ's sake. Get on to the guns – I'm going right through.'

Thereupon, putting on speed, he forced the tank forward through the French front line who were taking such shelter as they could, lying behind folds of ground, hummocks of grass and any cover as presented itself, and opening up a very heavy fire on the advancing German troops. With the appearance of the tanks the enemy forces, about the strength of a couple of battalions, wavered. Asser's crew had a very high reputation for gunfire, having in fact been Bion's previous crew before he had been promoted to the rank of section commander. Their fire was accurate and their spirits in the ascendant after the experiences of the morning. The machine-gun fire which the tank brought to bear made the enemy forces waver, and finally the line dropped. At this point the French began to advance in short rushes, a section at a time, but the Germans kept up a withering fire upon them. Asser decided to go forward and to cruise at speed along the front of the German line wherever he could find it. There was some risk attached to this because the enemy might have a field gun in support in the approaches to the village, and a direct hit from that at such close range would be the end of the tank. However, whether it was the operation of his tank or some other factor that played its part, it was not possible to say; some of the Germans began to retreat, others began to throw up their hands and come towards the French troops. At this they were greeted by a burst of machine-gun fire from their own troops further over on the right flank of the advancing French. Nevertheless there was nothing to stop them; panic had set in, and many of them gave themselves up calling out, '*Kamerad*', and trying desperately to persuade the French not to shoot.

It was now midday, and the sun blazed down on the entire scene, which was nevertheless becoming confused because of the smoke from fires where shells had hit village houses and ammunition dumps that lay concealed there. Asser drove his tank forward down the main street of the village, having given the crew instructions to be careful with their ammunition, but even so to open fire on every window and door that they could see, and to take no chances whatsoever.

The position was extremely confused: the enemy in the village were fighting desperately; at one point a party led by a young officer came out of a side alley and threw themselves on the tank; some even clung to the projecting barrels of the Lewis guns and attempted to weigh them down so that they would fire into ground; some had succeeded in clambering on to the top of the tank. For a moment the situation looked very black indeed. Luckily for Asser and his crew, the enemy's excitement seemed to be too great for them to use their common sense, and the roof of the tank was providentially cleared by one of the Germans, who released a bomb, which blew him and his companions off the roof.

'We mustn't let that happen again', said Asser. 'Can't we lob a bomb or two out of the ports, the pistol ports?'

This was done, and after a moment or two the attack melted away.

'I think we'd better keep to the middle of this street', said Asser. 'It's evident that this is pretty heavy stuff that's going on here.'

By this time the forward French troops were running for shelter from one house door to another. By degrees the situation became less confused, and Asser turned off down the left, where he had seen a German field-gun firing. He opened fire on this with his 6-pdr before the enemy was clearly aware of his presence. The gun crew surrendered at the sight of this unexpected opponent.

The sergeant reported that there were only a few more rounds of ammunition left and some twenty 6-pdr shells.

'My God, this is a sticky business', said Asser. 'I don't know what we can do about it. If we start withdrawing now, the French will feel that we have let them down – and of course they haven't any ammunition that fits our guns, so there's nothing much we can do about it. We'd better stop firing and simply rely on bashing into houses and suchlike, and fetching down walls wherever there seems to be any opposition. We'll keep our fire in case we need it. If we get another packet like that lot that came at us down the alley, we shall need everything we've got.'

For the next half-hour Asser's role was uneventful. Bursts of machine-gun fire, signs of confused fighting came from various parts of the village, but ultimately it was subdued and their senior French officer, a colonel, appeared. After a few words with Asser, congratulating him with great courtesy and civility on the help that he had given the French troops, he told him that he would no longer need his services, as according to orders it was now time that he stopped. Asser told him that he had no further orders, that he would be very glad to stay and assist, except that he had no ammunition and thought that he had better proceed to his starting-point. Whether the interpreter was able to make his remarks clear was not altogether certain because the interpreter simply repeated the colonel's statement that he no longer wanted Asser's services and that Asser could therefore proceed to the rallying-point that had been laid down for the company. Asser therefore turned his tank and made towards the Amiens–Roye road at the pre-determined point for the tank rendezvous.

'Just keep to your guns and keep a sharp look-out', he told the tank crew. 'We may still come across some bits and pieces as we go.'

6

Major de Freine, the Company Commander of C Company, had arranged to have his forward H.Q. in the Battalion H.Q. of the

1st ____shire Infantry Battalion, which was in the front line of trenches. He would have these H.Q. entirely to himself as soon as the attack started, because the Battalion H.Q. of the 1st ____shires would move forward at zero hour. He had taken the precaution to move in to some effect. He was a man fond of his creature comforts; in particular, he was extremely fond of port. He had therefore arranged for a case of his favourite drink to be available at the H.Q., together with his mattress.

He made himself comfortable. He was, in this respect at any rate, a good soldier and had no illusions whatsoever about regarding it as desirable to rough it when on active service. No officer who had had any experience of warfare made that mistake, and certainly de Freine was the last man to do it, even had he been an inexperienced officer. When Captain Cook came back to the H.Q., he descended into the depths of the dugout. It must at some time have been a German dugout, for no British infantry every dug so deeply or so securely, making a veritable fortresswork of what the British would ordinarily regard as a mere temporary entrenchment.

De Freine, in his own quiet way, had managed to arrange things previously with the infantry battalion commander, who, of course, would be moving out as soon as zero hour came; it was understood that he would take over possession of the dugout as soon as they left. In the meantime he was disposing himself in a corner, where he had a table and a couple of comfortable chairs, one for himself and one for Captain Cook, his second in command. There were also four runners available who shared the duties of the messengers to various parts of the front, at the same time acting as batmen to the Major. In addition to this, there was his own personal batman, whom he had somehow managed to bring into the army with him – one of his original retainers from his home in Ireland.

He did not believe in showing undue deference to the enemy; neither did he think that it was important to allow them to influence his movements too much. 'Give them an inch and they take an ell' was his motto in this respect, and in one particular way he was adamant. Some creature comforts he knew he would have to surrender; after all, war was an unpleasant business in which you had to bow to the elements of wind and rain, even sometimes to the enemy, but on one point at any rate he would make no concession, and that was with regard to his port. He was a connoisseur of port; he therefore had with him in the dugout a case of port, and, of course, if he was going to have port, it was essential that he should have good glasses. There were accordingly the appropriate glasses, very fine, beautifully polished and waiting to be used.

He listened to Cook's report approvingly. 'Very good, very good', he murmured gently. 'One of the most important things y'know, Cook, is that the British officer should always be imperturbable. Imperturbability is the hallmark of a gentleman, and certainly of an officer in war.

'Good God', thought Cook, 'he seems to have a good deal on board already. He doesn't often launch out into these moral disquisitions unless he has had something to drink. Anyhow, he has chosen a very good spot to be imperturbable in', as his eyes wandered to the heavy beams and rafters of the dugout, which must have been at least twenty to thirty feet below the surface.

'I take it all our tanks are in position, Cook?'

'Yes, sir', replied Cook, 'I have been along the line, and they are all there. Captain Bion put down the tapes with Captain Carter.'

'Very good', said de Freine rather drowsily. 'I always say it is a very important thing to give your officers plenty of scope for initiative. The consequence is that they learn how to take responsibility, and this young fellow, Bion, who really didn't know very much about things – well, I'm very pleased with him. Honestly I think I'm in some respects at any rate responsible for his development; if he hadn't had me as his Company Commander, I very much doubt whether he would have learnt to take the initiative. Very clever of him, don't you think, Cook, to have got all those compass bearings and to have led the tanks into their proper positions? I'm sure I couldn't do it even if I tried.'

At this point de Freine's eye caught sight of an officer, a mere captain, presumably the adjutant of the outgoing battalion, who was very beribboned. Shading his mouth with his hand, he whispered to Cook, 'Who is that fellow over there, that chap who is so very highly decorated?'

Cook told him that he did not know but assumed that it was either one of the company commanders or the adjutant of the battalion. He added that he looked as if he had seen a good deal of service and said that it was extraordinary how these infantry fellows managed to last out so long and how much strain of fighting they seemed to be able to stand.

'My dear fellow, I'm sure you are right', said de Freine. 'I don't think I could possibly disagree with you at all – they are extremely gallant fellows. God bless the infantry. Naturally, I never had anything to do with them myself, being in a cavalry regiment, but I think the wretched fellows are really quite, quite splendid. I'm not sure though that I would altogether agree with you. I always used to tell my son, John, that if you see a man with more than two rows of ribbons, you can be tolerably certain he's a waster, and I don't think this fellow is any exception. After all, I never saw such a horrible-looking moustache. He must be a ranker – that's the kind of thing that only sergeant-majors wear, and if you watch him I think you'll notice that he is doing a great deal too much "sir" and "yessir" and "no sir". The hallmark of a British officer, y'know Cook, is im-pert-urb-ab-il-ity, and I don't think he is showing himself to be at all imperturbable, not if he is showing so much deference to his commanding officer. But, y'know, I don't like being too hard on a fellow who is just going to go over the top; I daresay he has got a bit of wind up, don't you?'

Cook, who was wondering whether it was the aristocratic, fox-hunting breeding, or the deep dugout, or the fine port which contributed most to this rare blend of imperturbability valued so highly by de Freine, did not feel that it was necessary for him to reply. Nor did he flatter himself that de Freine would be likely to pay any attention if he did.

Major de Freine was a formidable fighter. He differed, however, from other formidable fighters in that his view of what constituted the enemy was not entirely the conventional one. He regarded the Germans as definitely a pestilential nuisance; he felt that they had broken up the very pleasant life he led, and that their activities on the front were definitely dangerous, if somewhat ill-aimed and indiscriminate in their effects. He was not particularly disturbed by their shell or machine-gun fire. He considered that the people who were supposed to be on his own side were considerably more dangerous, because the personal relationship with himself made it possible for their shafts to be correctly aimed and therefore more damaging to his personality. It was as a result of one such contretemps that he found himself at the present time so very far forward. It was probably that in this particular action and at this particular hour he was nearer to the enemy than any other company commander in his or any other battalion. He had been at great pains to impress upon the Colonel that he proposed to take up his position at the advance H.Q. at the very earliest hour. The Colonel had not pressed him too much as to the nature of the advance position he proposed to occupy, but applauded his decision as being well in accordance with the traditions of an officer; and one, moreover, who was not merely by courtesy known as a gentleman. He had been adversely criticized by his previous battalion commander: on a trench raid that had to be carried out by a portion of his company, he had not been sufficiently far forward to give the necessary orders to his returning section commanders. This criticism he had taken in very bad part indeed. In fact he had gone so far as to call together his company officers, and with sundry gestures and movements of his head intended to indicate, and did indicate, that he did not propose to let the matter rest; he explained in terms unexceptionable as far as their wording was concerned but open to more criticism when their emotional accompaniment was taken into consideration, that he was sorry to hear that some of his officers had felt that they were insufficiently briefed about the action that had just taken place. He himself thought that he had made everything clear, and, of course, he quite appreciated that none of his officers themselves had been guilty of criticizing him. Still, he added, there were certain senior officers who had seen fit to criticize his conduct of the operation, and of course he fully appreciated that they had a perfect right to do so. These criticisms would, he felt sure – and he looked meaningfully around the room – be properly investigated in due course. He would not say anything more about the matter just then. The officers were dismissed, and for a month calm descended upon the battalion, in particular on C Company commanded by de Freine. However, at the end of that time a senior officer was returned to England – not Major de Freine, but the Colonel of the regiment.

The Colonel of the regiment at that time had been Lieutenant Colonel Burnett, DSO. He was a regular officer from what de Freine regarded as a somewhat obscure line regiment, and in any case the fact that he was a regular officer – what would nowadays be called a career officer – was no recommendation to de Freine, whose family had a long fighting history. They did not regard the profession of arms as one at which people earned a living – not, at any rate, if you were above the rank of, say, sergeant-major. He accordingly started with a considerable dislike of Colonel Burnett, whom he regarded as potentially an upstart and one of the class who were not likely to appreciate fully the importance and value of the landed aristocracy. He felt that the Colonel's enthusiasm for his battalion was slightly vulgar: he was always meticulously turned out, with brilliantly polished boots, and with an attitude that he was able to strike at will, which was always intended to convey dignity, a sense of his own importance and that of his regiment. All these points were noted by de Freine with a somewhat jaundiced eye. He also felt disinclined to tolerate Colonel Burnett's manners in the mess, regarding them as the outcome of his military training and not springing naturally from the depth of aristocratic breeding.

Somehow – nobody knew quite how – the impression spread through the battalion that there had been a vigorous battle waged off-stage. Nothing was said, the outward calm remained unrippled, and yet it was as if there was something in the air like the percussions of a distant bombardment, indicating that an action of great urgency and vigour was being fought out, perhaps in the precincts of the War Office. It was therefore popularly supposed that the Colonel's departure was directly related to activities on the part of de Freine, whose reputation as a dour fighter was thereby considerably augmented. He was a man who was never rude to any of his officers; no officer ever felt that he was spoken to except in the most friendly manner, and yet no officer ever believed for a single moment that he was on friendly terms with the Major – it would in any case have been a presumption to think anything of the sort.

A formidable weapon in de Freine's armoury was his unerring instinct that enabled him to detect a gentleman at sight. He certainly was supposed to have had plenty of practice in being able to learn what constituted a gentleman. Although he allowed it to be known that he was a simple bachelor looked after by his widowed sister, it also somehow became known – not, of course, through de Freine – that his widowed sister was the Countess of Battersea and that she, while having no political ambitions whatsoever, was always disposed to be friendly and to lay open her small country house for the benefit of sundry more important politicians who might be in need of a week-end's rest or recreation. It was supposed that their interest was predominantly liberal; on the frequent occasions when the P.M. himself was said to find a haven of rest there with perfect freedom from all political cares, nothing was ever discussed except music and literature, and then only in terms of the most brilliant and yet soothing conversation. However, as befitted a woman who protested that she was ignorant of all politics, she was not averse from arranging that her guests were not entirely of the same complexion. It was possible that the leader of the opposition might occasionally be there, perhaps even that his visit might overlap that of the P.M. In this way her innocence of intrigue in political matters enabled her to play the part of a hostess with an impartiality not open to other more politically engaged people. It was therefore improbable, in the event of a reversal of government, that there would be any reversal of the fortunes of the Countess of Battersea and her friends, amongst whom, of course, was included Major de Freine.

Obviously the popularly supposed action could not have taken place in a milieu such as that. But on the other hand it was equally obvious that many influential people, including some senior army officers, would be unlikely to believe that such a good, modest fellow with such a fine table, with such witty, entertaining companionship, could possibly be guilty of any kind of fault as an officer and a gentleman – certainly not the fault of cowardice. And yet, what possible explanation could there be for the charge brought against him, unless it was believed by Colonel Burnett that de Freine was absent from the proper rendezvous with his section commanders through some failure to do his duty? Such an explanation as that was unthinkable. It became even more unthinkable when Colonel Burnett played his cards so carelessly that it might be supposed he was even hinting at some failure of courage on the part of de Freine in that his presence was lacking at the crucial point in the battle. Colonel Burnett was, after all, only a line officer. Moreover, his substantive rank was that of captain, as became clear when one of the officers of the battalion on leave met him in Whitehall and found to his surprise, just as he was on the verge of saluting, that his late commanding officer occupied a rank junior to himself, he in the meantime having been promoted to the rank of major to another battalion. It was in discussing the aristocracy, of which Major de Freine was an exemplar, that a junior officer once said that it was an axiom of their code of honour that you should never kick a man unless you were quite sure that he was down.

The infantry officers and men were now standing about with equipment in full battle order, restlessly and nervously exchanging comments between themselves and looking for last-moment adjustments more as a method of keeping the tension at bay than because there was any real doubt about the readiness for battle. The Colonel came over to de Freine and told him to make himself at home. He said he half expected they would be thrown back again and would be glad if de Freine would keep the dugout warm, ready for their return when the enemy duly threw them out of their forward positions.

'I know this battle is supposed to be the battle to end all battles', he said caustically, quoting what was now almost an infantry slogan, 'but I dare say it will be very much like all the others, in which case we shall certainly be needing this dugout again. In the meantime I hope you will make yourself cosy.'

'Goodbye, my dear old chap', said de Freine, exactly as if he had known him all his life. 'I shall be following very shortly, as soon as the first wave of our tanks have gone through. I dare say your runners will be able to find me all right and let me know if there is anything you feel we can do.'

De Freine was not speaking the truth, but he was not lying. He felt that it was not possible to explain to infantry officers that he would probably remain stationed in the dugout for most of the battle, almost certainly having no reason to leave it unless the advance had been successful and the time had really come for him to take up his battle positions at the rendezvous, which was not due until 11.30 in the morning. He, for the same reasons, had taken care to hide his port glasses under the cover of some maps during the last feverish stages of the infantry preparations to leave the dugout and to take up their positions lying out in no-man's land in advance of the infantry trench works. It was not easy to detect where his sympathies lay, and sometimes it seemed as if he had none, but at any rate one thing was sure: his subterfuges and evasions were not dictated by any wish to make himself appear better than he was in the eyes of his fellow men.

All the infantry had now departed, except for a corporal and two unfit men, who were left to pack up the remains of the H.Q. kit and hold it in anticipation of orders for their disposal.

'It must be nearly time', said de Freine to Cook.

The latter, pale and tired, studied his watch. 'I make it two more minutes to go, sir, but I don't suppose we shall hear much of the bombardment from here.'

'No', said de Freine, 'I don't suppose so. Just a rumble at the very most, unless of course we get a direct hit. That may stir things up a bit.'

'The fog must be as thick as ever, sir', said Cook nervously. 'Just look at the stuff coming swirling down these dugout steps even now.'

The dugout had become noticeably more opaque in the last half-hour or so. Cook, still staring at his watch, said, 'Time', and at that moment the earth began to tremble and the rafters of the dugout began to creak in a way reminiscent of an old railway coach travelling on a practically disused branch line.

'It feels as if the whole thing is moving, sir, doesn't it? You might almost think it was in a train journey.'

'Yes, you might, but I don't think we are likely to travel very far even if we get a direct hit. This place is pretty solidly built. I don't believe even a 95 Howitzer would do us much damage. D'you know, Cook, I've half a mind to go and have a look. This sounds to me to be as fierce as anything we ever had in the Somme – and that was pretty big. I don't suppose there will ever be any more barrages of that size, but this can't be far off it.'

'I think I should stay down here if I were you, sir; after all, you never know – we might get through this time, and if the tanks do break through they'll want some orders from you this time, sir. So far, on the H.Q. staff we've had nothing to do in this war, but if we do get into the open country, then I take it we shall have to provide some orders of our own and not wait for brigade and divisional staffs to work. Hello – here comes the enemy barrage.'

A shell must have burst practically at the main entrance to the dugout. It made a peculiarly unreal screaming, whistling sound as the fragments echoed through the valley, and then all was lost in the infernal din of the answering gunfire.

I suppose you're right', said de Freine. 'Anyhow, here we have to stick for the next hour and a half, and pretty useless hulks we are. There's really absolutely nothing whatever we can do. There's no chance we shall find out anything about the tanks until we're able to get out of here and start towards our rendezvous. By that time we may know something from the infantry. Poor fellows: I know what it's like for them. I had it all at the Somme. Still, perhaps when our tanks go through the first wave they'll feel a bit better. At Cambrai they were certainly very grateful indeed; the infantry even said they would far rather be infantry than be inside our tanks.'

'And I think they're about right, sir. In our battalion we have so far had two people out of every three who went over the top killed in every action. I don't think you can do worse than that in infantry.'

'They are a good lot of fellows', said de Freine sentimentally, and then, 'Have some more port.'

7

Inside the tank, the noise of the 75-hp Ricardo engine was so deafening that it was practically impossible even to hear the shell bursts unless they were very near indeed, almost hitting the tank. On these occasions the danger communicated itself more by the wobbling of the walls of the tank, which suddenly seemed to lose all their rigidity and become flexible, than the actual noise of the explosion; in the din it was impossible to communicate except by shrieking the orders.

Hauser beckoned his sergeant towards him. 'Sergeant', he yelled, 'tell those bloody gunners to keep their fingers off the triggers – I can't have these damned idiots firing down on our own men. Remember, we don't get through the first wave of infantry until the green line, and that's not due for another half-hour.'

He choked and spluttered in the fog which swirled through the slightly open front flaps, now mingled with the smell of bursting cordite. Shrieking into the ear of his driver, he asked him if he could see the oil pressure gauges. 'I think that knock is worse than ever – it won't be long before the big end goes.'

Throughout the advance to the battle positions, Hauser's tank had been giving trouble, and it was feared that there was something wrong with the timing. The defect had apparently been remedied, and yet the knock persisted. They thought it might be due to excessive carbonization, but at the same time it was a disquieting symptom.

'I hope to God the damned thing doesn't choose this moment to conk out', said Hauser to his driver. 'Keep your eye on the oil pressure and let me know if anything odd happens. I'm not going to stay in this damned rat trap if it's going to get hit. The moment this thing stops, out we all get with our machine-guns. He beckoned to Sergeant Wilkins again to come forward. 'Sergeant, see to it that all the men are fully armed if I tell them to get out of the tank. We'll go forward as infantry. You can stay behind here with somebody, and if you feel like it you can light the dynamite charge.'

The dynamite charge was a fad of Hauser's; it had become an obsession. To him it was the latest sign of the idiocy of the Staff. The reason for it lay in the secrecy now surrounding the new tanks. It was supposed that they consisted of all the latest improvements in armour plate, in engine power and transmission. It had therefore been decreed that no tank was ever to be allowed to fall into enemy hands. This was, in any case, a standing order, but now in addition to everything else they had been told to carry a packet of dynamite to be exploded in the event of the tank being abandoned in the middle of an enemy position. Hauser caustically drew attention to the fact that they had been very careful to order the removal of the petrol feed system to minimize the risk of fire, but had not thought that it might be rather dangerous to carry dynamite, which could be detonated at any moment in place of the relatively harmless petrol.

The men were in battle order, and owing to the great heat inside the tank the sweat was streaming down their faces. Owing to the dense fog Hauser steered by compass bearing; at the same time, he had to keep the lights on inside so as to study the pressure gauges. The men's faces showed the pallor of weariness, which was not dissipated even by the excitement of battle; the skin glistened yellow in the murk of the dark shadows and the grey steelwork of the engine coping and the gun covers.

'It should be dawn now', said the driver.

'Yes, dawn on a lovely summer day, Corporal. Wouldn't you like to be going off on your bank holiday trip? It must be a bank holiday about now – not that I have the slightest idea what day of the week it is.'

A shell burst in the immediate front of the tank and forced showers of mud through the front flaps. Hauser spluttered and swore and wiped the blood off his face.

'Are you hurt, sir?' asked his corporal.

'No, dammit, not a bit – only some scratches. I've got this filthy mud all over me.' He had only received a flesh wound just below his right eye, but it was enough to make him order the flaps to be shut entirely. 'We can't have that kind of thing going on – we'll just have to go on with them shut. It doesn't make any difference – we can't see a thing anyway. Hello, hasn't the knock stopped?'

The corporal listened for a moment or two and then agreed that he could no longer hear it.

'Must have been that last shell', said Hauser. 'It seems to have done the tank a lot of good.'

'I think we're climbing, sir.'

'Well, it's about time we were', said Hauser. 'This is about the stage when we should be getting up onto the beginnings of the plateau on the other side of the Luce. Ought to open this flap slightly, because it's time we got to the green line, and we don't want to be running down any of our own infantry chaps.'

'Shelling is less intense too, sir.'

'Yes, but for God's sake don't say so or we'll get one whack on the roof. Hello – I believe the fog has cleared a bit, hasn't it?'

'Yes, sir, I think it has – it seems to be clearing very fast indeed. Look, sir, it's all clear now!' Sure enough, the tank was right out into the open.

There was no sign of the infantry for a moment or two, nothing but the blinding sun beating down on what appeared to be rolling grassland, and far away on the left was the stretch of the Amiens–Roye road with the poplars pointing the way.

'There go the infantry', said the driver, pointing to a small section of some twenty or thirty men who were making advance on his immediate right flank.

'Ah, yes', said Hauser, 'now we have to go right through them. I think I see one of their sergeants waving us on. Probably means nothing at all, except that he's bucked and excited to see us, but still I think we'll go through all the same. Just head for the left corner of that wood in front of you.' Hauser was pointing out a clump of trees that lay between him and the Amiens–Roye road and about 600 yards to his front. 'I wonder what happened to Greenwood Copse. We must have gone round the edge of it by this time; we were supposed to skirt past it. I can't say I remember coming under any machine-gun fire.'

'Perhaps our artillery shut 'em up after all, sir.'

'I suppose it's just possible. Anyway, I can't say I mind so long as we didn't get anything from them. I think we had better start opening fire on that wood when we get within a hundred yards or so. It wouldn't surprise me in the least if they hadn't got a field gun trained on us. If so, driver, it'll get right between us – the worst of sitting up in front like you and I do is that if anything is coming through the front, we're sure to get it. It makes me feel quite hollow inside merely to think about it. Do you think it will take top gear, Corporal?'

'It might, sir, but we're still on a bit of a slope.'

'Well, try it.' The driver put the tank into top gear. 'Now open up the throttle, full speed – yes, that's all right. We ought not to do this, really, you know. We're going miles in front of schedule. I don't know what we shall catch at this rate. But I'm fed up with waiting about in the middle of a thick fog without being able to tell what's going on, so we may as well pretend we're having a battle, if nothing else.'

'There are some Jerries coming in to surrender, sir.' He pointed over to the right flank, where about half a dozen grey-clad troops were coming, all with their hands held high above their heads.

'They look extraordinarily like ducks waddling along like that. I must say I wouldn't be sorry to see them doubling all the way to Berlin. Serve the bastards right. I've a jolly good mind to give them a burst of machine-gun fire, it would hurry them on a bit.' He beckoned Sergeant Wilkins to him. 'Sergeant, have a look through the back gun port and see if you can tell what our infantry are up to. The sergeant came back in a moment to say they were following up fast. 'Well, the main thing is that they should be here', said Hauser, 'then there's a sporting chance they will get these damned enemy fellows under cover as quickly as possible, otherwise we can't afford to let them get through and set up a machine-gun on the other side.'

'I don't think they look very much like fighting, if you ask me, sir – not that lot any way, they're going too fast.'

The sun was blazing down out of a clear sky. It looked as if there could never have been a fog or a mist anywhere on such a magnificent day. The whole countryside lay spread out in front of them like a map.

'It doesn't seem to be at all like a battle', said Hauser, 'not the kind of thing I'm used to. I remember once seeing in a pub in Norfolk a lot of pictures – of the South African war, I think. Anyhow, there were a whole lot of Redcoats in a decent line, and a whole lot of fuzzy wuzzies in a ragged line; at one point there was even a man who had been hurt. It gave me quite a shock. Still, I don't think it does to get too confident. Ask that damned fool Smith what the hell he thinks he's firing at, will you?' Hauser indicated his right-hand Lewis gunner who was blazing off a burst.

The reply came that he was aiming at a patch of chalk, which he suspected of harbouring a machine-gun.

'Oh, well, if it pleases him, I suppose it does no harm', said Hauser, and let him continue his short bursts. 'At the same time, we must remember, we may need some of this ammunition later on.' My God, he said suddenly to himself, I'm tired, tired, absolutely worn out. I'm fed up with the whole goddamn thing.

It was curious how suddenly the reaction set in; from one moment to the next, the elation changed to steady depression. It seemed so futile to be out in the open with such a complete and absolute breakthrough as this appeared to be. It was either a gigantic trap, or else it was The Victory for which everybody had been hoping. If so, The Victory was singularly unexciting.

'Sergeant Wilkins says, sir, that he can't see Mr Cartwright's tank anywhere. Oh, yes, I think he just says that he sees a tank going towards Berle au Bois, sir. That must be Mr Asser's tank. I don't know what has happened to Mr Greene. He ought to be up on our left somewhere, but he isn't in sight.'

'Better ask Sergeant Wilkins to keep a look-out for anybody else – there may be some of the tanks of B Company visible up beyond the Amiens–Roye road.'

Hauser now changed place with his driver and told him to start opening fire on the corner of the wood. He also gave orders to his 6-pdr gunners to open fire in the same direction together with the two flanking Lewis guns.

'We may just as well pretend we are dangerous', he said, 'otherwise they'll get their heads up and think they might as well take a shot at us. I bet there's some devil in there with a gun of some kind. It hardly seems possible they'd leave a wood like that empty.'

'Perhaps, sir, they think it's a bad place to be because it would be marked on the map and the guns would come down on it. They may expect our gunners to put their barrage down onto a corner like that.'

'They would certainly be right if it was the Greenwood Copse – they said they were doing the same sort of thing to all these woods where there might be any enemy positions, but I don't remember seeing much just here on the map except a gun position. Of course it's the gun position that's so hellish dangerous for us. If they start firing over open sights, goodbye to you and me, Corporal.'

This time it was evident that there was no more gun-fire. The British guns were silent, and no enemy shells were falling. Only in the sky were there a few bursts of white from the enemy anti-aircraft guns still trained on any reconnaissance planes that came over.

Hauser reached the wood without casualty and then proceeded cautiously across its front, still firing into the shrubs in case they should conceal any enemy. When he came up towards the left flank, he saw a couple of Germans looking at him curiously, standing up in the open. He gave them a burst with his Lewis gun, and they promptly put up their hands and began to run towards him. By this time the infantry had also come up with the tanks and had begun mopping-up operations – that is to say they were throwing the odd grenade down into any small trench or dugout where Germans might be sheltering. It appeared, however, that the wood was not fortified. Hauser looked at his watch and said it was three-quarters of an hour before he was due to report at the rendezvous where he should meet Major de Freine and get fresh orders as to what was to be done.

'It's an extraordinary thing', he said, 'but it really does look as if this time we had broken through. Must be some kind of fluke, but I suppose we had better go and pretend to get fresh orders to "exploit the situation", as they put it.'

'It's not time yet, sir', said the corporal driver.

Hauser glanced at his watch again. 'My God, nor it is. There's still another forty minutes to go. This means we shall have to go on patrolling up and down here. What I would like to do would be to stop the tank and have a jolly good look round. Look at all these fellows loafing around here – it's the infantry. They don't seem to have to take cover, and there isn't a shot of any kind being fired. I'd like to get some fresh air instead of sticking in this thing. But we can't leave the tank stationary anywhere in case the enemy have an anti-tank gun and register a direct hit on us. I don't want to get court-martialled.'

The sun still blazed down from an intense blue sky. On the left was the Amiens–Roye road, on the right and in front lay the tiny hamlet of Berle au Bois with the spire sticking up from amidst the trees, just as Asser had seen it on his approach. In front was the small copse that Hauser had been patrolling until the infantry came up and took it. Beyond that, as far as the eye could see, it seemed to be flat rolling country, with very few obstacles of any sort, quite untouched by shellfire and with every appearance of being ideal countryside for the use of tanks – so much so that at a later stage even the cavalry found the temptation for action irresistible and were duly launched, with appropriately disastrous consequences. For the time being, however, all was peaceful and quiet. The men were smoking cigarettes, obviously relieved to be able to walk about in the open without thought or care. Nevertheless, anxiety gnawed at Hauser's heart. He had not enough experience to know what to do. In this respect he was typical of all the officers in the British Army at this time. They had no experience whatsoever of open warfare, and at the same time found themselves now in a situation that was either a prelude to a disastrous counter-blow by the enemy, or was precisely the open warfare for which everybody had longed, for which everybody had planned, but for which nobody had apparently been trained.

Hauser's feelings were expressed by the thought that this was a moment of extreme danger. The British guns were moving up into position; this could always be told by the lull, there was nothing new about that; all troops were familiar with it in all previous battles where there had been any kind of British advance. The enemy guns were for the time being silent; whether because they were pulling back into new positions, or because they had been put out of action like the battery that Asser had come across, it was impossible to determine. But it was at precisely such moments that the enemy was likely to launch his most dangerous counter-attacks in the days of trench warfare, when, no sooner had a position been taken and before the infantry could consolidate it, the enemy launched an attack. The British were occupying trenches that were facing the wrong way and were therefore peculiarly susceptible to attack from the enemy.

Even Hauser's pessimism and gloom were not proof against the wonderful weather that had followed the fog-bound morning. Oh, blast the blue skies, he thought. I wish somebody would go and tell these infantry that there's a war on. I'm sure this is an extremely dangerous moment. 'Corporal, I think we had better take our tank about a hundred yards in front of the infantry and patrol up and down there slowly. So long as we keep going in second gear, it ought to be all right; I don't think the enemy would find it easy to hit us. We shan't be a sitting target, and at the same time it will help to keep down any odd Boche machine-gunner who might still be about the place. If we don't go any further than a hundred yards in front of the infantry, the sight of them will also persuade the enemy gunners not to open fire on us. Anyhow, I can't think of any other damned thing to do, so we might just as well do that. What the hell's the matter with you, Rice?' he suddenly interjected.

'I've got the itch, sir.'

'Well, keep the itch to yourself. It's your damned lice coming out to enjoy the fine day. Why didn't you shove your shirt into some petrol before we started? Nobody else has them, have they?' The rest of the crew looked somewhat shame-faced – they were not going to admit to lice at that moment at any rate. 'And what the devil do you mean by leaving your gun anyway?' said Hauser suddenly, waking up to the fact that Rice had, in his attempts to rid himself of the nuisance of the lice, dropped the handle of the Lewis gun. 'You chaps don't seem to know there's a war on.'

Truth to tell, the crew were worn out. They had had hardly any sleep at all for some four days, and the excitement and exhaustion of the morning, the great anxiety of the fog and the opening stages of the battle had been intensified by the extreme heat in the tank and the debilitation induced by the loss of fluid through sweating. It was possible that the carbon-monoxide fumes had also had their effect: in some tanks that had been carrying infantry forward, the infantry had had to be put out of the tank after twenty minutes of action because they were in a fainting condition; it had previously always been believed that it was not possible to become acclimatized to carbon monoxide, but this proved conclusively that the tank crews were able to do so and could stand anything up to seventeen hours of battle continuously in that poison-laid atmosphere. But the effects nevertheless told.

This sunny day, this lovely country, blast it, makes it impossible for anybody to believe this is a war, thought Hauser. I can't really blame these men. The only thing I can do is to blast them and keep them up to scratch. Nobody's going to believe me when I say there's a war on when everything all round us keeps telling them the war is over. Surely we ought to be *doing* something; surely there ought to be some sort of attempt to push further into the enemy territory. Why are we hanging about here on this so-called 'blue line' – our final front? If there was any kind of flexibility about our schemes we should be chasing the enemy. They told us in our operation orders that we should do this, but they said the same sort of thing at Ypres, where anybody who had had a look at the country could see perfectly well that you could chase nobody in that, not unless you were a bird. Now, here, where we have the ideal conditions, nobody thinks of translating the operation orders into terms of actual reality, so we hang about. I can't go forward – if I do, I'll certainly run into a field gun, and that'll be the end of the tank, and I shall be deservedly blamed – not that I mind much – for having risked the tank. What I ought to do is to go forward with the infantry, but who's going to tell the infantry to go forward? There's nobody to do it.

Sergeant Wilkins interrupted his reverie. 'There's something going on just behind us, sir. I think we ought to go back and look. It looks as if the infantry are under fire.'

Hauser turned the tank towards the right flank of the advance. Some infantry were lying, opening fire at a small scratch of chalk that lay exposed bare of green turf. Hauser directed the tank against this patch, and then scrambling towards the back opened the rear door in the hope of being able to talk to an infantryman. A sergeant came up and said they were under fire from a sniper probably located in precisely this patch. Hauser drove towards the patch, but the sight of the advancing tank must have been too much for the German; he came out with his hands above his head, looking extremely frightened and sheepish. The infantry then came up and took him prisoner.

False alarm, thought Hauser, but anyway the infantry ought to be doing this sort of thing – I hope it puts them on their toes and makes them realize there's still something going on. But I'm damned if I can see where a counter-attack can come from. There seems to be nothing at all here that could hide any enemy concentration. The only possible place is Berle au Bois, and we've seen Asser's tank go in there. The French troops must be up there too, judging by that scattered line; they're standing around in groups, so I think their front line must be in advance of that.

'Look, sir', said Sergeant Wilkins, 'The French have got a first line in front of those men over there – I think those are the support troops.'

'Then we'll simply do what I said first: get in front of our infantry and patrol slowly up and down in second gear; there's nothing more we can do. How much more time have we got?'

'Still half an hour, sir.'

'My God, I never knew anything like time in a battle. You feel it's about six o'clock in the evening, and you find it's half past ten in the morning. Then suddenly, when you've got used to the idea that time stands still, it's so desperately late that you discover you've missed a rendezvous you ought to have been keeping.'

At last it was time. Hauser turned the tank towards the wood where the rendezvous was to take place, then suddenly he changed his mind.

'Sergeant Wilkins, you take over command of the tank. I think it's ruddy silly they give orders for all our company tanks to concentrate in this one spot. We don't know what enemy guns are about, and we'd make an absolute sitting target if we had the whole bunch of our twelve tanks here and no protection against anti-tank fire. You keep patrolling this, and I shall go over to the rendezvous with Gunner Smith. If you feel things are getting very tricky, then come over to the wood with the tank.'

Hauser and his gunner went on foot over to the extreme left of the section front that had been appointed as the rendezvous for the company officers to receive further orders from Major de Freine. Hauser found to his surprise that the Colonel was there with his assistant adjutant, but otherwise was alone. Major de Freine had not arrived, nor had any of the other tank commanders, including Captain Bion. The Colonel asked Hauser why he was on foot, and he explained his reasons.

The Colonel turned away, thinking that Hauser was one of the few officers who had any real sense. He reflected: I believe this chap had more soldiering qualities than the rest of us put together. I myself ought to have thought of this, or at least one of the company commanders should. It's clear that in any company rendezvous we shouldn't have all the tanks together.

He turned to Hauser. 'Well, what sort of battle have you had? Any casualties?'

'No, sir, nothing at all. It's been as quiet as the grave. We've had nothing whatever to do. The first part of it was pretty dull – we couldn't see a thing – and the last part, when we could see everything, there was nothing to see, nothing but this damned scenery.'

'What's wrong with the scenery?'

'It just puts all these chaps to sleep, sir. Just look at them hanging around the place – the infantry as well. Anybody would think there are no enemy about, and yet they told us before this battle started that the enemy were concentrating for an attack on our position. It stands to reason there must be heavy concentrations *somewhere*. In this kind of weather and in this kind of country, with our troops used to nothing but the mud of Ypres and places of that kind, they seem to think the war's all over and it's just a bank holiday. They might be out on Hampstead Heath, the way they're going on.'

The Colonel looked at his watch. 'There's still a few minutes to go, but I can't understand why somebody else hadn't turned up by this time. I suppose you haven't seen Major de Freine or anyone else, have you?'

'No, sir, I haven't. The only person I've seen was probably Mr Asser, whose tank was over on the far right. He was last seen by Sergeant Wilkins driving for Berle au Bois.'

'Well, we had better just sit down and wait, then.'

'Yes, sir.' Hauser ordered Gunner Smith to act as sentry and to take up his rifle, keeping a sharp look-out while he and the Colonel lay on the grass and waited for the others to come up.

8

A fresh breeze blew, the fog disappeared, the sun beat down and the gun-fire stopped. Bion lay huddled in the shell-hole with the moaning boy beneath the shelter of his side. The waving poplars of the Amiens–Roye road stood revealed as tall grasses on the opposite side of the trackway in the brilliant, clear light. The transformation was so complete that the scene appeared to be utterly unrelated to the black night that had preceded it. Everything was quiet except for the moans that had now become more inarticulate. Occasionally he could distinguish the word, 'Mother', but that was all.

A party of stretcher-bearers came down the road with some wounded. He called to them, 'Will you take this man?'

'No, sir', came the reply, 'we haven't any stretchers left. Can he walk?'

'I don't suppose he can walk at all', said Bion, but one of them came over and, lifting Sweeting up, it appeared that some fresh reserves of strength were released in a body that seemed to be too torn and broken even to maintain life. Before he could realize what was happening, Sweeting, supported by two stretcher-bearers, was tottering down the road in the train of the small RAMC party towards the casualty station.

Well, thank God he's gone, thought Bion, filled with passionate hatred of himself for his hatred of the wounded man.

Time to go, he said to himself as he stretched out of his cramped position. Even the very grasses seemed to scare the life out of him. He worked his way over to the left flank. He thought, it's now far too late to make the rendezvous with Asser at the *estaminet* at Berle au Bois. I may just as well find out what has happened to Greene's tank, and Hauser's.

In the distance, towards the Amiens–Roye road, he saw a stationary tank; there was now apparently no fighting going on at all. The sun beat down, the trees waved gently in the stiff breeze. Walking across the springy turf without seeing any sign even of infantry, he felt totally lonely and lost. As he approached the tank, he was glad to see that there was somebody moving, and then as he came nearer he saw that the left tank track had been blown back and thrown right over the tail of the tank – obviously a direct hit.

Greene came up to him and said they had had no luck at all; they had got just as far as this a little while before the fog cleared, when the tank received a direct hit on the nose to the left.

'Anybody hurt?' asked Bion.

'No, except for Gunner Harrison – he's gone nuts.'

'Oh, what happened to him?'

'Well, I got him out of the tank after a while, but about ten minutes ago some of the Germans started coming back with their hands up, and he immediately got up and began blazing off at them with his revolver, yelling something about them being a lot of bloody, murderous bastards who had killed his brother. It put the wind up us, I can tell you. I had to tackle him in the end – I thought I was going to get a shot in my innards. However, we got him down in the end. He was a frightful sight, frothing at the mouth. I thought we were sure to get into very great trouble with him bumping off unarmed prisoners – almost certainly a first-rate scandal. There was no fighting going on, not a soul in sight except these poor devils.'

'What are you doing about your tank?' asked Bion.

'There's nothing much we can do.'

'Have you tried lifting the track back onto the sprocket and starting the engine? That might help to drag it back over the top.'

'No good at all, I'm afraid, sir. Even if we did that, I don't think we could do any more because these plates at the end here – ', he walked Bion back towards the broken end of the tank track, 'are all buckled and destroyed, and I think two of them are missing; I don't know where they've got to.'

'In that case you had better send a runner back to Company H.Q. to see if you can get hold of Williams.' Williams was the engineer officer whose job it was to take on heavy-duty work of this kind. 'Where are your crew?'

'I've got 'em over there in that shell-hole. I thought, just to be on the safe side, we'd better get our Lewis guns out and turn that into something of a strong point.'

'Quite right. I don't think there's likely to be any need for it, but at the same time it's just as well to take the ordinary precautions. What the hell's this – ?' Bion broke off and turned suddenly at the feel of a tug at his sleeve.

Kneeling on the ground by his side was a German soldier who had crept up unobserved. Tears were streaming from his eyes. *'Kamerad kaput, Kamerad kaput'*, he wailed. He insisted on trying to drag Bion by his sleeve to a nearby dugout, and for some reason Bion did not resist but allowed himself to be pulled in that direction. Into this small hole he was taken by the German, who pointed out to him another soldier, obviously dead, whose body was in the most fantastic position with his legs thrown back over his shoulders. The German insisted that Bion should put his hand on his heart. This he did in a perfunctory manner and shook his head indicating that the man was dead, which was in any case quite obvious. At this the German burst out into renewed floods of tears.

'Sir', said Greene, 'you shouldn't be in here; you don't know what sort of booby-trap these people might have got ready for you. I wouldn't trust the Boche, not even if he was dead. The only thing to do with him is to put another burst of Lewis gun-fire into him.' Greene was obviously very disturbed.

Bion saw the force of his argument. Feeling rather shamefaced, he straightened himself up and waved to the German to get back to the rear and surrender himself.

'Did you ever see such chaps as these, sir?' said Greene. 'There they are, a lot of bloody murderers if ever you came across any. They fight like hell; they haven't the slightest hesitation in sniping or shooting us down at any point; they're as treacherous as you damn well choose, and yet they burst into floods of tears when one of them is knocked out.'

'I wonder what the devil it's got to do with him, anyhow', said Bion. 'Is it his brother, or something of the sort?'

'Not a bit', said Greene, 'much more likely to be his tart, I should think. Anyway, can you beat it? One minute he's blazing away at our troops with his guns, the next he thinks he can grab hold of an officer and get him to come and sentimentalize with him over one of his dead pals. They're a treacherous lot of swine, sir. I don't think you should ever pay any attention to them like that. It's not our job, anyway.'

'When you have fixed up with Captain Williams about the tank, you had better leave it in charge of Sergeant Williams and the crew, and come on yourself to the rendezvous. We shall need you there to let you know what the next orders are. Maybe we shall be able to find another tank for you.'

Greene saluted, and Bion went off on his own to the rendezvous. He was angry with himself in that the episode had occurred in the presence of Greene; he was the last officer with whom he wished to discuss the ethics of war.

I don't believe the Boche are any different from ourselves, he thought. They go through the same thing, they live in the same danger, the same vile conditions and the same bloody awful staff, if only we knew it. Something has gone wrong with this war; it seems that all the decent people are fighting and killing each other, and all the wasters and war profiteers are sitting at home in Germany or England making the best of a very bad job – and it isn't a bad best from their point of view either – plenty of money, plenty of cars, safety, comfort, but here . . . here . . . Greene is right; it's not my job to be handing round buns and cups of hot tea. I'm supposed to be at the front, fighting a war – and now there's that damned rendezvous at Berle au Bois. Why didn't I make it? If it's all a matter of high ideals, why wasn't I there? What am I going to say about that? Held up in the barrage. Yes, but what the hell holds you up in the barrage? You can't get held up in a barrage. The only way you can get held up in a barrage is to be blown to smithereens or have the side ripped out of you by a shell splinter, like Sweeting.

Bion saw the body of an infantryman lying just to his right with his rifle beside him. That reminds me, he thought, and went over to the man and collected his ammunition and rifle. These revolvers are no earthly use. It struck him as queer that this was the first dead soldier he had seen that day. Usually he relied on being able to pick up a rifle very quickly right at the beginning of an action, since he found, as did most officers, that a revolver was more of a danger to the user than it was to the enemy; a rifle, on the other hand, was a very valuable weapon. He stuffed a couple of spare clips of cartridges into his pocket and went on.

In the meantime Greene also had his own thoughts. After sending a runner to Captain Williams to ask for his help, he turned to the German prisoner. 'Come on, Fritzi, time you did some work. It'll cheer you up.' He told the corporal to give him a grease gun and show him how to set about greasing the tank tracks. For his part, the German had settled down quite cheerfully and gladly to find that he was not going to be ill-treated in any way. He seemed to be a simple-minded man, quite content and happy provided he was given a job he could understand and had all responsibility taken from his shoulders by a senior.

'Haben Sie Schutzengrabenvernichtungsautomobil gesehen?' said Greene, airing his German. The prisoner looked up astonished by this amazing hybrid that Greene had picked up from some magazine purporting to show how ludicrous, how truly comic the Germans were and what a fantastic language they spoke.

'*Ja, ja*', he said, 'plenty of tanks, plenty of tanks', and went on with his polishing and greasing.

'I could do with a pint, Sergeant', Greene said, looking at the damage to the nose of the tank where the shell had shattered the track. 'It's just as well it got it right there – another inch or two and we should all have been for it. Doesn't do to think about these things too much, you know, Sergeant. Look at that poor chap, Gunner Harrison.'

'He was a very good man, sir', said the sergeant who rather resented the presence of Greene as a new officer. He had been with the crew or with the battalion since the arrival at Le Havre; to him the casualties were real people, whereas to Greene they were not much more than names.

'I suppose they'll call it shell-shock', said Greene, 'though I'm not at all sure that he hadn't got the right idea; it's no good being sentimental about these sods. I've lost a couple of brothers in this war, and I think we might just as well teach 'em what war is if they mean to fight us, that it's dangerous to attack our country again. Still – it's an absolutely marvellous day, and I can think of plenty of better things to do than to be waiting here, humbugging around this tank. But we don't know if the old Boche is finished yet. They could get back here quite easily; if they've got all these troops massed for an attack, they ought to be able to mount a counter-attack shortly. It seems as if our guns are moving up now, this is about the time they usually set about us. What I could do with, Sergeant, is a little bit more peacetime soldiering.'

'Yes, sir', agreed the sergeant, 'that's the thing – parades, a lot of them, hard work, knock off at twelve, and the rest of your day's your own, nothing at all to do. That's my idea of war, not this kind of thing.'

Greene ruminated, 'I don't think much of these people who go in for religion and philosophy and that kind of thing. It seems to me they miss a great deal of what is actually happening. Look at today – can you beat it? Marvellous sun beating down, lovely green trees, even green grass everywhere. If I were at the seaside now, I'd be having a fine time – I wouldn't even mind being down at Brighton, though mind you, that's not my idea of a good spot. I like to be somewhere lonely in the country or at some small seaside place, a village. You can have plenty of fun in a place like that; there are worse things, Sergeant, than sitting in a nice snug little pub knocking back a pint of bitter on a hot day and having a few words with the landlady, or maybe her daughter.'

When Greene spoke of philosophers and religious people, Bion was not very far from his mind. He felt no sympathy at all with people of that type and made no secret of it – at any rate to himself in the privacy of his own thoughts.

'I can't say I've ever held with parsons and such-like', he continued to his sergeant. 'My wife – and she's a pretty shrewd judge of character – says whenever she sees one of them parson blokes, "There goes one of them sly, preaching buggers" – a very good description, don't you think, Sergeant?' He looked at his watch. 'Tell Haley and Cooper to get out there with their Lewis gun, right over there, just by that shell-hole about fifty yards to the right of the road. We may as well have sentries posted. They can keep a look-out and see if there is any sign of enemy counter-attack. I can't see that we'll be caught by surprise because our front lines are now miles away, but still, it's all part of the book, isn't it?'

The sergeant detailed the two men for the job and returned to Greene, who continued, 'We've got to stand up for decency and all that; we can't allow people like these Fritzis to overrun the world – I daresay they'd make a pretty mess of our country if they ever got inside it.'

'I don't know, sir', said the sergeant. 'Sometimes I wonder – would it make any difference to us? There are always people who have to govern us, and I don't think the German authorities would be any worse for simple people like me and my family and kids than the ordinary policeman and government nowadays. Sometimes the governments we get are less our friends than our enemies anyway. They make a good thing out of it, but if we do anything against the law, laws made by the wealthy, then we're for it. We'd be no worse off under the Germans.'

'Don't you believe a word of it, Sergeant. D'you think you'd be able to sit in your little pub, or go off to watch your local football match, or go out with your wife, or pick up a pretty girl when- ever you felt like it? Not a bit of it. The people swaggering around would be the Fritzis, like this chap here, in smart German uniforms. They'd be the ones who had the pick of the girls; you wouldn't catch any girl going out with a mere slave of the Germans – and that's what you'd be by that time.'

'I don't suppose we'd starve, sir.'

'I daresay not, but you'd have to work hard: you'd be going off to your factory shifts, and there'd be no trade unions or anything of that kind. Your foremen would be people working with the Germans, or they'd be German themselves; all the cushy jobs, all the plums would go to the Germans. If you saw a fine car go by, there'd be a German in it; if you saw a pretty girl well dressed, out with a man, she'd be with a German. You'd soon get fed up with a position of that kind. At present you can have your grouse, but you wouldn't be able to do it then, not unless you wanted to be a member of some kind of revolutionary movement – and that wouldn't be a comfortable life.'

He broke off suddenly. 'Hello, what's going on up there?' He pointed into the intense blue of the sky.

'Looks as if the ack-ack have got another of their planes', said the sergeant. 'Yes, I think it is, sir, I think it's a wing coming down, yes, yes, that's it, sir, they've hit one of the Boche planes.'

'What makes you think it's a Boche plane, Sergeant?'

'Well, he's too far over our lines for it to be one of ours, sir.'

'You don't know where their line is. If it is one of our guns that's been firing, that's the second time in this battle they have hit one of the enemy planes. That must be a record.' The anti-aircraft guns were not popularly supposed to be able to hit anything.

The wing of the plane swirled uncertainly down to the ground. 'Here's Captain Williams, sir.'

Williams looked at the shattered track. 'What's up, chum?' he asked Greene. 'Won't it go?' A few minutes' examination of the sprocket and the track satisfied him. 'I'll see what I can do for you', he said. 'We may have a few spare plates that would do the trick, but I'm not at all sure we shan't find the sprocket is out of alignment, and in that case it may well turn out to be a heavy workshop job. However, it will take me about an hour before I can let you know about that, and it will take another hour after that if we can do anything. If we can do it, you'll be able to go forward straight away. You were damned lucky, weren't you? Anybody hurt?'

'No, one chap threw a fit, that's all, but we got him under control, otherwise everybody is right as rain. A few scratches and splinters. I must say, it shook us up a bit, though – it was too close for pleasure. Luckily I had the flaps shut at the time.'

'Another six inches to the right', said Williams, 'and that would have been a case of *dulce et decorum est pro patria morir* for you.'

'I don't know what you mean, sir, but I'm sure you're quite right.'

'Have you seen the enemy about at all?' asked Williams.

'I think he's gone up to the rendezvous – there's supposed to be a conference on . . . oh, I'm sorry, you mean the real enemy. I thought you meant the Colonel. No, we haven't seen any at all. We've just been riding forward nicely and quietly until that chap, whoever it was, managed to blow our track off. There must be some about somewhere; in fact, we've just collected one here to do a spot of spit and polish on the tank, as you can see', and he pointed to the German prisoner.

'Well, I must be off', said Williams.

'Me too', said Greene. 'I shall leave Gunner Smith here in charge of the tank.' To Smith he said, 'Have a jolly good look-out and see nobody pinches the whisky. It doesn't matter a damn about anything else, but we mustn't lose the whisky, whatever happens.' He turned to Williams. 'I'm going forward to the rendezvous now, sir. Captain Bion told me I had better be there in case they want me to go into action again. I hope to God it will be with another tank and not with infantry.'

9

As Bion walked forward in the blazing heat, he thought he heard a voice hail him and looking round found it was Carter. The two of them walked together.

'So, you've managed to survive this far', said Carter. 'I see you picked up a rifle as well.'

'I always do – a revolver's no damned good', said Bion, and the two of them walked on. 'I think I want to go further over to the right flank. I'd like to know what has happened to Asser's tank.'

'What has happened to your section so far?'

'I don't know anything at all about Hauser; he seems to have disappeared. Greene is over there on the left; I've just been talking to him. His tank got a direct hit, and they're out of it for the time being. Williams is having a look at it. Cartwright's tank got a direct hit right at the start – I was nearby at the time. The whole thing simply went up in one crash. That leaves us with Asser unaccounted for. I hope he's all right, at any rate.'

'We've got plenty of time', said Carter, 'I'm just working my way forward to the rendezvous. I haven't seen anything of the Colonel because I was separated off at the beginning to go and see whether the A Company tanks got into action all right. I'm jolly grateful to you for those compass bearings. We seem to have had the tanks pointing in the right direction, as far as I can make out.'

'Yes, thank God', said Bion remembering his unpleasant experience at the mud track. He had almost forgotten the agonies he went through at that time; his fears about the direction of the battalion attack seemed now to be completely unreal.

'I wish I could find somewhere to dump my tunic', said Carter. 'This heat is terrific, it's all I can manage to stop from melting away into a drop of butter.'

'I shouldn't think you carried much fat', said Bion looking at the spare figure enviously.

They walked in silence for a few minutes. Then, 'Carter, I'm fed up with this war.'

'You don't say so', said Carter sarcastically. 'I thought most people had come to that conclusion long ago – within about the first five minutes. I certainly felt that way when I was handed a white feather within about three or four months of the beginning of the war – things were pretty poisonous then. And even now, if you go home on leave in London, it only takes you a few minutes to find out how ghastly the whole business is.'

'Yes, but I wasn't meaning that', said Bion. 'I mean out here; it's just about damned murder. I've been lying next to a runner who had part of his innards blown out.'

'I don't think that's much to worry about; it's the kind of thing one would expect. One expects to find casualties, one expects to find that the thing is murder, that's exactly what it's intended to be. It's organized in order to be murder. The main thing is to be sure you murder *them*, and not our own lot', said Carter, thinking once more about the failure to establish the correct compass bearings at the start of the action. 'I don't think I mind much, so long as I'm out here. There's a good deal of nonsense about it, of course: the odd whoring and so on in the back areas, a good deal of boring talk in the mess, and a lot of anxiety and a hell of a lot of wind-up when it comes to a battle. But at least one is with decent people.'

'I don't see why you say the people are any more decent than they would be in peace-time.'

'Ah, but they are', said Carter. 'You can say what you like about war. When you're faced with the possibility of being blown to bits at any moment, it jolly soon brings out the worst or the best in men.'

'I don't agree. Look at Quainton – he was a decent fellow if ever there was one.'

'Yes', said Carter somewhat noncommittally.

'Well, didn't you think so?'

'Yes, I did; he was an extremely decent fellow, but I don't think I put quite such a high value on him as you did. He was a charmer, he got on extremely well with everybody, and I know Colonel Burnett was extremely impressed by him, but look what happened to him. He goes into action just once, goes home on leave, and then he cracks up.'

'That's true. I must say I found that a bit of a shock, but at the same time we don't really know what happened, and we didn't hear anything from Quainton ourselves.'

'You saw the letter he wrote to Broom; it was a damn silly sort of letter. You'd think a chap who had his head screwed on straight wouldn't write like that, and he wouldn't write to Broom.'

'Something must certainly have happened to him, because when we went into action at Ypres, that show on September 29th, I had him near me, and I must say I was very glad to have him by my side. He seemed to me to have the root of the matter in him. I know his faith in God, and the confidence that it gave him, spread to me and brought me a good deal of relief too.'

'Faith in God?' said Carter doubtfully, 'I don't know much about that – I think I'll put my faith in the decent people who have the guts to stand up to things and are able to think clearly in a nasty mess. The important thing in this business is to be able to do your job, however sick you're feeling.'

'I agree', said Bion, 'but you've got to have more than that; I should have thought you must have faith in something. I don't see how you can possibly do without it. At the same time, I don't know how you, or anybody else, as a decent Christian manages to put up with this filthy mess out here.'

'But I'm not a Christian, I never have been. I put my faith in something better than that.'

'Well, then, what are you fighting for?'

'What I'm fighting for is really quite simple. I've had a lot of experience in Malaya; I've seen the way business is done there; I know our people by and large – crooks though they often are – are those on whose word you can rely. I know all about their failings; I know about the way someone, as likely as not, makes a hash of a business contract and something turns out to be defective. But on the whole when one of our commercial people says they'll deliver an order, they deliver it. When you're dealing with the Japanese or the Boche, they're as crooked as hell; even some of the Yanks we had dealings with can't be relied on – the're treacherous, they haven't got the same business standards. You fellows who live at home in England don't really know; you think that all people, every nation, is as good as every other. That's not my experience at all.'

'Yes, but I think it's just as true to say that you, Carter, because you live in Malaya, get an exaggerated idea of things in England.'

'There's some truth in that, but on the other hand I don't spend the whole of my time in Malaya. I have to come back to England from time to time and keep contact with our head office. I do work there, and I'm convinced that there's a standard of decency and honesty that just doesn't exist in many of the people I have dealings with.'

'I think you're being very narrow-minded.'

'I've seen far too much of it for that, and I'm a lot older than you, Bion.'

'How old are you?'

'Well, to tell the truth, I'm forty-six – not officially, mark you. I swore that I was thirty-five. I didn't bother much about dyeing my hair after the first interview. Even then they looked at me a bit oddly, I'm bound to say. I'm not a chicken, as you can see.'

'Why did you join up?'

'Because I felt the country was in great danger, and I think it would be a very grave thing indeed for the world at large if the British predominance were to disappear. For all I know, it will disappear anyhow – all good things come to an end sometime. But I don't think it's any good deluding ourselves; if the British fail, then something good will go out of international life, and people will find those who take their place are no more honest – and in my opinion a great deal less honest – and a great deal more unpleasant to get on with than the British have ever been. The real trouble with our country at the present time, if you'll excuse me saying so, is that a lot of you people who have been to public schools are chock full of high ideals, but you haven't got them geared to the realities of the situation. You're brought up on all this idealism about the poor and the depressed classes and the need to carry the white man's burden; the whole affair is absolutely riddled with guilt. You don't see what it's really like in the places where these jobs are done. But if you get out into the wilds, the so-called 'outposts of

Empire', you get a chance of seeing what human beings are really like. Even in this war some of the scrubby tricks you're complaining of aren't at all peculiar. They're not caused by war; it's just the war that shows them up. It shows you what people are really like. The human being is a nasty and dangerous animal. One of the reasons why he's supreme over other animals is because he is infinitely more dangerous than any tiger or wild beast possibly could be. Murder, hatred and lust – those are the predominant features. It's true they have some sort of intelligence, some kind of development of brain power, and that means they have ideals, they want to be kind to each other. I suppose it starts off with their being kind to their young, or wanting to, and then it extends to other people. But you've only got to scratch the surface – get people into a situation where there's a shortage of food, and you'll soon see what lies underneath. I can tell you, it isn't pretty; it's a case of every man for himself. I've got no illusions about this war: the Boche and others are out to get as much loot as they possibly can, and if we don't defend ourselves but take up the attitude that we are all miserable sinners, then we shall go down, we shall have failed in our job.'

'But how are we to know that? We're bound to think in that way.'

'Well, then, if we're bound to think in that way, better think in that way. What other way are you going to think?' Carter looked at Bion critically but not unkindly. They shouldn't send these youngsters out here, he thought to himself. They're fit for nothing except getting killed, or possibly getting the VC, and then they crack up. After all is said and done, what else can you expect of them? There should be a rule that nobody is allowed to come out to the front until they are at least twenty-one. I'd make it older myself.

They were now making their way over to the right flank and had got to within three or four hundred yards of Berle au Bois when heavy gun-fire broke out. There was a clump of trees beyond the village, possibly a mile distant; the shell-fire had broken out afresh, and the shells were bursting in this wood, throwing up huge clods of black earth with occasional puffs of white from what appeared to be shrapnel shells.

'I don't know who the hell's guns those can be', said Carter. 'It seems that some sort of resistance must be going on there.'

A moment or two later the fringe of the wood was peopled with a mass of men moving in an indeterminate manner. It was not at first possible to make out what the uniforms were.

'My God, I think they're Boche', said Bion.

Carter got out his binoculars and looked. 'Yes, they are. They're massing – here they come!'

Gradually a small bunch of the enemy detached itself from the right flank and dashed forward; a bit later some more in the centre. They started coming forward in short rushes.

'It looks to me as if this is their counter-attack developing', said Bion. 'I wonder how much of it there is. If it's only this bit, there can't be much more than a brigade in the attack. They'll have to mount something a good deal more massive than that if they're going to have any effect.'

'Yes, but we don't know what's over on the left of the copse', said Carter. 'You see there, that's a crest of a rise and as far as I can see – ', he started fumbling with his maps, 'there's a considerable dip there. We can't tell from here how many more troops might be lying there; it could be anything up to two or three divisions, if our staff were right in saying that the enemy were preparing to attack on this sector. This may be it, real trouble.'

The two of them watched anxiously, and then as bullets began to come over, they made a much more cautious forward advance, still working their way towards Berle au Bois, which remained quite peaceful.

'It seems pretty clear' said Carter, 'that there aren't any enemy in Berle au Bois anyhow. The whole of this lot is in the sector that's nothing to do with us; that's where our reserve troops should be going through to attack. They're supposed to be halted here on the green line, which runs through to the wood where we should be meeting. I hope to God our support troops have got up there, because this may develop into something very ugly.'

'Those must be our shells bursting in that wood, then. I don't know if they've started up because the enemy have commenced their counter-attack, or if the gunners have spotted a concentration in the wood and have opened fire first.'

'Well, it's much of a muchness', said Carter. 'It seems to me they've got their front lines out, otherwise we shouldn't be getting their advancing troops coming towards Berle au Bois like this.'

'I wonder where the devil Asser is. He might be able to do something about it.'

'No, he wouldn't', said Carter, 'it would be very risky. I wouldn't send him forward if I were you, even if we do find him. Remember, that's the French Front.'

'Yes, Foreign Legion', said Bion.

'At this point we're not supposed to be doing any more attacking with the French. They're going forward without tanks.'

'Yes, but it might be a good thing to lend them one of ours if the enemy attack gets really serious.'

'I think you ought to get permission from Major de Freine before you do anything of that kind. We have our job to do on this front, and at this point we definitely have to keep in with the 42nd Division and not get mixed up with the French. After tomorrow we may get more orders, but just now it would only create confusion, and the French might even shoot up our tank if we sent it in there.'

'Anyway, I can't see any sign of Asser. It looks as if the enemy attack is petering out a bit; they're meeting very heavy machine-gun fire. It sounds as if those are the French guns now, don't you think?'

'Yes, though I can't see where anybody is. All we're getting here are a few riccos flying about from the enemy fire – and their fire is very ragged and poor anyway.'

It was a rash remark. A sudden burst of machine-gun fire came so close that they were both glad to have the opportunity to flatten out in a shell-hole just in front of them.

'I don't like the sound of this at all', said Bion.

'Nor do I', said Carter. 'That burst of machine-gun fire was altogether too close, and yet on the right the French are obviously holding them. I never heard such a concentration of machine-gun fire.'

The rattle of the machine-guns was continuous – there was nothing ragged about it. It did not seem to either of the two officers that the enemy could advance into the face of such an intensity of fire, and yet somewhere a German machine-gunner must have managed to creep up, perhaps towards their left.

'It would be just as well to keep our heads down for a minute or two', said Carter. 'There must be some chap who had got round on the left flank. Funny thing is, that wood seems to be pasted by our heavy guns; all that stuff looks like ours rather than the French', but just at that moment there broke out a great furore from their right and behind them.

'It sounds like a whole lot of biscuit tins being slammed together', said Bion.

'That's the French 75', said Carter. 'They always make that infernal din. They sound like toy ones, but my goodness they can fire fast. Yes, now you can see the shrapnel bursting – and H.E. They must be sending over mixed H.E. and shrapnel, right along the edge of the wood there. That's a pretty good barrage they're putting down there; it must be one that hasn't been registered at all. The French must have got their guns up into their advance positions by this time. I don't think the Boche are going to have it all their own way by any manner of means.' There were a number of flares and star shells being fired. 'It's a funny thing how the French always seem to do that all night and all day; they go in for an enormous amount of these light signals. You'd think it wouldn't be much use in daytime, and yet you can distinguish them pretty well. There can't be much doubt about what the signals mean if you know the code.'

Out in front of Berle au Bois, towards the enemy counter-attack, they could distinguish two or three French infantry wandering about.

'I don't think I want to stay stuck in this confounded hole', said Carter, 'it's too ignominious altogether. If those chaps can walk about out there, there can't be much wrong with our doing it.'

'Anyhow', said Bion, 'we had better get on because we've got to work out how to get to the meeting. It's time we were shifting over. I wish I'd found Asser, all the same; I'd like to know what has happened to him. Come on, then.' They left the shell-hole and started walking over to the left in the direction of the Amiens–Roye road and their rendezvous.

'My God, they're letting that wood have it now', exclaimed Carter.

The gunfire was certainly intense. They could see huge branches and even trees uprooted, turned over on their sides and occasionally tossed up into the air. Great clods of earth were flying from the wood, and it was evident that heavy Howitzer guns had been trained onto it as well as the field artillery, which was maintaining a steady drum of fire on the wood and its immediate foreground where the enemy counter-attack seemed to have fizzled out. Then they noticed that a few enemy began to run back again towards the wood.

'I can't say I envy them if they're going to go back there for shelter', said Carter. 'They would do better to stay where they are.'

'Well, *some* of them seem to think they would do better to come forward', said Bion as he saw small parties begin to run towards the French lines with their hands above their heads. 'I don't think it can be the genuine counter-attack – just a local affair.'

In another ten minutes they had reached the trench that formed the advance company H.Q. There they found Major de Freine already installed with the Colonel, Asser and Hauser.

10

The small group of officers stood in the cool of the shade of the trees fanned by the breeze, which was now blowing steadily. They did not say very much to each other; they were all gazing intently at the spectacle set out before them like a vast panoramic film drama. The fact that reserves had been so conspicuously lacking in every action with which they were acquainted made it hard to believe in the reality of this scene as it unfolded. Never before had there been reserves, certainly not reserves brought up with such massive efficiency and in such great force.

The tanks were displaying into battle order, and for the first time the officers had an impression of what it might be like for an enemy if they found themselves attacked by formations that came on in the order they were supposed to do according to the textbooks. The rest of the troops still remained in column of route; obviously the Amiens–Roye road was not sufficiently wide to be able to bring forward the troops and also to carry the returning stream of empty lorries going back after having delivered their goods. Therefore the whole plateau was studded with columns, at a distance of some three hundred yards between each, advancing independently of roads in order to get forward as quickly as possible. This, combined with any lack of response from the enemy, led to a peculiar sense of exhilaration – or at least it potentially did so, for while there were ejaculations of surprise at this sight, there was also a heavy dragging at the heart, as if all felt that the event had occurred too late. Had this happened years before, then it would have chimed in with the enthusiasm, the sense of mission and crusade that had animated the early armies. As it was, the feelings of elation conflicted with the tide of depression and disillusion, which struggled at the same time for expression because it could at last find some relief from the evils that had originally caused it and that were no longer operating. This must have contributed to the somewhat grim, rigid, set expression with which these officers stood and watched the oncoming flood.

At last the Colonel turned to Major de Freine and his fellow officers, and for a while his face had lost the harassed, neurotic look that it had been wearing for some weeks past; he seemed able to be more human.

'I don't think I need to tell you one part of the operation orders at least. There, as you can see for yourselves, gentlemen, is the 1st Battalion going through. We are therefore relieved. At the same time, it must be understood that every tank is to be put into fighting condition at once; all the greasing up, all the reloading with ammunition has to be done before any man gets any rest. You had better serve food, of course – that has to be a priority, because they have not had any decent meals, and I think it is safe to say now that you can produce heated food on dixies and so forth. Nevertheless you should still preserve all precautions with regard to aeroplane observation and the possibility of bombing attacks. In any case', he said, turning back towards the enemy front, 'you can see we are observed'; waving his arm, he pointed to the row of enemy observation balloons, which seemed to be extremely near, as was always the case with the German army. 'You may be sure', he continued, 'they will be passing back all the information they can about our doings. I don't imagine it will be very cheerful information from the point of view of the German staff, but I doubt they have really got the troops now to be able to do much about it.' He nodded to de Freine who seemed to have something he wished to say.

'What has happened to the enemy attack that was being amassed against Amiens, sir?'

'I don't know', said the Colonel. 'Have you chaps seen many prisoners? I heard some report from Divisional H.Q. that a great many guns and men had been taken.'

De Freine, looking at the other officers interrogatively, seemed to invite comment, but nobody could say very much.

'I think, sir', said Hauser, 'that the fog was so thick that it was impossible to see what was going on. I haven't seen any prisoners.'

Asser said that he had seen some handfuls of enemy troops giving themselves up, but that was with the French Front; he didn't know anything about what had been going on 'on our own corps front'.

'Of course, I haven't yet had any orders from Division', said the Colonel, 'so I can't really tell you anything official about it, but it doesn't seem to me that they have got very much of a chance – I think they've been caught out very badly indeed. I did hear some casual talk that the Australians at Villers-Plouich had had difficulty on their extreme left flank, but that is to be expected in view of the fact that the troops on their left were not due to attack at all in this battle, and presumably they had to throw back a defensive left flank, but I haven't heard that they had any trouble in taking their objectives. If that is so, it seems pretty clear that the advance has been quite general along the whole front. No doubt I shall be able to tell you more later. In the meantime I must go and find out more of what has been happening – I'm going to Divisional H.Q. first, and then on to Army Corps. You know how to get in touch with us, Major de Freine. Well, good luck you fellows, you've done extremely well.' He turned on his heel and with the adjutant, and Carter who joined them, went off towards the left flank.

De Freine decided to waive his usual procedure. He was accustomed at this stage in an action to be welcoming back the officers and men from the usual abortive offensive with a glass of port and some murmured condolences and congratulations, interspersed with gentle suggestions of 'gallant fellows' and 'brave men'. But on this occasion it was obviously not quite what was required. He therefore turned to his section commanders, saying they had heard what the Colonel's orders were – the tank crews must immediately get ready to prepare their tanks for action and remain at their particular stations. This order was queried by Hauser, who suggested that they should find specific positions in which the tanks would be secure from observation.

'Oh yes, of course', said de Freine, 'I was taking that for granted. You must all get your tanks under the shelter of trees and report at once to the section commanders, who will, of course, report to me the exact location of every tank.' He drew Hauser aside. 'Hauser, you will have to give up your tank. I think Greene had better take it over with his crew. Your men can go into the company reserve for the time being – they deserve a rest in any case. I want you to take over Homfray's section – you'll be sorry to hear that he was killed. Bion, I'm afraid you must reconcile yourself to losing Hauser. I am sure you will be very sorry to see him go, but just as pleased as I am that at last he has the promotion he very much deserves. I think you said you actually saw Cartwright's tank hit, didn't you?'

'Yes, sir, I had just got out of it.'

'Poor fellows, no chance for any of them, of course.'

'None whatever, sir. They were obviously all killed practically instantaneously. I don't think they were even trying to get out of the tank. Some of them were blown through the door when it was blown off its hinges, and others over the top of the sides when the roof caved in. I don't think they can have lived long enough for any of them to have tried to make an attempt at escape.'

'Who was the sergeant?'

'Sergeant O'Toole, sir, my old tank sergeant.'

'What a pity, he was a very good man. He was extremely disillusioned and upset because he was not promoted to Company Sergeant-Major. There was nothing I could do about it; I think he would have made an extremely good one, but we had to take over Sergeant-Major Cannon from A Company, who had been due for promotion much longer.'

'Yes, sir, I know how he felt. He even said, poor devil, that he didn't want anything from this action except six feet of earth.'

'I think his nerve must have gone', said de Freine.

'It's very likely, sir. He had had continuous action since the time the battalion came out here.'

'Well, for that matter, so have you, but you don't show any signs of cracking up, I'm glad to say.'

Bion did not believe him. He felt that people who cracked up were merely those who did not allow the rest of the world to . . .

[*Ends here – no more written.*]

AFTERMATH

Parthenope Bion Talamo

'Had everyone gone mad?' (p. 69). This question came to Bion's mind while commenting on what should have been one of the more peaceful and less frightening moments of his war years, the Christmas 1917 break from fighting, and refers to the brutish behaviour of men off duty. He gives it no immediate answer, but reading *War Memoirs* makes me wonder whether he did not perhaps spend a good portion of the rest of his life exploring the avenues of enquiry that it opened up, as he moved through the study of history to teaching, medicine, psychotherapy and finally psychoanalysis and the psychoanalytically informed study of groups.

The diaries themselves are almost raw material, with hardly any emotional or intellectual elaboration, a far cry indeed from the war poems of Owen or Sassoon. Even the later versions of the same experiences delineated in Bion's autobiographical writings (1982, some parts of 1992) do not seem to have undergone great changes. It is interesting to note that some episodes are carried over almost unchewed and apparently undigested into *A Memoir of the Future* (1991), as though no further working-through were possible.

As far as *A Memoir of the Future* is concerned, this technique is justified by the fact that Bion was trying to present the reader with raw, basic, almost primitive experiences that had been dealt with at the time of their occurrence by a mind that was recognized as being ill-equipped to do so. In several places in the diaries he complains of the fact that he (and others) had not the mental equipment of a professional soldier, which, he seems to have felt, would have given him some sort of protection from the full blast of war. But the reason he uses these episodes in *A Memoir of the Future* is to show up the co-existence of regressed states of mind, together with more sophisticated ones. It is illuminating to compare his Diary description (pp. 119–120, this volume) of gaining some comfort from lying on the bank 'just as if I was lying peacefully in someone's arms', having in the previous sentence said that he felt just like a small child 'that has had rather a tearful day and wants to be put to bed by its mother', with the slightly defiant proclamation in *Cogitations* (1992, p. 166): 'Winnicott says patients *need* to regress; Melanie Klein says they *must not:* I say they *are* regressed. . . .' Reading his *War Memoirs*, one feels that he had had first-hand experience of what he was talking about.

This vision of the mind as a palimpsest with a continual potentiality for almost instantaneous regression can be seen to tie up to the theory of beta-elements, a continuous flow of unprocessed pre-mental sensory data, which then have to be subjected to alpha-function in order to be used for thinking at all, in the sense that these two theories deal with the rock bottom of mental and pre-mental life. I also feel that it is no mere coincidence that although the diaries were dedicated to his parents, it is his mother alone who is invoked every now and again as reader, as though Bion felt that she was a fundamental participant in an internal dialogue. It is perhaps not too fanciful to suppose that the fact that he had not 'written letters' during the war had not only been part of a desire to spare his mother pain, but was also an unconscious attempt to preserve her in his own mind as a container as undamaged as possible by hideous news, and hence as a part of the personality capable of alpha-function.

It is interesting to note that Bion never gave a central role to problems connected to aggression or death in his psychoanalytic theorizing. When he did deal with problems of warfare (rather than aggression) in his adult writings, it was almost as though he were forced into doing so by external circumstances (having been called up as an army psychiatrist in 1940), and at first his approach tended to be remarkable for its pragmatism rather than for its theory (1940, 1943). His later theorization of group dynamics (1948, 1952) made use of the idea of the proto-mental as the matrix sustaining basic-assumption phenomena; and again I suspect that the experience of panic described in the Diary, his awareness of the contagious effects of high or low morale, his attempts at a rough sort of 'behaviourist' group therapy, as well as his perception of the disaggregating effects of boredom and complete lack of discipline, all formed part of the real personal emotional experience on which his theories lie.

The 'madness' that Bion speaks of and describes as having experienced on more than one occasion (the two episodes described on pp. 90–91 and 103, this volume, are cases in point) and the loneliness he suffered (p. 74) were to some small extent ameliorated by the contrasting experiences of deep comradeship and real affection. He mentions Short's gratitude to him just as he is leaving at the very end (while being unrelentingly bitter over the ingratitude of the 'Great British Empire'). This more loving side of human relationships even in warfare comes out very clearly in the only episode that Bion quotes as feeling that it had done him credit – that is, his taking hot tea and stew up to the men of his section doing duty as infantry in the front line (p. 83). It is in fact clear throughout the diaries that he was capable of caring for his men, and his most scathing comments are reserved for those officers and staff who were not. To my mind, the capacity for love that can sometimes be found in group behaviour appears later on in Bion's work under the guise of the terms 'compassion' (1992, p. 125) and 'concern' (1992, pp. 247–248), and his experience of it is part of the mental humus from which the theories of L, H and K links were to grow.

It would, of course, be an excessive simplification to say that Bion became an analyst 'because of' his war experiences – in fact, it might be equally true to say that he became one in spite of them; notwithstanding his exposure to mindless stupidity and the brutality of war, he still felt that there was enough goodness in mankind (and that it was thought-provoking enough) for it to be worth dedicating his life to the study of people. Since no decision can be made on the matter, perhaps it is more useful to think of his Tank Corps life as having combined with many other pieces in a mosaic that led to a certain sort of evolution. One thread in this strand that can be picked out, however, is the recurring theme that underlies the Diary of the individual who is both part of his group, in tune with it, and against his group, at war with it and with himself, which in later psychoanalytic writings is carried over to illustrate the mental workings of the individual and his internal group. Another aspect of Bion's personality that appears clearly in the Diary and which was never to leave him was his remarkable capacity both for curiosity and for enquiry, supported by acute observation, even when the subject matter for investigation was painful or literally terrifying.

Although the comments Bion makes on war, aggressiveness, courage and cowardice are scattered throughout his works in a somewhat haphazard way, and after *Experiences in Groups* (1961) he never attempted any systematic approach to these problems, Bion continued to buy books on warfare, histories of war, memoirs of partisan warfare and so on right up till his death, as though the subject were never far from the surface of his mind, perhaps constituting, in its social and individual components, a great unsolved puzzle.

Turin, May 1997

REFERENCES

Bion, W. R. (1940). The "war of nerves". In: E. Miller & H. Chrichton (Eds.), *The Neuroses in War*. London: Macmillan.
Bion, W. R. (1943). Intra-group tensions in therapy. *Lancet* (27 November): 678–781.
Bion, W. R. (1948). Experiences in groups. *Human Relations, I–IV*. Reprinted in: *Experiences in Groups* (pp. 29–137). London: Tavistock Publications.
Bion, W. R. (1952). Group dynamics: A review. Reprinted As: Re-view: Group dynamics, in: *Experiences in Groups* (pp. 141–191).London: Tavistock Publications.
Bion, W. R. (1961). *Experiences in Groups*. London: Tavistock Publications.
Bion, W. R. (1982). *The Long Week-End: 1897–1919 (Part of a Life)*, ed. F. Bion. Abingdon: Fleetwood Press. Reprinted London: Karnac, 1991.
Bion, W. R. (1985). *All My Sins Remembered/The Other Side of Genius*, ed. F. Bion. Abingdon: Fleetwood Press. Reprinted London: Karnac, 1991.
Bion, W. R. (1991). *A Memoir of the Future*. London: Karnac, 1990.
Bion, W. R. (1992). *Cogitations*. London: Karnac. New Extended Edition, London: Karnac, 1994.
Campbell, C. (2009). *Band of Brigands: The First Men in Tanks*. London: HarperCollins.
Liddell Hart, B. H. (1959). *The Tanks: The History of the Royal Tank Regiment and Its Predecessors, 1914–45, Vol. 1*. London: Cassell.
Souter, K. M. (2009). The *War Memoirs*: Some origins of the thought of W. R. Bion. *International Journal of Psycho-Analysis, 90*: 795–808.
Wilson, G. M. (1929). *Fighting Tanks: An Account of the Royal Tank Corps between 1916 and 1919*. London: Seeley, Service & Co.
Winship, G. (1999). Review of W. R. Bion, *War Memoirs 1917–1919*. *Psychoanalytic Psychotherapy, 13*: 93–95.

INDEX

A Company, *passim*
Addison, J., 94
Admiral's Road, 21–22, 27
Agincourt, Battle of, 196
Aitches [Company Commander], 107, 108, 111, 114, 120, 127, 137, 140, 142, 151–155, 159, 169, 185, 188
Allen [Gnr.], 6, 55
Allen A. E. [L/Cpl.], 6, 27–29, 43, 50, 55, 61
alpha [α] function, x, 300
Amiens, France, 71, 76, 113, 118, 192
    Battle of, 118, 192, 202, 205–298
        8 Aug. 1918 [map], 118, 122
        10 Aug. 1918 [map], 136
        22 Aug. 1918 [map], 138
        attack, 22 Aug 1918 [photograph], 147
Amiens–Roye road, 114, 123–127, 135, 213, 239, 245, 250, 259, 270–273, 278–279, 293–294
Anvin, France, 9
Arras, France, 12, 108
Asquith, H. H., 199
Asser [Lieut.], *passim*
Australian Army Corps, 212, 221, 239
    9th Army [photograph], 169

Bagshaw [Capt.], 7, 27, 28, 55, 65, 76
Bailleul, France, 79, 81–84
Bairnsfather, B., 6
Bapaume, France, 42, 139
Bargate [Maj.], 40, 51, 63, 65, 76, 80, 83–87, 107

Barr, P. [company reconnaissance officer], 162, 164, 167, 175, 185, 186
basic-assumption phenomena, 300
battalion, entraining [photograph and diagram], 19
Battersea, Countess of, 264–265
battle, devastation after [photograph], 69
B Company, 6, 39, 46, 65, 83, 88, 98, 114, 125, 129, 150, 154–155, 164, 173, 175, 185, 188, 238, 272
Beaumetz, France, 10, 187
Beaumont Hamel, France, 39
BEF: *see* British Expeditionary Force
Bellenglise, France, 157, 164, 167, 173
Berle-au-Bois, France, 108–111, 245, 251, 253, 272–293
Berry, W. H., 149
beta element(s), x, 300
Binyon, L., 2, 208
Bion, Francesca, *née* McCallum, ix, 8, 2, 192, 206, 253–257
Bion/Bion Talamo, Parthenope, ix–x, 299–302
Bion, Wilfred R., decorations:
    Distinguished Service Order [DSO], 74
    Légion d'Honneur, 153
Black Watch, 37, 50
Blangy, France, 76, 150
Boer War, 190
Bohain, France, 185–186
Bonsey, E. K., 37

305

Bottomley, H., 59
Boulogne, France, 75, 149
Bourlon Wood, France, 254, 257
Bournemouth, 244
Bovington, 8, 196, 243
Bovington Camp, 8
Bridges [2nd Lieut.], 82–84
Brisleux-au-Mont, France, 40
British Expeditionary Force [BEF], 153
British Front, June–July 1918 [map], 109
British Infantry Rifle, compared with German anti-tank rifle [photograph], 115
British shell-burst, effects of, on German Outpost party [photograph], 125
Brooke, R., 208
Broom [tank commander], 211, 212, 214, 228, 288
Broomback [sergeant instructor], 243
Broome [2nd Lieut.], 7, 35
Buchanan [runner], 84, 139, 153
Burnett [Lieut. Col.], 8, 263–265, 288
Byng, Sir J., 225

California, 192
Cambrai, France, Battle of, 8, 55, 63, 65, 71, 73, 113, 134, 169, 180, 196, 204, 214, 222, 224, 229, 249, 251, 254, 268
   Cambrai Front [photograph], 73
   defensive wire at [photograph], 65
Cambrai Salient, 53
Campbell, C., vii
Campbell, R., 108
Canadian Army Corps, 212–213, 256
Canadian Division, 239
Canadian infantry, 133
   in Dodo Wood [photograph], 131
Canadian Tank Battalion, 135
Canal du Nord, France, 162, 164, 165 [photograph], 167
   banks [photograph], 170, 173
   entrance to tunnel [photograph], 175
Carter [Capt.], 55–60, 76, 83–86, 98, 120, 139–143, 148, 151, 152, 175, 188, 215, 220–224, 228, 229, 235–242, 261, 286–296

Carter, B., 80
Cartwright [officer], 110, 125, 210, 211, 230, 234, 235, 243, 272, 286, 297
Casualty Clearing Station, 17
C Company, *passim*
Chasseurs Alpines, 213
Chatigny, France, 256–257
Cheshire Regiment, 97, 101, 106
Chinese Wall, 93–95, 99
   position [map], 94
Christmas 1917, 63–70
Clifford [Capt.], 44, 55–65, 73, 76, 87, 202
Cohen [tank commander], 7, 21, 28–29, 37, 50, 198, 204
Coldstream Guards, 52–53, 63, 78, 108, 110, 137, 142, 200, 204
Colman, M., 37
Colombe, P. M. V., 6, 35, 49, 55
container:
   mother as, 300
   and contained, ix
Cook [Capt.], 65, 67, 76, 80, 97, 98, 107, 110, 127, 131, 133, 135, 151–154, 202, 206, 260–262, 266, 267
Cook [Maj.], 220
Cooper [Gnr.], 284
Corbie, France, 137
Craig [Maj.], 188
Croix de Guerre, 214, 219, 228
Curzon, G., Lord, 199

Damery, France, 133, 134
Dawson, 185
D Battalion, 56, 74, 142
DCM: see Distinguished Conduct Medal
de Coverley, Sir R., 94
de Freine [Maj.], 8, 40, 63, 206, 238, 259–268, 273, 277–278, 292–297
Derby Trench, 46
Dessart Wood, France, 61
Dickebush Lake, 25
Distinguished Conduct Medal [DCM], 190
Distinguished Service Order [DSO], viii, 39, 74, 76, 117, 150, 152–154, 202, 209, 210, 239, 263

INDEX   307

Dodo Wood, France, 121, 131
  Canadian infantry in [photograph], 131
Drocourt–Quéant Switch, 150
DSO: *see* Distinguished Service Order
Duke of Cornwall's Light Infantry Band, 101
Dunkirk, Belgium, 189

Edwards [Capt.], 39, 49
8th Tank Battalion moving forward for attack [photograph], 169
Ellis, General, 74, 77
English Farm, 21, 25, 27
Erin, Central Workshops at, 10
Étaples, France, 73
Expeditionary Force Canteen [EFC], 97, 112

Fairbanks [Commander], 76
fascine(s):
  attaching [diagram], 42
  use of [diagram], 41
field guns, 36, 51, 224, 249
5th Battalion, 147, 151, 157
  tanks [photograph], 157
51st Division, Highland Territorials, 38, 39, 55, 65, 111
52nd Division, 134
1st Battalion, 65, 126, 135, 256, 295
1st French Army, 113
1st Tank Battalion, 114
Flanders, Battle, 23
Flesquières, France, viii, 39, 44, 46, 48, 55, 254
  village [photograph and diagram], 55
Flims, France, 61, 63
Foch, Marshal F., 134
Fonsomme line, 173, 185
Foreign Legion, 213, 253, 292
Forman [Cpl.], 7, 49, 50, 55
42nd Division, 292
Foster [soldier], 35, 37
4th Battalion, 61, 67, 142, 147, 148, 151
4th British Army, 113
4th Tank Brigade, 73
French Division, 239

French First Army, 241
French 75-mm field gun, 86, 104, 293

Gallipoli, 219
Gatehouse [Maj.], 51, 65, 106, 151–155, 187
George, L., 199
George V, king, 59
German anti-tank rifle, compared with British Infantry Rifle [photograph], 115
German 5.9-inch field gun, 59, 86, 94, 96, 101, 103
German pill-box, 30, 56
  [photograph], 33
G.H.Q. Reserve, 77
G.O.C. Tank Corps, 74
Gouzeaucourt, France, 52, 200
Grand Ravine, 44, 46
Gray [Sgt], 49
Greene [Lieut.], 50, 196, 221–227, 272, 279–286, 296
Greenwood Copse, 214, 270, 272
Grenfell, J., 208
group therapy, 301

Haig, D. [Gen.], 113, 135, 151
Haley [Gnr.], 284
Handley Page bombers, 119, 213, 214, 233, 244
Hankey [Col.], 57, 73, 107
Happy Valley, 142, 143, 149, 150
Harrison [Gnr.], 65, 110, 153, 233, 242, 279, 282
Harrison [L/Cpl.], 110
hate [H], 301
Hauser [officer], 55–61, 73, 87, 98, 99, 102–106, 111, 121–129, 134, 137, 139, 151, 175, 178–180, 185, 204, 211–214, 222–224, 233, 235, 239, 240, 268–279, 286, 294, 296, 297
Havrincourt, France, 42, 43, 50, 51, 56, 61
Havrincourt Wood, 42, 51, 56, 61
Hayler [Cpl.], 110
Hayler [Gnr.], 6, 35, 46, 110
Hazebrouck, France, 16, 17, 78, 204
Henry IV, 193
Henry V, 225

308　INDEX

Henry V, king, at Agincourt, 196
Hindenburg, P. von [Gen.], 163
Hindenburg Line, 42, 152, 155, 169, 173, 184
Home [Brig. Gen.], 225
Hotblack [Maj.], 117, 215–218, 221, 228, 236
Howitzer(s), viii, 21, 63, 244, 267, 293
　5.9-inch, 59, 86, 94, 96, 101, 103
　6-inch, 242
　9.5-inch, 214
Huntlatch [Maj.], 151

Irish Guards, 108
Iron Division, 213, 215

Jamieson Elles, H. [Brig. Gen.], viii
Johnson [tank commander], 73, 111, 123, 125

King's Own Light Infantry [KOLI], 100
King's Own Yorkshire Light Infantry [KOYLI], 101
Kitchener, H. H. [Field Marshal], 23
knowing [K], 301

La Lovie, France, 20, 86
La Vacquerie, France, 53
Legion d'Honneur, 153, 219
Le Havre, France, 9, 107, 196, 197, 282
Le Tréport, France, 76
Lewis gun(s), viii, 12, 15, 48, 49, 77, 80, 82, 88, 100, 106, 113, 145, 200, 241, 258, 272–275, 280, 284
Liddel Hart, B. H., viii
Llewellyn [Capt.], 129, 154
love [L], 301
Luce, river, France, 114, 117, 120, 209, 215–217, 230, 239, 242, 250, 270
Lustleigh, Devon, 149, 150

Mackenzie [Col.], viii, 50, 51
madness, 90–91, 103, 301
Malaya, 222, 224, 288, 289
Marcoing, France:
　57.C.N.E., 57
　[map], 44

Mark IV tank, description, 12–14
Martha Louise Farm, 30
masturbation, 203
Maudesley Hospital, London **3**: 198
McNeil ['Sapper'] [Col.], 80
Méaulte, France, 53, 61, 63, 71, 73, 76, 139, 142, 149, 201
Merlimont Plage, France, Tank Gunnery School, 9, 10, 73, 74, 151
Merlincourt, 76
Messines, France, 90
Messines Ridge, 231
Meteren, Belgium, 81–87, 153
　position [map], 81, 85
Metz, France, 42, 43
Middlesex pioneer battalion, 80, 83
Military Cross [MC], 51, 86, 111, 154, 155
Millekruisse, Belgium, 98, 102, 103, 155
Milton, J., *Paradise Lost*, 243
Mont des Cats, Belgium, Trappist Monastery at, 86
Mont Kemmel, Belgium, 95–100, 221
　enemy advance in capture of [map], 100
　May 1918 [map], 99
Mont Noir, Belgium, 88
Mont Rouge, Belgium, 88
Morgan [Maj.], 221, 240, 241

New Zealand Army Corps, 212, 221, 239
9th [Lowland Scottish] Division, 88
Nixon [Capt.], 74, 151, 153, 155, 157, 159, 169
North Midland Division, 203
No. 5 Infantry Track, 22, 33, 36, 199

O'Kelly [Col.], 76, 126, 151, 152, 154
Oosthoek, Belgium, 17, 20, 21, 25, 35, 38, 86
Oosthoek Wood, 35, 38
open warfare, 128, 274
O'Toole, B. [Sgt], 6, 33, 50, 110, 125, 244, 297
Ouderdom, Belgium, 98
Owen [2nd Lieut.], 7

Owen, W., 7, 35, 299
Oxford University, vii, 2, 195, 199, 201, 202
    Queen's College, vii, 2, 192, 193, 194, 202

Parkins [soldier], 77
Parvillers, France, 133, 134
Passchendaele, Belgium, 17, 21
Pelcappelle road, 38
Pell [Gnr.], 46, 48, 49
pill-box, German, 30
    [photograph], 33
Plateau, 40, 63
Plumer [Gen.], 225
pre-mental life, x, 300
proto-mental, as matrix sustaining basic-assumption phenomena, 300

Quainton [tank commander], 7, 28, 29, 33, 50, 53, 61, 65, 67, 71–74, 110, 198, 201, 204, 228, 287–288
Queen's College, Oxford, vii, 2, 192–194, 202

Rawlinson [army commander], 225
regressed states of mind, 300
Reid [Sgt], 8, 33, 35, 37, 179, 180, 184
Reigersburg Château, 21, 25, 35
Restaurant du Cathedral, 71
Reynolds [battalion workshops officer], 137
Rhine, 163, 173, 250
Ribécourt, France, 44, 67, 200
    attack [photograph], 67
Rice, K., 275
Richards [soldier], 125–131
Richardson, W. [Gnr.], viii, 6, 48, 50, 55, 198
Richthofen, M. von [Red Baron], 147
Robinson [Sgt], 110, 111, 125
Roisel, France, 152
Royal Army Medical Corps [RAMC], 279
Royal Engineers [RE], 160, 164, 169
Royal Horse Guards [RHG], 151
Royal Scots, 93, 96, 97

Royal Tank Regiment, 2
Roye, France, 211, 245

Sandhurst, 225
Sargent, J. S., 111
Sassoon, S., 299
schizophrenic-type reaction, 195
Seaforth Highlanders, viii, 39, 49, 51, 55
Sequehart, France, 173, 175, 178–186
Shakespeare, W.:
    Henry IV, 193
    Henry V, 225
Shaw, G. B., 2
shell bursting [diagram], 142
shell-shock, 35, 48, 61, 74, 283
Shorncliffe camp, 189
Short [Corp.], 181–184, 189, 301
6th Seaforths, 39, 55
Smith [Cpl.], 106, 234, 272, 277, 286
Smith [Gnr.], 277, 278, 286
Soissons, France, 231
Somme, France, 39, 40, 53, 67, 139, 200, 255, 267
    Battle of, 53, 69, 147
S.O.S. signal lights, 83, 96, 102, 103
Spree Farm, 21, 22, 25, 28, 29
star shell(s), 10, 252, 293
Steenbeck stream, Belgium, 22, 201
St. Jean–Wieltje road, 36
Stokes [soldier], 50, 198
Stone [Cpl.], 243, 244
Sutherland, G., 83, 86
Sweeting [Gnr.], 123, 243–246, 278, 279, 282

tank(s):
    breaking through German wire [photograph], 65
    camouflaged [photograph and diagram], 20
    crossing trench [photograph], 117
    direct hit on, 35
        [photograph], 133
    entraining [diagram], 11
    5th Battalion [photograph], 157
    flaps [diagram], 13
    male [diagram], 7
    Mark V Ricardo, 110, 268

tank(s) (*continued*):
  MK IV female [photograph and diagram], 14–15
  moving forward for attack female [photograph], 169
  parked on night of 29/30 Sept. 1918 [map], 158
Tank Corps, 8, 76, 77, 117, 135, 236, 301
tank warfare, 233
Tara Hill, 160, 162, 163
  [map], 160–161
Times, The, 208
Tincourt, France, 74, 75
trench warfare, 274
Trescault, France, 42, 46
21st Division, 101
24th Division, 165

Valenciennes, France, 187
VC: *see* Victoria Cross
Very lights, 10, 53, 67, 74, 83, 90, 98, 102, 157
Victoria Cross [VC], viii, 51, 107, 135, 154
Villers-aux-Erables, France, 114, 117, 126
Villers-Bretonneux, France, 136, 137, 241
Villers-Plouich, France, 44, 57, 73, 296
  Front [map], 63

Wailly, France, 10, 12, 16, 38, 39, 63, 73, 187
warfare, 134, 253, 274, 300–302

Watts, I., 108
Western Front, 38, 149, 150, 210, 231
Whyte [soldier], 111
Wieltje, Belgium, 21, 22, 27, 33, 36
Wieltje–St. Jean road, 22, 27
Wilkins [Sgt], 269, 271, 272, 276–278
Williams [Capt.], 281, 282, 285, 286
Williams [engineer officer], 280
Williams [Sgt], 281, 286
Wilson, G. M., viii
Wilson, President W., 187
Wilson [tank commander], 43
Windle [Capt.], 99, 155, 159, 162, 163
Winnicott, D. W., 300
Wipers [Ypres], 197. *See also* Ypres
Wool, Dorset, 8, 12, 194, 196
Wytschaete, Belgium, 88, 89, 93, 95, 97
Wytschaete–Mont Kemmel, position, April–May 1918 [map], 95
Wytschaete Ridge, Belgium [map], 89, 93

Yates [2nd Lieut.], 219, 220
Y.M.C.A., 67
Ypres, Belgium, Battle of, 16–42, 56, 61–65, 73, 79, 134, 139, 143, 201, 202, 224, 229, 233, 236, 253, 276, 278, 288
  battlefield [photograph], 25
  light railway at [photograph], 23
Ypres Canal, Belgium, 27
Ytres, France, 42, 43, 53

Zonnebeke, Belgium, 21, 133